AMERICAN CHURCHES AND THE NEGRO

OTHER BOOKS ON RACE
BY THE SAME AUTHOR

Negro Life in the South

Present Forces in Negro Progress

The Negro From Africa To America

Race Relations (*With Chas. S. Johnson*)

An Analytical Index of DeBow's Review
(*A source book on information on the
Old South and Southwest*)

AMERICAN CHURCHES
AND THE NEGRO

AN HISTORICAL STUDY
FROM EARLY SLAVE DAYS TO THE PRESENT

By

W. D. WEATHERFORD, Ph.D.
Vice chairman Trustees of Berea College

THE CHRISTOPHER PUBLISHING HOUSE
BOSTON, U. S. A.

DEDICATED TO A GREAT CO-WORKER
JULIA MCCRORY WEATHERFORD

TABLE OF CONTENTS

7

INTRODUCTION

In his latest book, *American Churches and the Negro*, Dr. Willis D. Weatherford makes a ringing challenge to the churches not only to catch up with the Constitution as interpreted by the decisions of the United States Supreme Court but also to fulfill their own professions of faith based on the teachings of Jesus, who would have us all become more truly the children of God and the brothers of all people. He is troubled in mind and spirit that the churches, which should have prepared the way, are lagging behind the decision of the Court. This is true of the churches, south, north, east and west. It has been trenchantly observed that eleven o'clock on Sunday is the most segregated hour on the weekly calendar of American life.

By his long life of eighty years of thoughtful study, scholarly research, and religious leadership in the Southern colleges and universities, he is equipped to make his findings first-hand out of the stuff of his own life and convictions. In his various and vigorous life he has been International Secretary of the Y.M.C.A. in the Southern colleges and universities; founder and president of the Blue Ridge Southern Assembly, founder, president and professor of the Y.M.C.A. Graduate School, erstwhile affiliated with his alma mater, Vanderbilt University, from which he had received the A.B. and Ph.D. degrees; visiting professor at Fisk University and colleague of his friend, Professor and President Charles S. Johnson, an eminent authority on patterns of racial segregation. He has long been a trustee of Berea College, one of the earlier pioneers in non-segregation in higher education in the South.

His books on the Negro in Southern life were studied in voluntary classes by many more than a score of thousands of students in Southern colleges and universities. In his scholarly and pioneering part in the reorientation of youthful minds, he stirred the conscience of generations of youth into social thinking and action. Sometimes the youthful disciples, as fitting tribute to his teachings, adopted a speed beyond the not less effective pace of the master teacher for changing old *mores* toward new customs of a long unprepared and fearful people. He was in the forefront of those who prepared college youth for a new era in interracial relations of the beloved people of his own South. The dynamic influence of this man, unresting in his eighty years, has reached across all the States from the Potomac to the Rio Grande and down the decades to these years of epochal decision of the Court.

In his latest timely book, Dr. Weatherford has brought to life from old forgotten records, the place of Negro slaves in the churches of the Old South. He reminds us that in many Southern churches the White master and Negro slaves were members of the same church and shared in the sacrament of communion equally at the same table.

A dominantly White church in Virginia had a Negro minister. In Charleston, S. C., a good number of representative White people asked to be admitted to a Presbyterian Negro church ministered to by Dr. John L. Girardeau. They were admitted on the condition that they would not attempt to take over the management of the church.

He recalls, among the White leaders in the concern
of Southern churches for the spiritual equality and welfare of the slaves, such distinguished religious leaders as
the Episcopal Bishop Meade of Virginia, Charles Jones
of Georgia, and the Methodist Bishop Atticus G. Haygood of Georgia. He might have added as a coincidence
in names and an example of the concern that is not lagging but very immediate and valiant, the story of the
ministry today of the Reverend Charles Jones in Chapel
Hill, N. C.

Dr. Weatherford, with his many examples of religious equality in the pre-Civil War South, emphasizes
the fact that, with pioneering exceptions in a number
of Southern Catholic dioceses, Quaker communions, and
a few Protestant congregations, the churches today, in
their racially segregated membership, are not only lagging behind State institutions, but are also lagging behind the pre-Civil War Southern churches, with their
integrated memberships. On the basis of the facts established by Dr. Weatherford, we might say in general
that the Southern churches, which sanctioned slavery
and political inequality, practiced spiritual equality in
their integrated memberships. In the contemporary
South, the churches, which preach economic and political equality for all men, and religious equality in their
national and regional resolutions, mainly practice segregation in their local congregations. It may also be observed that, while the State in this regard is beginning
to "render unto God the things that are God's", the
churches, in their local congregations are continuing to
render unto Caesar the things that are no longer Caesar's.

Dr. Weatherford, with facts and faith, calls upon us
all in the churches not only to catch up with the State
but to lead the way in the building of spiritual com-

munions of equal freedom, dignity and opportunity in local congregations and in the world neighborhood of human brotherhood under the Fatherhood of one God.

FRANK P. GRAHAM *

* Former President of the University of North Carolina and now special representative of the United Nations.

FOREWORD

The Supreme Court of the United States in its famous desegregation decree of 1954 exploded a bomb which, in spite of the fact that all America knew well it must come, certainly shocked people out of their apathy and put them to hard thinking. The Church, which has sometimes agonized over the race problem, but more often has temporized, was brought up with a sudden shock and came to realize that the time was running out in which it could grapple with the problem, not as a follower, but as a leader of social action. Perhaps the time is ripe for a careful study of the historic action of the Church in its attitude toward the Negro.

In 1910, I wrote a book called *Negro Life in the South,* of which the publisher sold thirty thousand copies. It was used as a textbook in the voluntary study classes of the Student Y.M.C.A. and Student Y.W.C.A. It was also used in some of the young people's groups in the churches. In gathering the material for that book on race relations, I was fascinated by the many references to the interest of the early churches in the religious life of the Negro. I found one little volume, published in 1842 in Savannah, Georgia, by Rev. C. C. Jones, a Presbyterian minister, but also a slave owner, called *The Religious Instruction of the Negroes in the United States.* In it, Rev. Jones eloquently pleads the cause of the slave and his right to full religious life. He also gathered data showing the interest of many denominations in evangelizing the slaves. I also read the

13

little volume, *Our Brother in Black, His Freedom and His Future*, by Bishop Atticus G. Haygood of Georgia, one of the most eloquent appeals ever made for the religious freedom of the newly made freedmen.

I determined then that I would sometime assemble the records of all the leading denominations and their official actions and attitudes on this subject. It seemed to me then, and it seems to me now, that this record of the past, particularly that portion which refers to action before the Civil War, might throw considerable light on the pressing problems of the present. For there can be no doubt that our forefathers, who had colored people living in their homes and who often treated them as their own children, must have known the Negro more intimately than most of us of the present time who meet them only in casual business relations or as house help in our homes, which may or may not give us any intimate knowledge of the real Negro. It has been asserted times without number that the southern white man knows the Negro. I, as a southern white man who has given this subject more study than most and has worked long and faithfully to know him and help him, would deliberately challenge the accuracy of this statement, even if being willing to acknowledge that the southern white man should know the Negro much better than those who have not lived by his side. Even Rev. C. C. Jones, who owned slaves and lived with them, and who was an outstanding advocate of religious work for and with slaves, wrote in 1842, "Persons live and die in the midst of Negroes and know comparatively little of their real character." [1]

Certainly the present white man, even the southern

---

[1] C. C. Jones, *The Religious Instruction of the Negroes in the United States* (Savannah: Thomas Purse, 1842).

white churchman, is almost wholly ignorant of the facts of the churches' interest in the Negro during slavery. How many Episcopalians of the present day even know the name of Bishop Meade of Virginia, say nothing of his intense interest in and work for the religious instruction of slaves? How many South Carolina Episcopalians know that one of their most illustrious bishops, Bishop Bowen, labored in season and out to see that "Religious Instruction" was given to all "slave members of the Protestant Episcopal Church in the State of South Carolina?" [2] How many members of the Baptist Church know that at least two white Baptist churches in antebellum Virginia called Negro pastors? How many Methodists know that two of the most famous of the early bishops of that Church, Bishop William Capers of South Carolina, and Bishop Atticus G. Haygood of Georgia, gave a disproportionately large amount of their time through long and fruitful ministries to the service of the Negroes of their respective states?

Some years ago while speaking at the University of South Carolina, I was invited to speak at the eleven o'clock Sunday service of the Washington Street Methodist Church of Columbia, South Carolina. As I entered the vestibule of the church, I saw a large marble tablet dedicated to Bishop Capers as the founder of that church. In my introductory statement I remarked how happy I was to speak in a church founded by one of the greatest friends the Negro in the South ever had, and added that I suspected I was the only person in a group of more than a thousand Methodists gathered that morning who had ever read Wightman's *Life of William Capers*. I found no person, not even the pastor, who was willing to challenge my statement.

---

[2] Jones, *op. cit.*, p. 80.

How many Presbyterians know that Dr. John L. Girardeau of Charleston, South Carolina, one of the most scholarly and eloquent of Presbyterian divines, sometimes called the Spurgeon of America, organized and became pastor of a very large Presbyterian Church whose original members were drawn from the slave members of all the Presbyterian churches of the Charleston Presbytery, and that thirty-three of the most prominent white Presbyterians of the city asked for and were granted the privilege of joining this Negro church, after signing a pledge that they would never take the leadership and the management of the church away from the Negroes? [3] In this church both the white and the colored members sat on the same floor and were served the Holy Communion at the same time.[4] Facts like the above, and many more of similar import, showing the close relation between white and colored Christians in ante-bellum days are simply not known by present-day church members. Since most southern people have a high reverence for the great leaders of the Old South, and since most of us have a nostalgic appreciation of the finer elements in that old southern civilization, it seems reasonable to believe that a comparison of the attitude of the early leaders with the attitude of the average present-day church member might help to bring some sanity and poise into present-day thinking.

Pursuant to this thought, some years ago I visited the best archives of eight of the leading denominations and prepared a summary statement of the thought of these denominations about the Negroes as revealed in the official action of their several legislative bodies. It

---

[3] Blackburn, *The Life Work of John L. Girardeau, D.D., L.L.D.* (The Slate Company, 1916), pp. 82-84, passim.

[4] *Ibid.,* p. 44.

is a most revealing story. Perhaps each present-day church member who sees this volume will be interested to read the story of his own denomination's actions. This may give him a better understanding as he reads in the closing chapters some conclusions to which these comparisons have led the present writer.

My purposes, therefore, in preparing this historical statement have been four-fold. First, I wanted to find out just how much knowledge the early church members had of the Negro and how much real interest the churches had in introducing the Negro to the principles of Christianity. That this interest was very great the records prove to me beyond the shadow of a doubt. I have quoted extensively from these early documents rather than making simply a running comment drawn from them, because only thus it seemed to me could people be assured that I was stating the plain facts rather than trying to make a case for ante-bellum Christians. It seems so anomalous that people could have a deep religious interest in their slaves and yet still hold them as slaves that many people are inclined to discount that interest. But people often hold quite contradictory views without seeming to realize that they are contradictory. We ourselves hold very contradictory views. With our larger respect for personality, we would be shocked at the thought of holding any Negro as a slave. But we often treat Negroes with less respect than slaves. In a southern city recently the usher in one of the fashionable churches pleaded earnestly with certain very respectable and well-dressed Negroes not to attend the Sunday morning service of his church. Put beside that picture that of a group of the most highly respected planters of Charleston, South Carolina, joining a Negro church and worshipping each Sunday in a congregation where there were at least twenty Negroes (many of them slaves) to every white person in the congregation. And to heighten the contrasts, these Negroes in this ante-bellum Charleston church were the controlling element.

To be sure, this deep interest in the religious welfare of the slaves was affected in the last period of slavery by the rising tide of abolitionism in the North, which was producing discontent and restlessness among the slaves. This restlessness in time produced some of the ugliest forms of uprising of slaves, such as the Vesey plot in 1822, and the Nat Turner rebellion in 1831. These occurrences frightened some and dampened their enthusiasm, but all the churches continued right up through the Civil War to press for a vital religious program for Negroes. The College of Bishops of the Methodist Church, recognizing the harm the rising tide of fear might do to their practical mission program, addressed their Episcopal Letter of 1836 to this subject, saying that "The only safe, scriptural and provident way for us (the Methodists) to take, is wholly to refrain from the agitating subject." That they were in a measure able to reassure their members and continue their religious program is proven by the fact that at the next General Conference, that of 1840, a greatly increased number of Negro members (94,532) was reported.

During this agitation, the Baptists gathered in Charleston, South Carolina in 1835, and urged the legislature of that state not to pass laws restricting the liberty of worship of Negroes, and they also resolved that their own churches "use every consistent method to give them (the Negroes) the knowledge of salvation."

The branch of the Presbyterians later known as the Presbyterian Church in the Confederate States of America had as late as 1861, thirty-eight missionaries giving their full time to work among the slaves. The Methodists (South) at the opening of the war in 1860 had 335 full-time missionaries working among the slaves, led and directed by such illustrious men as William Capers (deceased 1855). Most of the southern denominations were very active in this work.

My second purpose in this book is to discover what evidence there is that the planters of the Old South understood their Negroes better than the present-day church members do. One thing is certain, as brought out by the study, that the planters and their slaves worshipped together. They belonged to the same church; in their services they sang the same songs (the spirituals were sung only in the fields and in Negro gatherings). In many cases they heard the same sermons; and often they partook of the Holy Communion together. Colonel Peyton, a large slave owner near Nashville, Tennessee, built an Episcopal chapel on his plantation. In this chapel on Sunday mornings, Col. Peyton's slaves occupied the entire first floor, while Col. Peyton's own family and other white people occupied the gallery. Col. Peyton himself was the precentor, and his daughter was the organist. In Charleston, South Carolina, Rev. John Bachman was pastor for many years of the St. John's Lutheran Church. Here in the 1850's he had a membership of 192 colored persons (many of them slaves) and 345 white persons, many of them slave owners. He preached regularly to the united congregation of colored and white and administered the Holy Communion to both groups at the same table. It would seem reasonable to believe that this intimate fellowship would produce a mutual interest and understanding.

In contrast to this situation, there is at the present time almost no common church life. Culver, in a recent study of this aspect of the race problem, estimates that only eighteen hundredths of one per cent of the Negro Methodists worship in churches which are predominantly white, and he thinks that the Methodists have a larger percentage of churches with Negro worshipers than would be found in other Protestant denominations.[5] It is often pointed out that the Catholic Church does better than the Protestant churches on integration. But, as Ralph Lord Ray points out in *The Christian Century* of May 30, 1956, 476,000 in a church of thirty-one million does not give very large opportunity for common fellowship.

The very rapid strides which nonreligious or secular agencies have made toward integrated or interracial interests and understanding in the last ten years would certainly call for a better understanding on the part of the churches. In particular, the Supreme Court decision of 1954, calling for integrated schools, would seem to force a new interest of the churches, if they wish to be leaders in human understanding and not reluctant and belated followers. Here the contrast between the ante-bellum church in the South and the present-day church is striking.

During the period of 1936 to 1946, when I was Head of the Department of Religion and Philosophy at Fisk University, I made it a practice to accept as many invitations as possible to speak in Negro churches. On the average, I must have spoken on at least twenty Sundays each year in some Negro church. It gave me a wonderful opportunity for first-hand observation. I have seen for myself what I had always heard—that religion has a large and central place in the life of the Negro

---

[5] Dwight W. Culver, *Negro Segregation in the Methodist Church* (Yale University Press, 1953), p. 143f.

people. I am sure I know the total impact of Christianity on American life better because of this rare experience. It is my hope that this study will show that a larger exchange of religious fellowship is in keeping with the very best traditions of the Old South.

Thirdly, I wanted to gather the most pertinent facts, showing what the major denominations are doing at present to express interest and concern for the religious life of those whom Bishop Haygood called "Our Brothers in Black."

Finally, and in the fourth place, I wanted to attempt an interpretation of what it seemed to me all these facts pointed to as a pressing demand for action in the present hour. If an enlarged understanding based on fellowship is really demanded by the facts, then how can the churches go about making such a fellowship possible? The closing chapter will attempt to deal with this problem.

After gathering the early historical material sometime ago, I submitted it to those whom I considered competent to judge of their value. I am deeply indebted to a number of persons who have read the manuscript for their respective denominations. Dr. Henry J. Cadbery of the Friends Service Committee read the chapter on the Quakers, and made many helpful suggestions. Dr. Fred Brownlee, of the American Missionary Association, read the chapter on the Congregational Church and wrote: "I have read every word with deep interest and concern." He added quite a list of suggestions. Two priests of the Order of St. Joseph under the suggestion of Rev. Edward V. Casserly read the chapter on the Roman Catholic Church and made extended and helpful comment. Rev. Robert D. Bedinger, former Superintendent of Negro Work for the Presbyterian Church, and Dr. T. H. Spence, of the Presbyterian Historical Foundation, went with me over the chapter on the Presbyterians and made extended comments. Dr. Bedinger asked to print this Presbyterian chapter in a pamphlet and said if permitted to do so he would put a copy of it in the hands of every pastor of a Presbyterian church. Dr. Ryland Knight, formerly pastor of a leading Baptist Church in Atlanta, and grandson of Dr. Ryland, President of Richmond College, and the first pastor of the original Negro Baptist Church in Richmond, Virginia, went over the manuscript on the Baptist denomination and made helpful suggestions. Mr. R. B. Eleazer, former Counsellor on Race Relations of the Methodist Board of Education, read with me the chapter on the Methodist Church. Dr Frank Loescher of the Friends Service Committee kindly read the entire manuscript and made valuable comments. Faculty members of the Department of Religion and Philosophy at Fisk read parts of the manuscript and made valuable comment.

Although I have not followed all the suggestions made, I have tried to profit by all of these helpful suggestions and many others too numerous to mention. I would not, however, want anyone to charge any of the shortcomings of this volume to any of these helpful advisers. I must take complete responsibility for the ideas set forth. I can only send them forth with the hope that there will be enough of solid truth and fairness of approach to commend the contents of this volume to careful consideration. Certainly the issue at stake is one of the most pressing of our generation. Probably no other subject calls forth as constant comment as does the race issue. Unfortunately, accurate information is not as widely disseminated as it should be. Still more unfortunately, many people are inclined to look back to what they think are the good old days of southern relationships, and they may be surprised to find what the attitude was in those good old days. If the worthy and interested attitude of our forefathers arouses in us some new and vital interest in proper relations between the races, then the effort in preparing this volume will have been more than repaid.

American Churches and the Negro

CHAPTER I

THE ATTITUDE OF THE EPISCOPAL CHURCH TOWARD THE NEGRO DURING SLAVERY

Not all the English who migrated to America in the early colonial days were members of the Established Church. "The famous colony of the Pilgrims at Plymouth, in 1620, was founded by independents or separatists, who believed that a true church is a body of Christians under the guidance of pastors elected by 'the Lord's godly and free people.' "[1] The Massachusetts Bay Colony was composed of English people who "were Puritans who sought to remain within the Church of England, but who wished to eliminate from it what they deemed corruptions and disorders."[2] They disclaimed any intention of separating from the Church of England. However, their clergy seem to have had a preference for congregational polity.[3]

The Rhode Island groups were radicals who were obnoxious to the Massachusetts Bay Colony. In Connecticut the same general attitude toward the Church of England prevailed as was found in Massachusetts.

In New York, settled by the Dutch, the Dutch Re-

[1] Latourette, *A History of the Expansion of Christianity* (Harper & Bro., 1939), Vol. III, p. 191.
[2] *Ibid.*, p. 191.
[3] *Ibid.*, p. 192.

formed Church was at first very strong, but later when England took over this colony the Church of England was given a preferred position. However, as late as 1701, there was no congregation of the Church of England outside of New York City.[4] Huguenots in considerable numbers, Quakers, Waldensians, and Lutherans were to be found in this early colony.[5]

In New Jersey Quakers early became very prominent. Huguenots and Dutch Reformed were also found. The religious conditions were so bad that the Society for the Propagation of the Gospel in Foreign Parts soon decided to send missionaries to establish the Church of England in this province. They likewise early sent workers to New York. Pennsylvania was primarily a Quaker colony. While religious toleration was declared, there were not many members of the Church of England to be found here. Mennonites, Dunkers, Dutch Reformed, Lutherans were also to be found in this colony. The first Baptist Church in Pennsylvania was organized in 1684.[6]

Maryland was founded by the Calverts, who were Catholics. Jesuits were in the first party that came out to this colony, and the colony was at first quite distinctly Catholic. But the founders soon found it expedient to grant religious tolerance, and other groups early began to come in. The Church of England soon became powerful, and in 1692, it was by law made the Established Church. Governor Nicholson encouraged the setting aside of glebes for the clergy and even the Calverts became members of the Established Church. "Rev. Thomas Bacon, ordained in 1744, came to Mary-

[4] Latourette, *op. cit.*, p. 194.
[5] *Ibid.*, p. 195.
[6] *Ibid.*, p. 203.

land in 1745 as Chaplain to Lord Baltimore. He was first located in Talbot County, but in 1747 he moved to Dover, some twelve miles distant. It was upon his entrance into this new field of labor that he began the work of laboring for the good of the Negro slaves about him." [7]

Bacon reported as follows: "Upon being appointed as your minister . . . I found a great many poor Negro slaves, belonging to Christian masters and mistresses, yet living in as profound ignorance of what Christianity really is, as if they had remained in the midst of their barbarous heathen countries . . . and considering them as part of my flock which the Almighty God had placed under my care, I began seriously to consider in what manner I could discharge my duty to them." [8] "Before the close of the third year a chapel was erected, and in 1749 he preached and published four sermons upon the great and indispensable duty of all Christian masters and mistresses to bring up their slaves in the knowledge and fear of God." [9]

"In 1642, Thomas Gerrard, a Catholic, whose wife, Susannah Snow, was Anglican, built a chapel on his manor of St. Clement for the use of Protestants and endowed it with a glebe of one hundred acres." This would be the first record of an Anglican endowment in Maryland.[10] "In 1654 William Marshall gave the milk and one-half the male increase of three heifers for the maintenance of a minister in the Neck of Wicoco-

---

[7] Jewett, *History of the American Episcopal Church* (New York: Osgood & Co., 1885), Vol. I, p. 317.

[8] *Ibid.*, p. 317.

[9] *Ibid.*, p. 317.

[10] Pennington, *The Church Historical Society*, Publication VII (Ocaldla, Florida, 1934), p. 24.

moco. This was the second endowment of the English Church in Maryland." [11]

Virginia was of course the first permanent colony, and the English coming to Jamestown in 1607 were members of the Church of England. Dale's Laws enacted in 1611 were very strict in their demand that everybody should attend morning and evening prayer. The Parish Church was one of the centers of social as well as religious life. "In this edifice all the people of the entire parish were supposed to assemble every Sabbath morning, and as there was a considerable penalty for remaining away, it is probable that few who were without a good reason to be absent failed to attend." [12] Governor Berkeley in 1671 wrote concerning the quality of ministers sent out by the Church of England: "But of all commodities so of this (the ministers) the worst is sent us." [13] "In 1860 there were said to be forty-eight parishes served by 35 ministers. In 1784 when the church was disestablished, ninety-five organized parishes, and a dozen or more nominal parishes existed." [14] All ministers were paid in tobacco which was really legal tender at this time. In 1750, the price of tobacco rose very high due to a scarcity of crop. A relief act was passed allowing the vestry to pay in terms of the old price, but a bitter protest was made and the law was promptly annulled. [15]

The Church of England was not only the established church of Maryland after 1692, and in Virginia from

---

[11] *Ibid.*, pp. 26, 27.

[12] Bruce, *Social Life in Virginia in the Seventeenth Century* (Lynchburg: J. P. Bell, 1927), p. 244.

[13] Tiffany, *American Church History, The Episcopalians* (New York, 1895), p. 32.

[14] Latourette, *op. cit.*, p. 207.

[15] Tiffany, *op. cit.*, p. 43.

the beginning, but it was the established church in North Carolina, South Carolina, and Georgia.

In Charleston, in 1680, "A piece of land was granted by private parties, Reginald Jackson and his wife, Millicent, as a site for the erection of a building in which the services of the Church of England were to be celebrated. In the following year a church of black cypress upon a brick foundation, large and stately, was built and was called by the name of St. Philip.[16] Samuel Marshal was made rector and paid 150 pounds per year, and the Assembly directed that a Negro man and woman and four cows and calves be purchased for his use, and paid out of the public treasury." [17]

In 1689, Henry Compton, Lord Bishop of London, instituted the practice of appointing commissaries who would exercise delegated authority in the colonies. The first commissaries were James Blair, appointed in 1689, and Thomas Bray, appointed in 1696. These commissaries were to exercise ecclesiastical authority in places that were too far removed from the Bishop's Consistory Court to be summoned there.[18] The appointment of Thomas Bray had very far-reaching consequences. Although appointed in 1696, he did not go out at once. He undertook to find ministers who would go but found only poor men responded. These men Bray knew could not secure books which would keep them alive and growing. So he reported to the Bishops the condition he found, and suggested that a library for each such minister was indispensable. The Bishops evidently agreed, for Bray was soon at work raising funds for his new

---

[16] Tiffany, *op. cit.*, pp. 224-225.

[17] *Ibid.*, p. 225.

[18] Pennington, *The Church Historical Society*, Publication No. VII (Ocala, Florida, 1934), pp. 6-7.

venture. Princess Anne, of Denmark, after whom An-
napolis was named, gave him one of his first large contributions. These libraries were to be located in the
rectory, and a later plan by Bray made them lending
libraries. Bray thus became the father of the library
movement in America.[19] Out of this movement grew
Bray's Society for Promoting Christian Knowledge, and
in 1701 the Society for the Propagation of the Gospel
in Foreign Parts, usually known as the S.P.G.[20] This
Society became the active agent of the Church of England
in the colonies. For more than eighty years, from 1702 to
1782, the majority of the Church of England missionaries
in the American colonies were chosen, sent over, and in
great measure supported by the S.P.G. Three hundred
and nine men were employed during that period in the
Society's Service in America. The colonies of New
England received eighty-four; New York, fifty-eight;
Pennsylvania and Delaware, forty-seven; New Jersey,
forty-four; South Carolina, fifty-four; North Carolina,
thirty-three; and Georgia, thirteen.[21]

The program of the Society for the Propagation of
the Gospel in Foreign Parts divided its work into three
branches: First, "the care and instruction of our people
settled in the colonies," second, "the conversion of the
Indian savages," and third, "the conversion of the
Negroes."[22] The first missionary sent out was Rev.
Samuel Thomas, sent to work with Yammosee Indians
in South Carolina, but the Governor, Sir Nathaniel
Johnson, sent him to care for the people on the branches

---

[19] Pennington, *op. cit.*, p. 10.
[20] *Ibid.*, passim.
[21] *Ibid.*, p. 41.
[22] C. C. Jones, *The Religious Instruction of the Negroes in the
United States* (Savannah: Thomas Purse, 1842), p. 9.

of the Cooper River with headquarters at Goose Creek.[23] He reported to the Society that he had taken much pains also in instructing the Negroes and taught twenty of them to read.[24] Dr. Le Jeau (sometimes spelled Le Jeon or Le Jan) who succeeded on Rev. Thomas' death in 1706, found "parents and masters indued with much good will and a ready disposition to have their children and slaves taught the Christian Religion. "He instructed and baptized many Negroes and Indian slaves." His communicants in 1714 included seventy English and eight Negroes.[25] Le Jeau died in 1717, and was succeeded by Rev. Ludlam, who said many of the Negroes understood English well, and "if the masters of them would heartily concur to forward so good a work, all those who have been born in this country might without much difficulty be instructed and received into the church." [26] However, all found some masters objected to religious instruction of their slaves lest on becoming Christians and receiving baptism they might claim their freedom. Le Jeau wrote that there were notable exceptions to this attitude and that many masters and mistresses zealously seconded his efforts to evangelize their servants. Le Jeau in order to allay the fear of masters that baptism would free their slaves required all slaves before baptism to subscribe to the following declaration: "You declare in the presence of God and before this congregation that you do not ask for the Holy Baptism out of any design to free yourself from the duty and obedience you owe to your master while you live; but merely for the good of your soul and to partake of the grace and

---

[23] *Ibid.*, p. 10.
[24] Jones, *op. cit.*, p. 10.
[25] *Ibid.*
[26] *Ibid.*

blessings promised to the members of the Church of Christ." [27]

Le Jeau said that, "Masters were generally of the opinion that a slave grows worse by being a Christian." [28] There was objection to allowing them to assemble together because "they would thereby have an opportunity of knowing their own strength and superiority in point of numbers." [29] In 1712, the Assembly passed a law for the better governing of Negroes and slaves. It provided: "Since charity and the Christian religion which we profess obliges us to wish well to the souls of all men, and that religion may not be made a pretense, to alter any man's property and rights, and that no person may neglect to baptize their Negroes or slaves, or suffer them to be baptized, for fear that they should be manumitted, and set free, be it therefore enacted that it shall be and is hereby declared lawful for any Negro or Indian slaves or slaves, or any other slave or slaves whatsoever, to receive and profess the Christian faith and be thereunto baptized. But that notwithstanding such slave shall receive and profess the Christian religion and be baptized, he or they shall not thereby be manumitted or set free of his or their owner, nor shall master or mistress, lose his or their civil rights, property, and authority over such slave or slaves, with respect to his or their servitude, they shall remain and continue in the same state and condition that he or they was in before the making of this act." [30]

An act was passed in 1710 which provided for the erection of a church at Goose Creek, but in 1720, it was

---

[27] Jewett, *op. cit.*, Vol. I, p. 380 (quoting S. C. MSS pp. 242-243).
[28] Jewett, *op. cit.*, p. 382.
[29] *Ibid.*
[30] *Ibid.*, p. 383.

declared that the church was in such bad condition that a new church must be erected, "therefore, an additional duty was laid for the purpose of completing the church on rum, brandy, and other spirits and on Negroes imported for sale." [31]

The S.P.G. established a catechetical school in New York in 1704, it being computed that there were 1500 Negroes there at that time. Mr. Elias Neau, a French Hugenot, was appointed catechist. He conformed to the English church and became one of their most noted teachers. "Nothing is more praiseworthy, either in the history of the Venerable Society (S.P.G.) or of the annals of Trinity Church (of New York) than the care and attention given to the Indian natives and the Negro slaves of New York. During its connection with the province the Venerable Society employed sixteen clergymen and thirteen lay readers for the helpless and ignorant classes. Trinity Church from the very start maintained and persuaded the Venerable Society to maintain catechists and schoolmasters for Indians and Negroes." [32] We have reports of a Mr. Honeyman, sent out by the S.P.G. to Providence, who baptized two Negroes in 1724. [33]

About this time we find in the records of the Society this statement: "It is a matter of commendation to the clergy that they have done thus much in so great and difficult a work. But alas! what is the instruction of a few hundreds in several years, with respect to the many thousands uninstructed and unconverted." [34]

Dr. Gibson, the Bishop of London to whom the

[31] Jewett, *op. cit.*, p. 383.
[32] Tiffany, *op. cit.*, p. 177.
[33] Jones, *op. cit.*, p. 13.
[34] *Ibid.*, p. 14.

religious care of the plantations was committed, wrote
two famous letters in 1727, one to the masters and mistresses on the plantations and the other to the missionaries. These letters were an earnest plea for the salvation of their slaves. The one to the masters said in part,
"The care of the plantations abroad being committed
to the Bishop of London, as to religious affairs, I have
thought it my duty to make inquiries into the state of
Religion in those parts; and to learn among other things,
what number of slaves are employed within the several
governments, and what means are used for their instruction in the Christian faith. I find the numbers are prodi-
giously great, and am not a little troubled to observe
how small a progress has been made in a Christian country toward the delivering of those poor creatures from
the pagan darkness and superstition in which they were
bred, and making them partakers of the light of the
gospel and of the blessings and benefits belonging to
it." [35] He then goes on to enumerate the difficulties that
are supposed to make the work impossible; first, that
most of the slaves were adults steeped in superstition
before being brought to America; second, that they cannot speak or understand the English language; third,
that some of the masters deliberately hinder their slaves
from being instructed in the Christian faith, partly because they do not want to give them time, and partly
from lack of interest. The fear that baptism may liberate
the slaves is discussed and he says, "The freedom which
Christianity gives is a freedom from the bondage of sin
and Satan and from the dominion of men's lusts and
passions and inordinate desires," but as to bondage, "it
makes no manner of change in it."

---

[35] Jones, *op. cit.*, p. 16.

He further reminds them that as Christian masters they must remember that they have a great opportunity to extend the Kingdom of Christ, and they must remember that the slaves are men and women with souls capable of being made eternally happy. He exhorts the masters most of all that they teach the slaves by their own Christian example.[36]

To the missionaries he writes on the same day, May 19, 1727, that he has written to the masters urging their cooperation, and he cannot conceive that he really needs to urge the missionaries to have zeal in this work. However, he admonishes them not to think themselves too busy in other tasks to give time to the slaves; he urges those ministers who themselves own slaves to use their best endeavors to instruct them in Christian faith; and adds that all Christian schoolmasters help in this great work.[37]

Bishop Berkeley went in person to the colonies and was in Rhode Island from 1728 to 1730. He finds that most of the Negroes do not secure religious instruction, and that there is an "ancient antipathy and irrational contempt for the blacks." He finds also the old notion, that baptism and slaves are incompatible, is still abroad. He said, to answer this, he had gotten the King's attorney and the Solicitor General to send signed statements to the colony of Rhode Island, saying that baptism did not free slaves.[38]

Bishop Sicker, in 1741, reports that in forty years great multitudes of Negroes and Indians had been brought over to the Christian faith.[39] A most remark-

---

[36] Jones, *op. cit.*, pp. 16-25.
[37] *Ibid.*, pp. 25-27.
[38] *Ibid.*, p. 28.
[39] *Ibid.*, p. 29.

able record of a single parish is given by Mr. Bishop,
late secretary of the American Church Institute for
Negroes, where he says he saw in the register of Bruton
Parish (Williamsburg, Va.) thirty-three pages consecu-
tively devoted to the entry of the baptisms of Negro
servants and children extending from 1746 to 1797 and
containing 1122 names.[40] Bishop Bratton thinks the first
reported Negro Episcopal Church was organized in
Philadelphia in 1791.[41]

During the entire colonial period there were re-
peated efforts to have a resident bishop or bishops in the
colonies. The northern colonies seemed much more
eager for this than were the southern colonies. The
northern ministers were more staunch loyalists than were
the southern ministers, though many southern clergymen were loyalists in spirit. However, the pressure in
the South was such that the Church on the whole was
pro-revolutionary.

Monross thinks this attitude in the South was largely
due to the friction between the planter class and the
proletariat or common man who were in the great majority and because they envied and hated the planters
who were Episcopalians, were opposed to the growing
power of the Episcopal Church, and most of all opposed
to any bishop of the Established Church who would
become a charge upon the community. Virginia early
deprived the church of its glebes.[42] In South Carolina
fifteen out of twenty Church of England clergymen

---

[40] Rt. Rev. T. D. Bratton, *Wanted: Leaders* (New York, 1922), p.
181.
[41] *Ibid.*, p. 181.
[42] Monross, *History of the American Episcopal Church* (Morehouse Publishing Co., 1835).

were pro-revolutionary.[43] James Madison in Virginia, later the first bishop of Virginia, was a revolutionist, and Robert Smith of South Carolina, also later a bishop, was banished by the British because of his revolutionary tendencies.[44] In all the southern states the Church was disestablished either during the revolution or immediately following.[45] Maryland deprived the clergy of any public support in 1779.[46]

In 1780, a small group, clergy and laymen, assembled in Maryland and voted to call the body which it represented the Protestant Episcopal Church.[47] Out of a rather difficult struggle, particularly between Connecticut and the other colonies, the American Church finally achieved unity in 1789.[48]

In 1791, a group of Negroes in Philadelphia founded a benevolent society, "bought a lot, erected a building which they called St. Thomas and by an almost unanimous ballot voted itself into the Episcopal Church, upon three conditions named in their petition to Bishop White. These were: First that they should be received as a body; secondly, that they should forever have local self-control; and thirdly, that one of their number should be chosen as lay reader, and if found worthy, be regularly ordained as their minister. Bishop White accepted their conditions and on July 17, 1794, St. Thomas Church was formally opened for services. Absolam Jones was chosen for ordination and ordained a deacon in 1795, and priest

---

[43] *Ibid.*, p. 181.
[44] Monross, *op. cit.*, p. 182.
[45] *Ibid.*, p. 183.
[46] *Ibid.*, p. 186.
[47] *Ibid.*
[48] *Ibid.*, p. 199.

shortly after—the first Negro ordained in the Episcopal Church in America." [49]

Following the organization of the American Church there was a considerable period of weakness and depression. Tiffany, in his history of the Protestant Episcopal Church calls it a "Period of suspended animation and feeble growth." [50] But so far as the records go there was no slackening of interest on the part of the Church in Negro religious life. By 1810, the Church in South Carolina could report 193 colored communicants in Charleston alone, 120 in St. Philips, and 73 in St. Michaels.[51] In 1817, South Carolina reported 328 colored Episcopalians.[52] In 1823, we find Bishop Dehon, of South Carolina, of whom it was said: "In his own congregation he was the laborious and patient minister of the African; and he encouraged among the masters and mistresses in his flock that best kindness toward their servants—a concern for their eternal salvation." [53]

In this same year, Rev. Dr. Dalcho, of the Episcopal Church in Charleston, published a pamphlet on "Practical considerations founded on the scriptures relative to the slave population of South Carolina." His purpose was "to show from the scriptures of the Old and New Testaments, that slavery is not forbidden by Divine Law, and at the same time to prove the necessity of giving religious instruction to our Negroes." [54] Dr. Dalcho tells us he had 316 colored communicants and 200 children in the colored Sunday School. In 1833, Rev.

---

[49] Bratton, *op. cit.*, pp. 181-182.
[50] Tiffany, *op. cit.*, Ch. 14.
[51] Jones, *op. cit.*, p. 58.
[52] *Ibid.*, p. 62.
[53] *Ibid.*, p. 69.
[54] Jones, *op. cit.*, p. 69.

Joseph Walker, of Beaufort, South Carolina, reported 57 Negro communicants and 234 members of the colored Sunday School.[55] In that same year, Bishop Ives of North Carolina urged upon his convention the importance "of providing for our slave population a more adequate knowledge of the doctrines of Christ Crucified." [56] In 1834, the second annual report of the Liberty County (Georgia) Association, which was organized to give religious instruction to slaves, calls attention to the work of Bishop Meade, who was then Assistant Bishop of the Episcopal Church in Virginia. It says he had published an admirable pastoral letter to the ministers, members and friends of the Protestant Episcopal Church in Virginia, on the duty of affording religious instruction to those in bondage." [57] "In 1836, Bishop Meade collected and published sermons, dialogues and narratives for servants to be read to them in families." [58] In 1837, Dr. Gadsden (later Bishop), with others, published a Catechism to be used by Episcopalians in instructing their slaves in religion.[59] In 1838, the South Carolina Convention of the Protestant Episcopal Church resolved, "That it be respectfully recommended to the members of the Church who are proprietors of slaves individually and collectively, to take measures for the support of clerical missionaries and lay catechists, who are members of our church, for the religious instruction of their slaves. That it be urged upon the rectors and vestries of the country parishes to exert themselves to obtain the

---

[55] *Ibid.*, p. 74.
[56] *Ibid.*, p. 75.
[57] Harrison and Barnes, *The Gospel Among the Slaves* (Nashville: Publishing House of the M. E. Church South, 1893), p. 80.
[58] *Ibid.*, p. 82.
[59] *Ibid.*, p. 83.

services of such missionaries and lay catechists." [60] In 1841, Bishop Meade made an extended report to the Virginia Convention on "the best means of promoting the religious instruction of servants" and Bishop Gadsden of South Carolina spoke at length in his Episcopal Address of the fact that they had many masters in the Church whose slaves were not yet Christians and that "To make these fellow creatures, who share with us the precious redemption by Jesus Christ, good Christians, is a purpose of which the church is not and never has been regardless." He continued in his address to say, "I speak more particularly of those the smoke of whose cabins is in sight of our ministers who live on the same plantations with members of our church." He reminds them that twenty-two out of thirty-one Episcopal churches in the Convention have colored members—a total of 869. He tells them these churches have fifteen Sunday Schools for Negroes with 1,459 scholars, that there are two missions to Negroes embracing 1,400 in their congregations, and that eight of the clergy preach regularly on plantations in addition to their own colored congregations. He commends the churches for their baptism of colored children and tells them 159 colored children had been baptized in one diocese during that year.[61]

This is a fairly typical report of the activities of Episcopal churches. In the annual report of the Association for the Religious Instruction of Negroes in Liberty County, Georgia, one can find some indication of the pervasiveness of this work among Episcopalians. In the diocese of Alabama twelve out of eighteen par-

---

[60] Harrison and Barnes, *op. cit.*, p. 83.
[61] *Ibid.*, pp. 86, 87.

ishes reporting contain notices of attention to the Negroes. Bishop Otey of Tennessee and Mississippi writes, "The work in which you have been so long and so arduously engaged is one which deeply interests me"; one planter in Mississippi offered $500 and board annually for the services of an Episcopal clergyman on his plantation; Bishop Elliott of Georgia said he had full opportunity to work on plantations but that it was difficult to get workers to devote themselves to this work; the settled clergy of the diocese of South Carolina were said to include servants in their regular services, and Bishop Whittington of Maryland claimed that half of his clergy "reported Negro baptisms, marriages, and funerals." [62] Some illumination is thrown on the attitude and work of the Episcopal Church by a picture drawn by a Miss Kate Conyngham who came from Connecticut to be governess to the daughter of Colonel Peyton at Overton Lodge, near Nashville, Tennessee, in 1853. She attends the Episcopal service on the plantation and writes home as follows:

> The second Sunday after I came here I was invited to attend service in the chapel with the family. Upon entering it, I found the body of the floor occupied by the black men and women of the plantation, seated in chairs with the utmost decency and quiet, and all neatly and cleanly attired. We took our seats in the gallery, while Isabel (Col. Peyton's daughter) placed herself at the organ to play a voluntary. Until the old gentleman who officiated entered, I had time to look at the interior of this bijou of a church. On the right of the chancel was an exquisite group of statuary, executed in Italy expressly for this chapel by the colonel's order, at an expense of $800. It represented the Madonna and her child. On the opposite side was a table of the purest white marble, surmounted by

---

[62] W. D. Weatherford, *The Negro From Africa to America* (Doran, 1924), p. 317.

a dove with its wings extended. It was a memento of the death of a little son of the colonel. There were no pews in the body of the church, only low chairs of oak, a chair to each worshiper, with an aisle between.

The service was very solemn, and my Puritanic objections to praying from a prayer-book, have been wholly removed by this day's experience. The singing was very remarkable. The African women all sing well, having harmony with it, the effect was very fine. "Is it possible," I asked myself, "that these are slaves? Is it possible that this rich voice which leads in such manly tones is their master's? Is it possible that the fair girl who united, by an accompaniment upon the organ, her praises with theirs, is one of the 'haughty daughters of the South?'" [63]

We must now look briefly at the struggle in the Episcopal Church over slavery. Like all the other churches its membership was divided on the question of whether slavery was right or wrong. We have seen that the southern parishes and dioceses were very zealous in their effort to give religious instruction to slaves. But many of these churchmen owned slaves and felt they had done their whole Christian duty when they cared for their moral and religious life. The matter of the attitude of the Church officially was sharply brought out by an incident in connection with theological training. In 1839, Alexander Crummell, a colored man, applied for admission into the General Theological Seminary and took up residence in the Commons. Although there was no specific ruling against his entry, the Bishop advised him to withdraw from the Commons and attend classes as a visitor. This Crummell refused to do on the grounds of self-respect. The matter finally came to the

[63] Weatherford and Johnson, *Race Relations* (D. C. Heath and Company, 1934), p. 174 (quoted from Joseph H. Ingraham, *The Sunny South*, or *The Southerner at Home*, pp. 67, 68).

Bishops and all except Bishop Doane sustained the resident Bishop.[64] This incident drew attention to the growing tension in the Church, but fortunately the Church remained united right up to the Civil War. When the southern states seceded, Bishop Meade of Virginia and Bishop Otey of Tennessee opposed the move but joined with their states in loyal support once this step had been taken. Bishop Wilmer, in his Reminescences, speaks of Bishop Meade and Robert E. Lee as men who loved the Union with a deep devotion.[65]

In 1861, the representatives of the Episcopal Church in South Carolina, Georgia, Florida, Mississippi, and Texas met in Montgomery, Alabama, and resolved, "That an independent church was necessary." After drawing up a tentative constitution and canons, they adjourned to meet in October. In accordance with this action, ten bishops convened at Columbia, South Carolina, and Bishop Meade was elected Chairman. The constitution was adopted and submitted. The church was to be called the Protestant Episcopal Church in the Confederate States. R. H. Wilmer was elected Bishop of Alabama and consecrated by Bishop Meade. But the Church of the North refused to concede that the Church was divided. In the convention held in 1862, the names of the southern dioceses were called just as if their representatives were expected to be present. Bishop Hopkins of Vermont claimed that the southern states had a right to secede if it seemed to their best interest. There was less of harsh criticism of the southern states than had been expressed in some other church bodies. This irenic

---

[64] Wilberforce, *History of the Protestant Episcopal Church in America* (New York: Thomas Whittaker, 1887), p. 32.

[65] Wilmer, *The Recent Past* (New York: Thomas Whittaker, 1887), p. 32.

temper helped much to smooth ruffled feelings and bring
the southern dioceses back. Before the convention of
1865, Bishop Hopkins, who had become the presiding
bishop, wrote letters to all the southern bishops inviting
them to the convention and assuring them of a warm
welcome. The Bishop of North Carolina responded.
When the convention opened the secretary called the
names of all the southern dioceses just as in 1862. Tennessee, North Carolina, and Texas responded.

Bishop Wilmer of Alabama wrote a full and irenic
letter to Bishop Hopkins explaining why he could not
answer his call. He calls Bishop Hopkins' attention to
the fact that he (Hopkins) has referred in his letter of
1861 and in the letter of 1865 to the Protestant Episcopal
Church in the Confederate States as a schismatical move.
This Bishop Wilmer denies and holds that it was just
as legitimate as the separation of the American Church
from the Church of England. He claims it is a division
of legislative function but not a separation from the
Church. He also denies that it was a *wilful and needless
separation*. He further calls attention to the fact that
those who had organized the Church in the Confederate
States had been called "rebels and traitors." He therefore thought it wise to wait and see what the temper
of the general convention would be.[66]

Bishop Atkinson and Lay from the South did attend
the general convention, but before doing so assured
themselves that the action of the Southern Church in
electing Wilmer Bishop of Alabama would be ratified.[67]
The fact that some of the southern bishops did attend
the convention eased the tension in the North, and the

---

[66] Wilmer, *op. cit.*, pp. 153-165.
[67] *Ibid.*, pp. 148, 149.

fact that Bishop Wilmer's election was accepted as valid, eased the tension in the South, so that the way was open for a gradual reunion, and the Protestant Episcopal Church in the Confederate States, by inertia ceased to exist. Most Episcopalians prefer to claim that the church never was divided. That, one can interpret to his own liking, but at least the division was quickly healed, if it did exist. On this point Monross gives a full discussion in his *History of the American Episcopal Church.*

Bishop Bratton, in his volume on *Wanted: Leaders,* points out that a number of independent Negro Episcopal churches had been organized before the Civil War, such as St. Thomas in Philadelphia, 1791; St. Philips Church in New York, 1819; Christ's Church in Providence, R. I., 1843; St. Luke's in New Haven, 1844; Calvary Church in Charleston, 1849; St. Matthews in Detroit, Michigan, 1850; St. Stephens in Savannah, Georgia, 1856; and others.[68] This tendency was more marked after the Civil War. "The Negroes themselves had spoken by their actions, in refusing any longer to attend the white man's services. Plainly this indicated a desire for churches of their own, with local self-government such as had already been found palatable in political life." [69] Bishop Bratton quotes Bishop Howe as saying to his convention in 1873, "Let a missionary jurisdiction be erected by the General Convention with express reference to these people, and let a missionary bishop be consecrated who will give his whole time and thought to this work; who as the executive, not of a single diocese but of the whole Church, shall organize congregations, provide them with church schools and pastors, and in due time raise up from the colored people themselves,

---

[68] Bratton, *op. cit.,* pp. 181-185.
[69] *Ibid.,* p. 192.

deacons and priests who shall be educated men, and competent to the work of the ministry, and I cannot but think good would result." [70]

About 1873, a controversy arose in the Church, not as to the Negro's full membership, but as to his franchise in the deliberations of the Church. To the Negro, his standing in the Church was closely connected with his right to attendance and vote in the General Convention. South Carolina partly met this by establishing "in 1888 a separate Archdeaconry, where voice and vote and conference with the Bishop would be free." [71]

The question was also up as to the ability of the newly emancipated Negro to measure up to the priesthood. "Prior to 1865 only fourteen Negroes had been ordained to the priesthood." [72] Bishop Bratton says that of twenty-seven Negro clergy ordained between 1866 and 1880, seventeen were in the South, but while assuring the Negro he was welcome in the Church, it did not bring numbers of members into the Church.[73]

Bragg, one of the historians of the Negro's part in the post-war Church, admits that "in all the southern country the Episcopal Church was the only religious body of white men setting an example of absolute equality in the family of Jesus Christ." [74] But Bragg feels that there was a growing fear on the part of white Episcopalians lest the Church might be flooded by Negro members. The storm broke when St. Mark's Church in Charleston, South Carolina, asked to be admitted into

---

[70] Bratton, *op. cit.*, pp. 192, 193.
[71] *Ibid.*, p. 196.
[72] *Ibid.*, p. 196.
[73] *Ibid.*, p. 197.
[74] Bragg, *History of the Afro-American Group of the Episcopal Church* (Baltimore: Church Advocate Press, 1922), p. 150.

full union with the Diocesan Convention.[75] In 1883, the Sewanee Conference was held to try to arrive at some settled policy on the question of extension of the Church among Negroes. Unfortunately, no Negro delegates were present in this meeting.[76] "The Sewanee plan authorized the segregation in any diocese of the colored people under the direction and authority of the diocesan, with such missionary organization as might be necessary for its purposes. The Negro Conference of colored clergy and laity, which assembled in New York City, the month previous to the assembling of the General Convention, presented a united front against the Sewanee Canon, and appointed a committee to attend the General Convention and exert every means in their power to defeat the proposed canon." [77]

The Sewanee Canon was defeated, but due to the spirit of the grandfather clauses in politics, Bragg thinks, many dioceses began to act on the implication of the Sewanee Canon.

"The Church Commission for Work Among Colored People was created by the General Convention in 1886." [78] While the work immediately began to make progress, it seemed pitiful as compared with what the Church was doing before the Civil War.[79] In Florida by 1922, there were missions all the way from the northern border to Key West. By this same date North Carolina had thirty-nine Negro congregations. Maryland had sixteen; South Carolina had twenty-five congregations

---

[75] Bragg, *op. cit.*, p. 151.
[76] *Ibid.*, p. 151.
[77] *Ibid.*, pp. 151, 152.
[78] *Ibid.*, p. 198.
[79] *Ibid.*, p. 198.

and thirteen schools by 1922. Virginia had forty-three churches; Georgia had twenty-two.[80]

The growth of Negro ministers and of Negro membership tended to emphasize the discrimination and brought the Church face to face with the race problem. Negro churches and ministers felt they were discriminated against and southern white churches and ministers felt it would be wise to give a Negro episcopate and separate churches to the Negro people. This was resisted by the General Convention where the northern vote was in the majority. Finally, however, some of the northern dioceses found the work too heavy for one bishop so they were willing to elect suffragans, who would have seats with the House of Bishops, but not votes, and with no assurance that they would succeed to the Bishopric on the death of the Bishop. This gave a way for Negroes to be elected as suffragans, which helped to satisfy the desires of the Negro churches. This ruling became effective for southern dioceses which desired to take advantage of it in 1918.[81] Bishop Bratton thought in 1922 that this did not fully satisfy the Negro churches but he did feel it was a long step toward bringing peace and harmony in the life of that section of the Church located in the South.[82]

At the present time the Church Institute for Negroes is the chief representative of the Protestant Episcopal Church in carrying forward this interest which has always characterized this Church. A fuller statement of the work of this Institute has been set forth in Chapter IX.

Thus, we see that the Episcopal Church has a long

---

[80] Bragg, *op, cit.*, pp. 199, 200.
[81] Bratton, *op. cit.*, p. 224.
[82] *Ibid.*, p. 224.

and continuous history of interest in and work for the religious instruction of colored people. After the Civil War it looked as if it would be the one church which would give the Negro full and equal privileges in his church life and activity. But the bitterness of the Reconstruction Period was too powerful. Perhaps it was too much to expect that any institution could go against the current so strongly flowing toward segregation. Like all the other churches, the Episcopalians had to succumb to the spirit of the times which led to discrimination and unhappy relations. But the spirit of good will seems to be growing again and the future may tell a more hopeful story.

CHAPTER II

THE ATTITUDE OF THE QUAKERS TOWARD THE NEGRO DURING SLAVERY

George Fox, the father and founder of Quakerism, was born at Drayton in the Clay, Lescestershire, England, 1624, and at the age of twenty-three (1647) "commenced his public appearance as minister of the Gospel, at Ducenfield, Manchester and places in the neighborhood." [1] From the very beginning, Fox had a deep social concern. In 1649, he writes: "About this time I was exercised in going to courts to cry for justice, in speaking and writing to judges and justices to do justly; in warning such as kept public houses for entertainment, that they should not let people have more drink than would do them good; in testifying against wakes, feasts, May games, sports, plays, and shows, which trained people up to vanity, etc." [2] So keen was this social sense in George Fox that Holder, the historian of Quakerism, could write: "The Quakers were pioneers in 1656 in every dominant reform normal men and women are fighting for in 1913." [3] "They demanded arbitration in place of war in 1660, political and religious freedom, and there is not a great moral reform from capital punishment to the equality of women, or the freedom of slaves to civic righteousness, worked for today by organ-

---

[1] *Friends' Library* (Joseph Rakestraw, 1837), Vol. I, pp. 22, 30.
[2] *Ibid.*, p. 32.
[3] Charles Frederick Holder, *The Quakers in Great Britain and America* (Los Angeles: The Neuner Company, 1913), Preface, p. 13.

ized forces, that the Quakers had not thought of, and were demanding from the housetops two hundred and fifty years ago." [4]

Our record of the part the Society of Friends, usually called Quakers, has played in the slave question begins with the journey of George Fox to the Barbadoes in 1671. He was accompanied on the journey by Thomas Briggs, William Edmunson, John Rouse, John Stubbs, Soloman Eccles, James Lancaster, John Cartwright, Robert Widders, George Pattison, John Hull, Elizabeth Hooten, and Elizabeth Miers.[5]

Soon after landing on the island he became deeply interested in the welfare of the Negroes, his first injunction being:

> "Respecting their negroes, I desired them to endeavor to train them up in the fear of God, as well those that were bought with their money, as them that were born in their families, that all might come to the knowledge of the Lord; that so, with Joshua, every master of a family might say: 'as for me and my house, we will serve the Lord.' I desired also that they would cause their overseers to deal mildly and gently with their negroes, and not use cruelty towards them, as the manner of some hath been and is; and that after certain years of servitude they should make them free." [6]

It is noted in the foregoing quotation that there was a tendency on the part of planters to make a distinction in the treatment meted out to slaves born in their own household, and those bought fresh from the slave ships. This same distinction was later made in the American colonies. George Fox stood strongly against this, claim-

---

[4] Holder, *op. cit.*, pp. 13, 14.
[5] *Works of George Fox* (Philadelphia: Marcus T. C. Gould, 1831), Vol. II, p. 108.
[6] *Ibid.*, p. 113.

ing that all were equally human. Naturally, criticisms arose, and we find Fox and a few other Friends drawing up a defense of the Society:

> *"For the Governor of Barbadoes, with his Council and Assembly and all others in power, both civil and military, in this island; from the people called Quakers."* [7]

The first protest derided the "scandal and lie" that the Quakers denied God and Christ Jesus, and the second protest denied that they were stirring up strife among the Slaves:

> "Another slander they have cast upon us, is, that we teach the negroes to rebel; a thing we utterly abhor and detest in our hearts, the Lord knows it, who is the searcher of all hearts, and knows all things, and can testify for us that this is a most abominable untruth. For that which we have spoken to them, is to exhort and admonish them to be sober, to fear God, to love their masters and mistresses, and to be faithful and diligent in their service and business . . . that they should not steal nor be drunk, nor commit adultery, nor fornication, nor curse, swear, nor lie, nor give bad words to one another, nor to anyone else: for there is something in them that tells them they should not practice these nor any other evils . . . We declare that we esteem it a duty incumbent on us, to pray with and for, to teach, instruct and admonish, those in and belonging to our families . . . This wicked slander (of our endeavoring to make negroes rebel) our adversaries took occasion to raise, for our having some meeting amongst the negroes; for we had several meetings with them in divers plantations wherein we exhorted them to justice, sobriety, temperance, chastity, and piety, and to be subject to their masters and governors. Which was altogether contrary to what our envious adversaries maliciously suggested against us." [8]

---

[7] Fox, *op. cit.*, p. 117.
[8] *Ibid.*, pp. 119, 120.

George Fox evidently made a great impression on the planters of Barbadoes for in 1676, under Governor Atkins, they passed a law, entitled "An Act to prevent the people called Quakers from bringing their negroes into their meetings for worship though they held these in their own houses." [9] Godwyn, the early historian of the Colonial Church, mentions an officious Quaker who had put into his hand "a petty Reformanda Pamphlet on this subject (slavery) in which the question was asked 'who made you a minister of the Gospel to white people only and not to the Tawnies and Blacks also?' " [10]

After Fox returned to England he wrote a letter back to Friends in Barbadoes in which he held up the Jewish law of liberation as a practice to be imitated.[11]

> " 'And if thy brother, an Hebrew man, or an Hebrew woman, be sold unto thee, and serve thee six years, then in the seventh year thou shalt let him go free from thee, and when thou sendest him out free from thee, thou shalt not let him go away empty: thou shalt furnish him liberally out of thy flock, and out of thy floor, and out of thy winepress, of that wherewith the Lord thy God hath blessed thee, thou shalt give it to him. And remember that thou wast a bondman in the land of Egypt, and the Lord thy God redeemed thee; therefore I command thee this thing today.' Deut. XV: 12, 13, 14, 15 . . . let me tell you, it will doubtless be very acceptable to the Lord, if so be that masters of families here would deal so with their servants the negroes and blacks whom they have bought with their money, to let them go free after a considerable term of years, if they have served them faithfully: and when they go and are made free, let them not go away empty handed."

---

[9] Clarkson, *History of the Rise, Progress and Accomplishment of the Abolition of the African Slave Trade by the British Parliament* (Philadelphia: James P. Parke, 1808), p. 110.

[10] Anderson, *History of the Colonial Church*, Vol. II, p. 495.

[11] Coleman, *A Testimony Against That Anti-Christian Practice of Making Slaves of Men* (New Bedford, Reprinted 1825), pp. 11, 12.

Mary Fisher and Ann Austin, two Quaker women, along with eight other Quakers landed at Massachusetts Bay, August 9, 1656. They were promptly put in jail and soon deported to England, but Christopher Holder and five comrades immediately prepared to go to America, for Quakers were never people to be intimidated. They landed in May, 1857, on Long Island. Sandwich became the pioneer Quaker town in America. The persecution of Quakers by Puritans does not make very happy reading.[12] But their number grew. In 1691, William Penn received his charter for Sylvania, to which the King added Penn's name making it Pennsylvania.[13] The first yearly meeting was held in Pennsylvania in 1681. A meeting was early established in Germantown for which we have perhaps the first official protest against slavery.[14]

"GERMANTOWN FRIENDS' PROTEST AGAINST SLAVERY, 1688.

"This is to Ye Monthly Meeting Held at Richard Worrell's.

"These are the reasons why we are against the traffic of menbody, as followeth. Is there any that would be done or handled at this manner? viz., to be sold or made a slave for all the time of his life? How fearful and faint-hearted are many on sea, when they see a strange vessel, being afraid it should be a Turk, and they should be taken, and sold for slaves into Turkey. Now what is this better done, as Turks doe? Yea, rather is it worse for them, which say they are Christians; for we hear that ye most part of such negers are brought hither against their will and consent, and that many of them are stolen. Now, tho they are black, we can not

---

[12] Holder, *op. cit.*, Ch. 17, 18.
[13] *Ibid.*, p. 498.
[14] Quoted from A. C. Thomas pamphlet, *The Attitude of the Society of Friends Towards Slavery* (Knickerbocker Press, 1897), pp. 295-297.

conceive there is more liberty to have them slaves, as it is to have other white ones. There is a saying, that we shall doe to all men like as we will be done ourselves; making no difference of what generation, descent or colour they are. And those who steal or robb men, and those who buy or purchase them, are they not all alike? Here is liberty of conscience, wch is right and reasonable; here ought to be likewise liberty of ye body, except of evil-doers wch is an other case. But to bring men hither, or to rob and sell them against their will, we stand against."

"Now consider well this thing, if it is good or bad? And in case you find it to be good to handel these blacks at that manner, we desire and require you hereby lovingly, that you may inform us herein which at this time never was done, viz., that Christians have such a liberty to do so. To the end we shall be satisfied in this point, and satisfie likewise our good friend and acquaintances in our natif country, to whose it is a terror, or faithful thing, that men should be handled so in Pennsylvania.

"This is from our meeting at Germantown, held ye 18 of the 2 month, 1688, to be delivered to the Monthly Meeting at Richard Worrel's.

> Garret Henderich
> derick up dengraeff
> Francis daniell Pastorius
> Abraham up Den graef

"At our Monthly Meeting at Dublin, ye 30—2 mo., 1688, we having inspected ye matter, above mentioned, and considered of it, we find it so weighty that we think it not expedient for us to meddle with it here, but do rather commit it to ye consideration of ye Quarterly Meeting; ye tenor of it being nearly related to ye Truth.

> On behalf of ye Monthly Meeting,
> Signed, P. Jo Hart.

"This, above mentioned, was read in our Quarterly Meeting at Philadelphia, the 4 of ye 4th mo. '88, and was from thence recommended to the Yearly Meeting, and the above said Derick, and the other two mentioned therein, to present the same to ye above said meeting, it being a thing of two great a weight for this meeting to determine.

Signed by order of ye meeting,
Anthony Morris.

"YEARLY MEETING MINUTE ON THE ABOVE PROTEST.

"At a Yearly Meeting held in Burlington the 5th day of the 7th month, 1688.

"A Paper being here presented by some German Friends Concerning the Unlawfulness of Buying and keeping Negroes, It was adjudged not to be so proper for this Meeting to give a Positive Judgment in the Case, It having so General a Relation to many other Parts, and therefore at present they forbear It."

In 1679 and 1690, we find George Fox writing back to Friends in America:

"In an epistle to Friends in America, concerning their Negroes and Indians, written in 1679, he says: 'All Friends, everywhere, that have Indians or Blacks, you are to preach the Gospel to them and other servants, if you be true Christians; for the Gospel of salvation was to be preached to every creature under heaven. Christ commands it to his disciples, 'Go and teach all nations, baptizing them into the name of the Father, Son, and Holy Ghost.' . . .

"And also, you must teach and instruct Blacks and Indians, and others, how that God doth pour out his Spirit upon all flesh in these days of the new covenant, and New Testament." [15]

"Let your light shine among the Indians, the blacks and the whites; that ye may answer the truth in them, and bring them to the standard and ensign, that God hath set up, Christ Jesus . . ." [16]

---

[15] Ed. Evans, Thos. and Wm., *Friends' Library* (Philadelphia: Joseph Rakestraw, 1837), Vol. I, p. 79.
[16] *Works of George Fox*, Vol. II, pp. 359-360.

In 1678 the women of the Society of Friends made a protest against cruelty, against lack of education of Negro children and care of the aged.[17]

In 1711, the Sandwich Monthly Meeting dealt with a woman who was a Quaker, and yet was reputed to be cruel to her slaves:

> "3/30/1711.—Whereas a woman Friend hath given over to hardness of heart to such a degree she hath been not only consenting but encouraging the unmerciful whipping or beating of her negro man servant, he being stript naked, and hanged up by the hands, in his master's house, and then beating him, or whipping him so unmercifully that it is to be feared that it was in some measure the occasion of his death that followed soon after, the which we do account is not only unchristian but inhuman for which cause we find ourselves concerned to testify to the world that we utterly disown all such actions, and particularly (sic) the Friend above mentioned." [18]

Up to the first part of the eighteenth century, the Quakers contented themselves with urging that the slaves be treated humanely, that they be given some education, that they be taught the Christian religion, and that after a reasonable period they should be given freedom. As we noticed in 1688, the Philadelphia Yearly Meeting refused to take action in the question of condemning all slavery. But by the end of the first quarter of the eighteenth century they were ready to condemn all importation of slaves.

In 1714, the Philadelphia Yearly Meeting wrote a rather sharp letter to London Friends in which they say:

---

[17] Minutes of Maryland Half Years Meeting of Women Friends, 1678. Quoted from *Jones Quakers in the American Colonies* (Macmillan, 1911), pp. 321, 322.

[18] Minutes of the Sandwich Monthly Meeting. Quoted from *Jones Quakers in American Colonies*, p. 156.

"We also kindly received your advice about negro slaves, and we are one with you that the multiplying of them may be of dangerous consequence, and therefore a law was made in Pennsylvania, laying a duty of twenty pounds upon every one imported there, which law the Queen was pleased to disannul. We could heartily wish that a way might be found to stop the bringing in more here; or at least that Friends may be less concerned in buying or selling of any that may be brought in; and hope for your assistance with the government, if any farther law should be made, discouraging the importation. We know not of any Friend amongst us, that has any hand or concern in bringing any out of their own country; and we are of the same mind with you, that the practice is not commendable nor allowable amongst Friends; and we take the freedom to acquaint you, that our request unto you was, that you would be pleased to consult or advise with Friends in other plantations, where they are more numerous than with us; because they hold a correspondence with you but not with us, and your meeting may better prevail with them, and your advice prove more effectual." [19]

In 1727, the Nantucket Meeting passed the following minutes:

"It is the sense of this meeting that the importation of Negroes from their native country and relations,* is not a commendable nor allowable practice and that practice is centured by this meeting." [20]

From this data on the Monthly and Quarterly and Yearly Meetings began to take strong stands against buying and selling of slaves. In 1729, the Chester Monthly Meeting:

---

[19] *Brief Statement of the Rise and Progress of the Testimony of the Religious Society of Friends Against Slavery and the Slave Trade* (Philadelphia: Joseph and William Kite, 1843), p. 11.

[20] Nantucket Monthly Meeting, *Book of Discipline* (Providence: John Carter, 1785), p. 101. (The * after the word relations refers to a footnote, "This intended as slaves or against their consent." Note also that Negro is here first spelled with a capital.

" 'offer to the quarterly meeting, that inasmuch as we are restricted by a rule of discipline from being concerned in fetching or importing negro slaves from their own country, whether it is not as reasonable we should be restricted from buying of them when imported; and if so, and the quarterly meeting see meet, that it may be laid before the Yearly Meeting for their approbation and concurrence.' The substance of this minute was adopted by the quarterly meeting, and sent to the Yearly Meeting of that year, (1729), which deferred the consideration for one year, and in 1730, issued the following advice.

" 'The Friends of this meeting resuming the consideration of the proposition of Chester meeting, relating to the purchasing of such negroes as may hereafter be imported; and having reviewed and considered the former minutes relating thereto, and having maturely deliberated thereon, are now of opinion, that Friends ought to be very cautious of making any such purchases for the future, it being disagreeable to the sense of this meeting. And this meeting recommends it to the care of the several monthly meetings, to see that such who may be, or are likely to be found in that practice, may be admonished and cautioned how they offend herein.' " [21]

In 1713, Anthony Benezet was born in France and in 1731 he removed to America where he became a Quaker in 1736.[22] In 1720, John Woolman was born in Burlington County, West Jersey. These two men were destined to become two of the greatest influences in American Quakerism, and more than any other persons were to influence the policy of the Quakers toward slavery.[23]

In 1742, a small storekeeper at Mount Holly in New Jersey, a member of the Friends Society, sold a Negro

[21] Rise and Progress of Religious Society of Friends, pp. 13, 14.

[22] Wilson Armistead, Anthony Benezet (London: A. W. Bennett, 1859).

[23] John G. Whittier, The Journal of John Woolman (Boston: James R. Osgood and Company, 1876).

woman and requested his clerk, John Woolman to make a bill of sale for her.

"On taking up his pen, the young clerk felt a sudden and strong scruple in his mind. The thought of writing an instrument of slavery for one of his fellow creatures oppressed him. God's voice against the desecration of his image spoke in his soul. He yielded to the will of his employer, but while writing the instrument, he was constrained to declare, both to the buyer and to the seller, that he believed slave-keeping inconsistent with the Christian religion." [24]

In 1746, Woolman began preaching and soon made a preaching tour in Maryland, Virginia, and North Carolina. At this time he records in his journal:

"Two things were remarkable to me in this journey: first, in regard to my entertainment; when I eat, drank, and lodged free-cost with people, who lived in ease on the hard labour of their slaves, I felt uneasy; and as my mind was inward to the Lord, I found, from place to place, this uneasiness return upon me, at times, through the whole visit. Where the masters bore a good share of the burthen, and lived frugally, so that their servants were well provided for, and their labour moderate, I felt more easy; but where they lived in a costly way, and laid heavy burthens on their slaves, my exercise was often great, and I frequently had conversation with them, in private, concerning it. Secondly: this trade of importing slaves from their native country being much encouraged amongst them, and the white people and their children so generally living without much labour, was frequently the subject of my serious thoughts; and I saw in these southern provinces so many vices and corruptions, increased by this trade and this way of life, that it appeared to me as a dark gloominess hanging over the land; and though now many willingly run into it, yet in future the consequence will be grievous to posterity; I express it as it hath appeared to me, not at once, nor twice, but as a matter fixed on my mind." [25]

---

[24] Whittier, *op. cit.*, pp. 10, 11.
[25] *The Works of John Woolman* (Philadelphia: Joseph Crukshank, 1775), pp. 23, 24.

Returning from his preaching tour he was again asked (1753) to draw a bill of sale for slaves which he records:

"About this time, a person at some distance lying sick, his brother came to me to write his will: I knew he had slaves and asking his brother, was told he intended to leave them as slaves to his children. As writing is a profitable employ, and as offending sober people was disagreeable to my inclination, I was straitened in my mind; but as I looked to the Lord, he inclined my heart to his testimony: and I told the man, that I believed the practice of continuing slavery to this people was not right; and had a scruple in my mind against doing writings of that kind: that though many in our society kept them as slaves, still I was not easy to be concerned in it; and desired to be excused from going to write the will. . ." [26]

"Near the time the last mentioned friend first spoke to me, a neighbour received a bad bruise in his body, and sent for me to bleed him; which being done, he desired me to write his will: I took notes; and amongst other things, he told me to which of his children he gave his young negro: I considered the pain and distress he was in and knew not how it would end; so I wrote his will, save only that part concerning his slave, and carrying it to his bedside, read it to him; and then told him in a friendly way, that I could not write any instruments by which my fellow-creatures were made slaves, without bringing trouble on my own mind. . ." [27]

The method of persuasion used by John Woolman and other Quakers, in dissuading their fellow Quakers from owning slaves is well set forth in a passage from the Journal, 1757:

"After some further conversation, I said, that men having power, too often misapplied it; that though we made slaves of the negroes, and the Turks made slaves of the Chris-

---

[26] *The Works of John Woolman* (Philadelphia: Joseph Crukshank, 1775), pp. 34, 35.
[27] *Ibid.*, pp. 42, 43.

tians, I however believed that liberty was the natural right of all men equally: which he did not deny; but said, the lives of the negroes were so wretched in their own country, that many of them lived better here than there: I only said, there is great odds in regard to us, on what principle we act; and so the conversation on that subject ended; and I may here add, that another person, some time afterward, mentioned the wretchedness of the negroes, occasioned by their intestine wars as an argument in favour of our fetching them away for slaves: to which I then replied, if compassion on the Africans, in regard to their domestic troubles, were the real motives of our purchasing them, that spirit of tenderness being attended to, would incite us to use them kindly; that as strangers brought out of affliction, their lives might be happy among us; and as they are human creatures, whose souls are as precious as ours, and who may receive the same help and comfort from the holy scriptures as we do, we could not omit suitable endeavors to instruct them therein: but while we manifest by our conduct, that our views in purchasing them are to advance ourselves; and while our buying captives taken in war animates those parties to push on that war, and increase desolation amongst them; to say they lived unhappy in Africa, is far from being an argument in our favour. . ." [28]

In 1754, the Philadelphia Yearly Meeting issued a letter which is supposed to be from the pen of Anthony Benezet. We give excerpts from it:

"Dear Friends. It hath frequently been the concern of our Yearly Meeting, to testify their uneasiness and disunity with the importation and purchasing of negroes and other slaves, and to direct the overseers of the several meetings, to advise and deal with such as engage therein; and it hath likewise been the continued care of many weighty Friends, to press those that bear our name, to guard as much as possible, against being in any respect concerned in promoting the bondage of such unhappy people; yet as we have with sorrow to observe, that their number is of late increased amongst us,

---

[28] *The Works of John Woolman* (Philadelphia: Joseph Crukshank, 1775), pp. 58-60.

we have thought proper to make our advice and judgment more public, that none may plead ignorance of our principles therein; and also again earnestly exhort all, to avoid in any manner encouraging that practice, of making slaves of our fellow-creatures.

"Now, dear Friends, if we continually bear in mind the royal law of 'doing to others as we would be done by', we shall never think of bereaving our fellow-creatures of that valuable blessing, liberty, nor endure to grow rich by their bondage. To live in ease and plenty, by the toil of those, whom violence and cruelty have put in our power, is neither consistent with Christianity nor common justice; and we have good reason to believe, draws down the displeasure of heaven; it being a melancholy, but true reflection, that where slave keeping prevail, pure religion and sobriety decline; as it evidently tends to harden the heart, and render the soul less susceptible of that holy spirit of love, meekness and charity, which is the peculiar character of a true Christian. . .

"And we likewise earnestly recommend to all who have slaves, to be careful to come up in the performance of their duty towards them; and to be particularly watchful over their own hearts; it being by sorrowful experience remarkable, that custom, and a familiarity with evil of any kind, have a tendency to bias the judgment, and deprave the mind; and it is obvious, that the future welfare of these poor slaves who are now in bondage, is generally too much disregarded by those who keep them. If their daily task of labour be but fulfilled, little else perhaps is thought of; nay, even that which in others would be looked upon with horror and detestation, is little regarded in them by their masters, such as the frequent separation of husbands from wives, and wives from husbands, whereby they are tempted to break their marriage covenants and live in adultery, in direct opposition to the laws both of God and man. . .

"And dear Friends, you, who by inheritance, have slaves born in your families, we beseech you to consider them as souls committed to your trust, whom the Lord will require at your hands; and who, as well as you, are made partakers of the Spirit of Grace, and called to be heirs of salvation. Let it be your constant care to watch over them for good, instructing them in the fear of God, and the knowledge of the gospel of Christ, that they may answer the end of their creation, and God be glorified and honoured by them, as well as by us; and so train them up, that if you should come to behold their unhappy situation in the same light that many worthy men who are at rest have done, and many of your brethren now do, and should think it your duty to set them free, they may be the more capable to make a proper use of their liberty. Finally, brethren, we intreat you in the bowels of gospel love, seriously to weigh the cause of detaining them in bondage. If it be for your own private gain, or any other motive than their good, it is much to be feared, that the love of God and the influence of the Holy Spirit is not the prevailing principle in you, and that your hearts are not sufficiently redeemed from the world; which that you, with ourselves, may more and more come to witness, through the cleansing virtue of the holy spirit of Jesus Christ, is our earnest desire." [29]

In 1760, the Nantucket Meeting passed a resolution not only warning against owning slaves, but urging that all Quakers should be free from reaping any profit from the system.

"2. We fervently warn all in profession with us, that they be careful to avoid being any way concerned in reaping the unrighteous profits of that iniquitous practice of dealing in Negroes, and other slaves; whereby, in the original purchase, one man selleth another as he does the beast that perishes, without any better pretension to a property in him than that of superior force. . . . We therefore can do no less than with the greatest earnestness impress it upon friends every where, that they endeavour to keep their hands clear of this unrighteous gain of oppression. 1760." [30]

---

[29] *Rise and Progress of Religious Society of Friends,* pp. 17-21. Note 2.

[30] *Book of Discipline* (Providence: John Carter, 1785), p. 101, Note 2.

In 1758, the Philadelphia meeting practically ordered that all Quakers who continued to hold slaves should be disunited from the Society. In 1774, a committee of thirty-four Quakers drew up a statement of procedure with reference to the few remaining Quakers who held slaves:

"That such professors among us who are, or shall be concerned in importing, selling, or purchasing; or that shall give away or transfer any negro or other slave, with or without any other consideration than to clear their estate of any future incumbrance, or in such manner as that their bondage is continued beyond the time limited by law or custom for white persons; and such member who accepts of such gift or assignment, ought to be speedily treated with, in the spirit of true love and wisdom, and the iniquity of their conduct laid before them. And if after this Christian labour, they cannot be brought to such a sense of their injustice, as to do every thing which the monthly meeting shall judge to be reasonable and necessary for the restoring such slave to his or her natural and just right to liberty, and condemn their deviation from the law of righteousness and equity, to the satisfaction of the said meeting, that such member be testified against, as other transgressors are, by the rules of our discipline, for other immoral, unjust, and reproachful conduct.

"And having deliberately weighed and considered that many slaves are possessed and detained in bondage by divers members of our religious Society, towards whom labour has been extended; but being apprehensive that a Christian duty has not been so fully discharged to them as their various circumstances appear to require;

"We think it expedient that the quarterly meetings should be earnestly advised and enjoined, to unite with their respective monthly meetings, in a speedy and close labour with such members; and where it shall appear that any, from views of temporal gain, cannot be prevailed with to release from captivity such slaves as shall be found suitable for liberty, but detain them in bondage, without such reasons as shall be sufficient and satisfactory; the cases of such should be brought forward to the next Yearly Meeting for consideration, and such further discretions as may be judged expedient. And in the meantime, we think those persons ought not to be employed in the service of Truth. . . .

"Also that all Friends be cautioned and advised against acting as executors or administrators to such estates where slaves are bequeathed, or likely to be detained in bondage.

"And we are of the mind, that where any member has been heretofore so far excluded from religious fellowship, as the minute of this meeting, in the year 1758, gives authority; nevertheless, in case of further disorderly conduct, that they be treated with agreeable to our discipline." [31]

So faithfully did this meeting do its work that by 1783, there were no slave owners left in its membership.

"The following extracts will fully justify this remark. In 1776, Philadelphia Monthly Meeting replies to the query, 'that a considerable number of the slaves heretofore belonging to members of this meeting have been set at liberty.' A committee of that monthly meeting had been labouring since 1774, with those who held slaves, and in 1777, report is made that *a few* continue to hold negroes in slavery. The minutes of that meeting, from the year 1756 to the year 1783, exhibit an unremitted attention to this subject, in labouring first with those who bought and sold, and next with those who kept slaves. In 1778, seven members were disowned for the latter offence, and one in the following year. A much greater number emancipated their slaves so that in 1781, there was but one case under care; and in 1783, the meeting reported that there were no slaves owned by its members." [32]

John Woolman made a tour through Maryland, Virginia, and North Carolina in 1746, and a second tour in 1757. It is probably due to this fact that the Virginia Meeting in 1757 asked: "Are friends clear of importing

[31] *Rise and Progress of Religious Society of Friends*, pp. 25-27.
[32] *Rise and Progress of Religious Society of Friends*, p. 31.

or buying negroes to trade on; and do they use those well which they are possessed of by inheritance or otherwise, endeavoring to train them up in the principles of the Christian religion?" [33]

The Virginia Yearly Meeting of 1764, having had reports that there was a general deficiency in the instruction of Negroes, recommended to the Quarterly and the Monthly Meetings to take these unhappy people more immediately under their care, looking carefully after their clothing, their feeding, and their instruction. This meeting shows a very genuine concern. The question of forbidding members of the Society to own slaves was up in the Yearly Meeting in 1766, but referred to the Quarterly Meeting for consideration. It came up again in the Yearly Meeting of 1767 and finally in the Yearly Meeting of 1768 a rule of discipline was agreed on as follows:

". . .'The subject in regard to negroes being brought before this meeting, and duly and weightily considered, it appears to be the sense of the meeting, and accordingly agreed to, that in order to prevent an increase of them in the Society, none of our members for the time to come, shall be permitted to purchase a negro or other slave, without being guilty of a breach of discipline, and accountable for the same to their monthly meeting.' " [34]

In 1773, the Yearly Meeting urged the manumission of all female slaves as soon as they reached the age of eighteen, and all male slaves at the age of twenty-one. Each Yearly Meeting continued to urge that members free themselves from this evil practice. In 1781—

"A person not professing with Friends, having been appointed executor to a Friend's estate, had sold some negroes,

[33] *Ibid.*, pp. 51, 52.
[34] *Rise and Progress of Religious Society of Friends*, p. 53.

and two members, heirs of the deceased, had purchased them. The case being represented to the Yearly Meeting of 1781, it was recorded as the unanimous judgment of the meeting, that notwithstanding motives of humanity may have induced such purchases, yet they being contrary to our discipline, monthly meetings ought to receive no acknowledgment, short of the purchaser's executing manumissions for said negroes; also to continue it under their care, that the remaining heirs do not receive any part of the money arising from the said sales." [35]

By 1787, it seems from minutes of the meetings that the Society had practically freed itself in Virginia from any share in slavery.

The first mention I can find of a slave in Tennessee is that of an eighteen year old Negro boy belonging to Joshua Horton, who came to the Holston River in 1766.[36] When John Sevier moved to Nolichucky in 1788, he took slaves with him. The record of the court of pleas, Jonesboro, Tennessee, November Term, 1788, records the bill of sale of a slave woman, Nancy, to Andrew Jackson, then a young attorney of twenty-one. It is also known that General James Robertson brought slaves with him when he marched overland to the spot on the Cumberland when he laid the foundation for Nashville, and Colonel Donaldson, who brought the women and children in flat boats down the Tennessee into the Ohio and thence up the Cumberland to Nashville (landing April 24, 1780) brought slaves with him.

There were Quakers in east Tennessee who in the early nineteenth century became very active in opposition to slavery. One of them, Elihu Embree, published at Jonesboro, the first antislavery paper in the South known

---

[35] *Ibid.*, p. 55.

[36] Ramsey, *Annals of Tennessee* (Charleston: Walker & James, 1853), p. 69.

as the *Emancipator* in 1820. In 1821, the Tennessee Manumission Society, made up of Quakers, petitioned the state legislature of Tennessee as follows:[37]

". . .'that they have had that subject (slavery) under examination, and on the first proposition contained in said petition, to-wit: allowing masters, convinced of the impropriety of holding the man of color in slavery, to emancipate such, on terms not involving masters of their estates, provided such slave offered for emancipation is in a situation to provide for him or herself, express it as their opinion that it is consistent with the rights of freemen, guaranteed by the Constitution, to have, and exercise the power of yielding obedience to the dictates of conscience and humanity.

"That in all cases where chance or fortune has given the citizen dominion over any part of the human race, no matter of what hue and whose reflection has taught him to consider an exercise of that dominion inhuman, unconstitutional, or against the religion of his country, ought to be permitted to remove that yoke without the trammels at present imposed by law.

"Your committee beg leave to state that, while they feel disposed to amend the law and guarantee the right, they wish it not to be perverted to the use of the unfeeling and avaricious, who, to rid themselves of the burden of supporting the aged slave whose life has been devoted to the service of such a master would seize the opportunity of casting such on the public for support.

"Your committee beg leave further to state that very few cases have occurred where slaves freed in the State of Tennessee have become a county charge.

"On the second point, your committee are of opinion that it is worthy the consideration of the legislature, to examine into the policy of providing for the emancipation of those yet unborn. . . . Liberty to the slave has occupied the research of the moral and philosophical statesmen of our own and

---

[37] Patterson, *The Negro in Tennessee* (University of Texas Bulletin 2205, 1922), p. 84.

other countries; a research into this principle extends wide
into the evil, whose root is perhaps dangerously entwined
with the liberty of the only free governments. On a subject
so interesting, it cannot be improper to inquire; therefore, as
a question of policy, it is recommended to the sober consideration of the General Assembly.

"Your committee also advise a provision by law, if the
same be practicable, to prevent, as far as possible, the separating husband and wife.' "

This same Society addressed a letter to the churches
of the state as follows:[38]

"The Manumission Society of Tennessee wish to address
you again on the important subject of slavery. In calling
your attention to this subject, in which we feel a most serious
concern, we wish to use that sincerity and candor which
become friends travelling through a world of error and sin,
in which they are to make preparation for eternity. We
therefore beg you to pause a moment, and let us compare the
principles of slavery, as it exists among us, with the holy
religion we profess, and the divine precepts of our common
Lord. What is our religion? Our Divine Master had told us,
that the most prominent features were, to love the Lord our
God, with all our heart, mind, soul, and strength, and to love
our neighbors as ourselves . . .

"Now let us ask what slavery is, as it stands between
Africa, America, and the Supreme Judge of Nations. Is it
not injustice, cruelty, robbery, and murder, reduced to a
practical system? The dreadful answer is, that hosts of the
disembodied spirits of unoffending Africans have taken their
flight to eternity from the dark holds of American slave ships,
and their last quivering groans have descended on high to
call for vengeance on the murderous deed, that stained the
earth and ocean with their blood. When we ask what slavery
is, we are answered by the civil wars existing in Africa—by
the thousands slain by the bands of their brethren—by the
captive's last look of anguish at his native shore—by the

---

[38] Patterson, *op. cit.*, p. 85 (Footnote).

blood and groans of the sufferers on the seas—by the sighs
of men driven like herds of cattle to market—by the tears that
furrow the woe-worn cheek of sorrow, as oppression mould-
ers down the African's system."

The first mention of slavery in the Minutes of the
North Carolina Meeting is 1740.[39] In 1758, the question
was asked: "Are all that have Negroes careful to use
them well, and encourage them to come to meetings as
much as they reasonably can?"[40] The action in 1768
settles the question that Quakers could not buy Negroes
for the purpose of resale, and could not buy of Negro
traders, but does not specifically forbid owning slaves.[41]
In 1770, the Yearly Meeting asked: "Are all Friends
careful to bear a faithful testimony against the iniquitous
practice of importing Negroes, or do they refuse to
purchase of those that make a trade or merchandize of
them? And do they use those whom they have by inheritance or otherwise, well, endeavoring to discourage
them from evil and encourage them in that which is
good?"[42]

In 1772, it was noted that a Friend should not purchase a slave to keep husband and wife or parent
and child from being separated. In this same year
the North Carolina Yearly Meeting concurred with
Friends in Virginia in supporting a petition of the Virginia House of Burgesses to Great Britain to stop the
slave trade.[43]

---

[39] *A Narrative of Some of the Proceedings of North Carolina
Yearly Meetings on the Subject of Slavery Within its Limits.* (Greens-
borough, 1848), p. 6. (This is a very rare pamphlet in the library of
Guilford College to which I was given access.)
[40] *Ibid.,* p. 6.
[41] *Ibid.,* p. 6.
[42] *Ibid.,* p. 7.
[43] *Ibid.,* p. 8.

In 1775, the meeting went one step further and ordered that no Friend should buy or sell a slave without the consent of the Monthly Meeting.[44] The Meeting of 1776 declared: "It is the unanimous sense of the meeting that all the members thereof who hold slaves, be *earnestly and affectionately advised to clear their hands of them as soon as they possibly can*." [45] To this earnest request was added a threat suggesting disowning those who would not conform.

Progress in emancipation was set back (1777) by the state seizing and selling back into slavery a number of Negroes whom the Quakers had freed.[46]

The Friends protested against this and employed lawyers to defend their former slaves, paying six hundred pounds in lawyers fees.

In 1787, the standing committee of the North Carolina Yearly Meeting sent to the General Assembly of the State of North Carolina to be held at Tarborough the following:[47]

"The petition of the Yearly meeting of the people called Quakers, held at Centre in Guilford County—for North Carolina, South Carolina and Georgia—respectfully showeth:

"We believe that the emancipation of slaves is in no wise inconsistent with the principles of the present constitution and that it clearly corresponds with a declaration of the General Congress in these words, 'We hold these truths to be self-evident that all men are created equal, that they are endowed by their Creator with certain unalienable rights, that among these are life, liberty, and the pursuit of happiness, and to secure these rights governments are instituted among men.'

---

[44] *Ibid.*, p. 10.
[45] *A Narrative of Some of the Proceedings of North Carolina Yearly Meetings, op. cit.*, p. 11.
[46] *Ibid.*, pp. 11, 12.
[47] *Ibid.*, pp. 16-18.

"From full persuasion of these truths, as well as the obligation of the injunction of our blessed Lord, 'to do unto all men as we would they should do unto us,' divers of the members of our religious society, in order to preserve a conscience void of offence both toward God and toward man, have found themselves under the constraining necessity to yield up a considerable part of what (by the laws and customs of the country) was termed their property, and emancipate their negroes. Several so liberated have been afterwards seized and sold into slavery, and others remain liable to like treatment.

"Those things coming under our consideration, we have felt our minds deeply concerned for the welfare of our country; and being animated with love to mankind we believe it to be our religious duty to bring them to your view. Inasmuch as it is righteousness which exalteth a nation and sin is a reproach to any people will not such treatment of our fellow creatures incur the displeasure of what God who is our common Father and the rightful dread of nations?

"We are affected with sorrow that in this State there should remain in force laws whereby the civil and religious liberties of mankind are so frequently violated, while in every other State on this continent, except Georgia, there is an open door for such as choose to liberate their slaves.

"We do therefore earnestly request that you may take this subject under your serious deliberation and grant such relief as to you may appear just and reasonable. And we do most ardently wish that a total prohibition may be put to the importation of slaves into this State.

"Under sincere desires that divine wisdom may govern your deliberations for the welfare of the State, and to the peace of your own minds, we are your friends.

"Signed on behalf of the meeting, 31st day of 10th mo., 1787

LEVI MUNDEN, Clk."

In 1792, the minutes indicate that "No Friends import, buy or sell slaves, but a few yet hold them, some of whose cases were under care."[48] Practically every year the Yearly Meeting made new protests or memorials to the Assembly, but to no avail.

In 1809, the Yearly Meeting appointed a committee to receive slaves and hold them for the Meeting from those who might desire to be freed from their slaves.

". . . the Society went vigorously to work to carry out the idea; for we find in 1814 that more than three hundred and fifty negroes had already been transferred to the agents. In 1822, John Kennedy assigns thirty-six negroes to the committee; Joseph Borden assigns eighteen; and the heirs of Thomas Outlaw, fifty-nine. There were then four hundred and fifty in their hands. The gifts came from all parts of the Yearly Meeting, and persons other than Quakers began to make them assignments, for the Yearly Meeting of 1822 found it necessary to forbid the agents to receive negroes from any except members of Society."[49]

By 1814, it was stated "That nearly all the black people belonging to Friends of the Eastern Quarter had been transferred to the trustees appointed for the purpose."[50]

In the minutes of 1818 this standing Committee reports: "That they have used some exertion for the education of the colored people, some of whom can spell and read."[51] In this same meeting an appropriation of $1000 was made to the American Colonization Society,

---

[48] *A Narrative of Some of the Proceedings of North Carolina Yearly Meetings, op. cit.,* p. 19.

[49] Stephen B. Weeks, *Southern Quakers and Slavery* (Baltimore: The Johns Hopkins Press, 1896), pp. 226-227, passim.

[50] *Narrative of Proceedings of North Carolina Yearly Meetings, op. cit.,* p. 23.

[51] *ibid.,* p. 26.

just founded.[52] In 1822 the Committee for securing slaves for freedom reported they held 450.[53]

About this time the Yearly Meeting began investigating places to which freed slaves might be sent and Hayti in particular was investigated.[54] In 1834, the Eastern Quarter had sent 133 to the West.[55]

This pamphlet being quoted, published in 1848, reports that "There are at this time a few persons to whom our Society retains the legal right." [56]

In answer to question 6, the 1849 Yearly Meeting says: "Friends are clear of purchasing, disposing or holding mankind so as to prevent them from benefit of their labor, except of two instances of hiring of their holders, and two of holding, which are said to be under notice. Friends are careful to use those well who are under their care, endeavoring to encourage them in a virtuous life." [57] The answer to question 6 in the Yearly Meeting of 1850 says: "None held of slaves, so as to prevent them of the benefit of their labor." [58]

From this time on constant petitions were made to state and national governments, pleading for the freeing of the slaves.

Having freed its own membership from slave owning, the Society of Friends turned its attention to the freeing of slaves in the country at large. In 1790, an abolition society was formed in Virginia, with Robert Pleasants, a prominent Quaker of Henrico County, as

---

[52] *Ibid.*

[53] *Ibid.*, p. 28.

[54] *Ibid.*, pp. 30-33, passim.

[55] *Ibid.*, p. 38.

[56] *Narrative of Proceedings of North Carolina Yearly Meetings, op. cit.,* p. 40.

[57] Minutes of the North Carolina Yearly Meeting, 1849, p. 5.

[58] Minutes of the North Carolina Yearly Meeting, 1850, p. 4.

president. Many, though not all, of the members were Quakers. This society sent a message to the legislature of Virginia in 1791 against slavery. The president carried on extensive correspondence with such leaders as George Washington, Thomas Jefferson, James Madison, Patrick Henry. In 1741, North Carolina had passed a law (C24), an act concerning servants and slaves, in which section 56 said: "That no negro or mulatto slaves shall be set free upon any pretense whatsoever, except for meritorious services, to be adjudged by the county court and license thereupon." [59]

This law, which seems to have become a dead letter, was re-enacted in 1777 (at noted before), and the Courts of Perquimans and Pasquotank arrested negroes who had been liberated. Friends claimed this was an ex post facto law and employed a lawyer, paying him sixty-four pounds to fight the case.[60] The Friends won. But the legislature passed another law in 1779 which confirmed the re-enslaving of those freed through the action of the Friends. The North Carolina Yearly Meeting of Friends sent up another petition to the state legislature which is most remarkable:[61]

"The remonstrance and petition of the people called Quakers from the Yearly Meeting held in Pasquotank County, 'That your remonstrants feel their minds impressed with sorrow, that such injustice and cruelty should be perpetrated under sanction of law, in any Christian community, as have been exercised towards numbers of the African race of people in this State, who after they were emancipated from

---

[59] J. C. Hurd, *The Law of Freedom and Bondage in the United States* (Boston: Little Brown and Co., 1853), p. 295.

[60] Weeks, *Southern Quakers and Slavery* (Johns Hopkins Press, 1896), p. 210.

[61] *Ibid.*, pp. 220-222.

motives purely conscientious, have been taken up, without being chargeable with the commission of any offence, and sold into abject slavery, divers being thereby far separated from their nearest connections in life. We believe such proceedings to be contrary to the laws of nature; and that it will surely incur the wrath of the Almighty who is no respecter of persons, having 'made of one blood all nations of men,' and sent His son into the world that all might be saved; for 'He tasted death for every man,' agreeable to the holy scriptures so that all people, whatever their complexions may be, are objects of His mercy. For a legislative body of men, professing Christianity, to be so partial, as thus to refuse any particular people the enjoyment of their liberty, under the laws of the government wherein they live, even when the owners of such slaves are desirous, from religious motives, that they might enjoy their personal freedom, as the natural right of all mankind, is so incompatible with the nature of a free republican government, and repugnant to the spirit of the Christian religion, that the present case, perhaps, all circumstances considered, hath never been paralleled in Christiandom; yet we hope divine wisdom may enable this house to exercise the power vested in them, to the honor of the most High, and the welfare of the State, that piety and virtue may be promoted, and injustice with other vice and immorality suppressed. Therefore we earnestly entreat and request that you may please to give your attention to this important and interesting subject, and pass an act whereby the free citizens of this state, who are conscientiously scrupulous of holding slaves, may legally emancipate them, and the persons so liberated be under protection of law; such a reasonable request we hope will not now be rejected, as we have no motive herein but a sincere desire that mercy, justice and equity may be put in practice, and are respectfully your friends.' "

In consequence of the Ordinance of 1787 declaring all territory north of the Ohio river free territory, a general migration of Quakers from North Carolina, South Carolina, Georgia, and Virginia set in about 1800. Most of these Quakers went to Ohio and Indiana. The migration was meant as a protest against laws which they could not change.[62]

About this time there arose a movement among the Quakers which refused to use or buy articles produced by slave labor. We can quote only one plea, sent out by Charles Marriott, who gathered many other such appeals into a pamphlet printed 1835.[63]

"In the epistles of our Society, frequently published to the world, we have clearly and unequivocally, as a united body, declared our abhorrence of slavery. And to show that no specious pretext of good usage could warrant such a flagrant violation of natural rights, our own members, if guilty of such violation would be disunited from the Society. Is it, then, reconcilable with moral equity, and with our own consistency of character, to employ another to do an act which we ourselves cannot conscientiously perform? That this is done requires no other proof than the undeniable fact, that many amongst us are freely purchasing articles obtained (by our own declarations) through violence and injustice; in other words, such as are raised solely by the labour of slaves; for what, I ask, is the negro purchased, for what is he retained in slavery, but to obtain those articles?

"It may be said, that the articles alluded to are so numerous, and in such daily use, that in seeking to extricate ourselves we might become entangled in a labyrinth of scruples and be at last unable to *draw the line*. The case, it is admitted, is not without its difficulties. The difficulties, however, are more imaginary than real, if it can be shown that our religious Society has already *drawn the line*, and in a regulation respecting one of our own peculiar tenets, every article of which appears to apply with still greater force to this subject, I allude to our testimony against war. In war a variety of passions are strongly excited, while *revenge*, a principle deeply rooted in minds unsubjected by the influ-

---

[62] Holder, *op. cit.*, Ch. 24.

[63] An address to the Members of the Religious Society of Friends, On the Duty of Declining the Use of Products of Slave Labor. (New York: Isaac T. Hopper, 1835), p. 5.

ence of religion, urges retaliation for real or imaginary in-
juries; and the subsequent frequent recurrence of acts of
mutual aggression, seem to offer some apology for robbery
and murder. But in this case, there is not even the stimulus
or revenge, for it is not pretended that the negroes have in-
jured us. One mean, despicable passion, avarice, cold-hearted,
but vulture-eyed avarice, seizes his unresisting prey, and
devours for ages, insatiable as the grave."

The letters, pamphlets, and other documents sent out
by the Society of Friends trying to persuade all men to
free their slaves and governments to pass laws freeing
slaves, are so numerous that it is impossible to quote
them. One outstanding document prepared by the Annual Meeting of London, 1849, and presented in person
by representatives of the Society, to practically every
government in the civilized world, gives the spirit and
the attitude of the Quakers. The four commissioners
chosen to present this remarkable document to the President of the United States (Franklin Pierce) and to the
several governors of slave holding states were John
Chandler and William Forster, both ministers, and
Josiah Forster and William Holmes, elders in the Society. The account indicates they made their presentation in 1853 to Franklin Pierce, President of the United
States, Joseph Johnson, Governor of Virginia, Lazerous
W. Powell, Governor of Kentucky, Sterling Price,
Governor of Missouri, P. O. Herbert, Governor of
Louisiana, Governor Foote of Mississippi, Governor
Henry W. Collier of Alabama, Governor H. V. Johnson
of Georgia, Governor John L. Manning of South Caro-
lina, Andrew Johnson, Governor of Tennessee, David
S. Reid, Governor of North Carolina, Thomas S. Ligon,
Governor of Maryland. They also visited many of the
nonslaveholding states and made their presentation. They
also sent a written address to each of the judges of the

Supreme Court and to each legislature of the United States, two hundred and ninety, in number. It was a most ambitious undertaking and shows the great concern of the Friends on this subject:

"To Sovereigns and Those in Authority in the Nations of Europe, and in Other Parts of the World where the Christian Religion is Professed.

"*From the Yearly Meeting of the Religious Society of Friends of Great Britain and Ireland, held in London, 1849.*

"It having pleased the Lord to bring our fathers to a sense of the cruelty and wickedness of the African Slave-trade, and of the injustice of holding their fellow-men in Slavery, they were strengthened to act upon the conviction wrought on their minds: they set at liberty those they held in bondage, and in their faithfulness they enjoyed the answer of a good conscience towards God. In that love which comes from Him their hearts were enlarged in love to their neighbor, and they could not rest without endeavoring to bring others to that sense of justice and mercy to which the Lord had brought them. From that time to the present day we have felt it to be laid upon us as a church to bear a testimony against the sin of Slavery.

"We have believed it to be our Christian duty to represent the wrongs inflicted upon the people of Africa, and repeatedly to plead the cause of the Slaves in addresses to our own Government. We rejoice and are thankful at the progress which has been made in this country and in other nations, in this cause of righteousness. Hundreds of thousands of slaves have been restored to liberty, and many of the nations of the civilized world are now, to a large extent, delivered from the guilt of the African Slave-trade, a trade which the Congress of Vienna, in 1815, pronounced to be 'a scourge which desolates Africa, degrades Europe and afflicts humanity'; and for the suppression of which laws have been enacted. But our hearts are sorrowful in the consideration that this traffic is still carried on to a large extent; and that a vast amount of the population of the western world is still subject to the cruelty and the wrong of Slavery. We desire to cherish this sympathy, and that we may behold the increase of it amongst all men everywhere.

" .   .   .   .

"We are now assembled in our Yearly Meeting for the promotion of charity and godliness amongst ourselves, and, according to our measure, for the spreading of truth and righteousness upon the earth. The condition of the natives of Africa, as affected by the continuance of the Slave-trade, and that of the slaves in North and South America and on the islands adjacent to that continent, have again awakened our sympathy. We believe it to be a duty laid upon us to plead the cause of these our fellow men. We submit to the consideration of all those in authority in the nations which take upon them the name of Christ, the utter incompatibility of Slavery with the Divine law, . . .

"For the space of three hundred years, the trade in slaves has been carried on from Africa to the opposite shores of the Atlantic; and this traffic in the persons of men is still prosecuted with unrelenting and unmitigated cruelty: year by year, countless multitudes are torn from all that they hold dear in life, to pass their days in toil and misery. Men are still to be found so hardened in heart, so bent upon the gain of oppression, and so devoid of all that we deem the common feeling of humanity, as to spend their time and talents in pursuit of this criminal commerce. We forbear to enter in detail upon the large variety of human suffering, inseparable from this complicated iniquity. But we trust we do not take much upon ourselves in asking those whom we now address, to open their ears to the groaning of the oppressed, and to give themselves to sympathy with their sufferings; to think upon the war, and rapine, and bloodshed, attendant upon the capture of slaves in the interior of Africa—upon what they are made to endure in their transit to the coast, and in their passage across the ocean; and not to shrink from making themselves acquainted with the horrors and the loathsomeness of the Slave-ship; to follow the poor, helpless, unoffending Negro, if he survive the suffering of the voyage, and to think upon his condition when landed upon a foreign

shore, and entered upon a life of hard and hopeless servitude
—it may be—to be worked to death in his early manhood, or
to live to behold his children subjected to the same degradation and oppression as himself.

"   .   .   .   .

"Our sympathies are awakened not for the native African
alone, and the victims of the African Slave-trade, but we feel
for those who are living and labouring in a state of Slavery,
who were born in Slavery, and possibly may die subject to
its privation and its hardship. In those countries in which
this system is upheld by law, man is degraded to the condition
of a beast of burthen, and regarded as an article of merchan-
dise. The slave has nothing in life that he can call his own;
his physical powers, the limbs of his body, belong to another;
it can scarcely be said that the facilities of his mind are his
own. All that distinguishes him as a rational creature is, by
the law of the State, treated as the property of another. He
may be a man fearing God, and desiring to approve himself
a disciple of Christ—we believe that there are such,—whatever the consistency of his character as a Christian, and
however advanced in the cultivation of his mind, all avails
him nothing, he is still a Slave, and the law allows him nothing to look to in life but hopeless, helpless, friendless
Slavery . . .

"   .   .   .   .

"The Gospel of Christ is precious to us. Through the
mercy of God to our souls, we trust we are prepared, in
some degree, to appreciate the means which, in His wisdom
and love, He has provided for the redemption of the world,
and the reconciling of man to Himself. In the word of ancient
prophecy, Christ was promised, that in Him all the families
of the earth might be blessed. We cannot but entertain the
opinion that the enlightenment of multitudes of the inhabitants of Africa, and their participation in the privileges and
the consolations of the Christian religion, have been much
retarded by the evil deeds of many who have gone among
them; especially that the cruelty and wickedness of the
Slave-trade have done much to keep them in ignorance of
Him who died for them. In that love which extends over sea

and land, and seeks the happiness of the whole human race, we make our appeal to those with whom it lies; and respectfully press upon them to take their part, in accordance with the peaceable religion of Christ, in removing every impediment out of the way, that, through the grace of God, the African of every tribe and every tongue, may be brought to the knowledge of the Truth as it is in Jesus." [64]

The work of the Religious Society of Friends on behalf of the Negro is well summarized by the author of the pamphlet narrating the actions of the Yearly Meeting as follows:

"The patience manifested in this work is remarkable. The labors extended over a period of more than one hundred years. One step after another was taken, each approximating nearer and nearer, toward the ultimate object of completely undoing the heavy burdens and letting the oppressed go free! Attention seems first to have been directed to their religious instruction, then to trading in them with persons who dealt therein for the sake of gain. Soon Friends were prohibited from buying of any except members of Society—finally their slaves must be given up. One committee after another was appointed, deficient members were again and again advised and dealt with in love and tenderness. A very few were disowned. They mostly yielded to their conviction of duty. Truth and justice triumphed. Slaveholding in the Society was abolished." [65]

---

[64] *Proceedings in Relation to the Presentation of the Address of the Yearly Meeting of the Religious Society of Friends on the Slave Trade and Slavery.* (London: Edward Newman, 1854), pp. 5-9, passim.

[65] *A Narrative of Some of the Proceedings of North Carolina Yearly Meeting with Subject of Slavery Within its Limits*, p. 3.

CHAPTER III

THE ATTITUDE OF THE METHODIST CHURCH TOWARD THE NEGRO DURING SLAVERY

On October 14, 1735, John Wesley embarked for Georgia as a missionary. The motive which led him to this step was through hardship and privation that he might "save his own soul." [1]

Wesley stayed only a short time in Georgia and did little of value. Whitfield went to America just as John Wesley was returning, and his mission was much more successful.

John Wesley was deeply interested in humanity, and his attitude on slavery was in accordance therewith. He found not a few Negroes in the colonies interested in religion, and he declared the best way to reach them was to travel from plantation to plantation where the masters would permit, and to preach to and catechize the slaves.[2]

In 1771, Wesley wrote in his Journal: "I read a different book published by an honest quaker (supposed to be Benezet's book published in 1762) on the execrable sum of all villainies commonly called the slave trade." [3]

It is said that Nathaniel Gilbert, a prominent planter and political leader of the West Indies, spent two years in England 1760, and following. He had two of his

---

[1] McTyeire, *History of Methodism* (Nashville: Southern Methodist Publishing House, 1888), p. 72f.

[2] *Wesley's Journal* (Everyman's Library), Vol. I, p. 48.

[3] *Ibid.*, Vol. III, p. 461.

slaves with him. He himself met John Wesley and became a Methodist. His two slaves were baptized and
taken into the church by John Wesley. When Mr. Gilbert returned to his plantation in the West Indies, he
fitted up a room, placed a pulpit in it and was soon
branded as a madman for preaching to his own slaves.
When he died, (1774), he left a Methodist Church of
two hundred. Thus, was Methodism active among the
slaves in the 1760's.[4]

Whitfield, who followed Wesley in America, was
deeply interested in the Negro, but unlike Wesley, he
believed slavery was a blessing. He purchased a plantation of 640 acres and Negroes to work it in order that
he might support his beloved orphan asylum, Bethesda,
in Georgia.[5]

But Whitfield was a constant worker for the Negroes. At one time when he was very sick and reported
to be near death, an old Negro woman came and sat by
him and said: "Master, you just go to heaven gate, but
Jesus Christ said, Get you down, you must not come
here yet, but go and call some more poor Negroes." [6]

Philip Embury organized the first Methodist Society
in America at New York in 1766. While the Methodist
Church in America was not organized as an independent
institution until 1785, we find in the conference of 1780,
questions 16 and 17, and in 1780, questions 12 and 13,
and their answers, read as follows:

> "Question 16. Ought not this Conference to require those
> traveling preachers who hold slaves to give promises to set
> them free?
>
> "Answer. Yes.

---

[4] McTyeire, *op. cit.*, p. 326.
[5] *Ibid.*, p. 263.
[6] *Ibid.*

"Question 17. Does this Conference acknowledge that slavery is contrary to the laws of God, man, and nature, and hurtful to society; contrary to the dictates of conscience and pure religion, and doing that which we would not others should do to us and ours? Do we pass our disapprobation on all our friends who keep slaves, and advise their freedom?

"Answer. Yes.

"Question 12. What shall we do with our friends that will buy and sell slaves?

"Answer. If they buy with no other design than to hold them as slaves, and have been previously warned, they shall be expelled, and permitted to sell on no consideration.

"Question 13. What shall we do with our local preachers who will not emancipate their slaves in the states where the laws admit it?

"Answer. Try those in Virginia another year, and suspend the preachers in Maryland, Delaware, Pennsylvania and New Jersey." [7]

In the conference of 1785, which was the organization conference of the Independent American Church, the following very interesting action was taken:

"It is recommended to all our brethren to suspend the execution of the minute on slavery til the deliberations of a future conference; and that an equal space of time be allowed all our members for consideration, when the minute shall be put in force.

"N.B. We do hold in the deepest abhorrence the practice of slavery; and shall not cease to seek its destruction by all wise and prudent means." [8]

In the first regular session of the conference of the

---

[7] *Minutes of the Annual Conference of the Methodist Episcopal Church 1773-1828* (T. Mason & G. Lane—Mulberry St., 1840), Vol. I, pp. 12, 20.
[8] *Ibid.*, p. 24.

newly organized Methodist Church in America (1786), there were 51 churches reporting. Of this number, all but 15 reported colored members. Ten of these fifteen were located in the North where presumably there were no Negroes. The total number of Negro members was reported as 1,890. No mention is made of slavery and the rule against owning slaves was not called up.[9]

The conferences meeting for 1787 at Salisbury, N. C., Petersburg, Virginia, and Abingdon, Maryland, make no reference to slavery but do urge the spiritual care of the colored people.

"Question 17. What directions shall we give for the promotion of the spiritual welfare of the colored people?

"Answer. We conjure all our ministers and preachers, by the love of God, and the salvation of souls, and do require them, by all the authority that is invested in us, to leave nothing undone for the spiritual benefit and salvation of them, within their respective circuits or districts; and for this purpose to embrace every opportunity of inquiring into the state of their souls, and to unite in society those who appear to have a real desire of fleeing from the wrath to come; to meet such in class, and to exercise the whole Methodist discipline among them." [10]

The Minutes for 1787 report 3,893 colored members; for 1788, 6,545 colored members; for 1789, 8,243 colored members. The first general conference was held in 1792, and 16,227 colored members were reported. This number seems to be too high, for the succeeding years reported somewhat smaller numbers.[11]

Of this early period of work, Dr. Bangs says:

[9] *Minutes of the Annual Conference of the Methodist Episcopal Church 1773-1828* (T. Mason & G. Lane—Mulberry St., 1840), Vol. I, p. 26.

[10] *Ibid.*, p. 10.

[11] *Ibid.*, pp. 27-95, passim.

"At an early period of the Methodist Ministry in this country, it had turned its attention and directed its efforts toward these people, with a view to bring them to the enjoyment of gospel blessings. The preachers deplored, with the deepest sympathy, their unhappy condition, especially their enslavement to sin and Satan: and while they labored unsuccessfully by all prudent means to effect their disenthralment from their civil bondage, they were amply rewarded for their evangelical efforts to raise them from their moral degradation, by seeing thousands of them happily converted to God." [12]

It was claimed that the work for the Negro slaves added much to the labors of the ministers of the gospel, because the masters felt they could not allow the slaves to leave the fields, especially during the growing season. Hence, the ministers must duplicate their efforts by preaching to the slaves at night and catechizing them. Some of the masters objected to this work for the slaves at first, fearing it would have a bad effect on discipline. Gradually, however, it seems to have become a common opinion that religious instruction led to greater discipline rather than the reverse. Many masters therefore provided regular places for the slaves to assemble.

It was particularly noted at this early day that the preachers were extremely careful not to suggest the possibility of emancipation but only to emphasize the moral implications of the gospel.

In some of the northern cities churches were organized for the Negroes, with of course a white pastor in charge, but this pastor was often aided by such capable Negroes as might be trained as assistants. Many of these loyal workers were licensed as preachers and exhorters.

---

[12] For a full account, see Nathan Bangs, *A History of the Methodist Episcopal Church* (New York: Methodist Book Concern, 1839-1842), Vol. II, pp. 64, 65.

Throughout the South a custom began to develop of setting aside a special portion of the house as the quarter for slave worship. Many of the early churches provided a gallery for this specific purpose.

In 1801, the Discipline of the Methodist Church carried the following articles on slavery:

"Question. What regulations should be made for the extirpation of the crying evil of African slavery?

"Answer 1. We declare that we are more than ever convinced of the great evil of African slavery, which still exists in these United States, and do most earnestly recommend to the Yearly Conferences, Quarterly Meetings, and to those who have the oversight of Districts and Circuits, to be exceedingly cautious what persons they admit to official stations, to require such security of those who hold slaves, for the emancipation of them, immediately or gradually, as the laws of the States respectively, and the circumstances of the case will permit; and we do fully authorize all the Yearly Conferences to make whatever regulation they judge proper, in the present case, respecting the admission of persons to official stations in our church.

"Answer 2. When any traveling preacher becomes an owner of a slave or slaves, by any means, he shall forfeit his ministerial character in our church, unless he executes, if it be practicable, a legal emancipation of such slaves, conformably to the laws of the State in which he lives.

"Answer 3. No slave-holder shall be received into society, till the preacher who has the oversight of the Circuit, has spoken to him freely and faithfully upon the subject of slavery.

"Answer 4. Every member of the society, who sells a slave, shall immediately, after full proof, be excluded from the society; and if any member of our society purchase a slave, the ensuing Quarterly Meeting shall determine on the number of years, in which the slave so purchased would work out the price of his purchase. And the person so purchasing, shall immediately after such determination, execute a legal instrument for the manumission of such slave, at the expiration of the term determined by the Quarterly Meeting. And in default of his executing such instrument of manumission, or on his refusal to submit his case to the judgment of the Quarterly Meeting, such member shall be excluded from the society. Provided also, that in the case of a female slave, it shall be inserted in the aforesaid instrument of manumission, that all her children who shall be born during the years of her servitude, shall be free at the following times, namely—every female child at the age of twenty-one, and every male child at the age of twenty-five. Nevertheless, if the member of our society, executing the said instrument of manumission, judge it proper, he may fix the times of manumission of the female slaves before mentioned, at an earlier age than that which is prescribed above.

"Answer 5. The preachers and other members of our society are requested to consider the subject of negro slavery with deep attention; and that they impart to the General Conference, through the medium of the Yearly Conferences, or otherwise, any important thoughts upon the subject, that the Conference may have full light, in order to take further steps towards the eradicating this enormous evil from that part of the Church of God to which they are connected.

"Answer 6. The Annual Conferences are directed to draw up addresses for the gradual emancipation of the slaves, to the legislatures of those States, in which no general laws have been passed for that purpose. These addresses shall urge in the most respectful, but pointed manner, the necessity of a law for the gradual emancipation of the slaves; proper Committees shall be appointed, by the Annual Conferences, out of the most respectable of our friends, for the conducting of the business; and the Presiding Elders, Elders, Deacons, and the Traveling Preachers, shall procure as many proper signatures as possible to the addresses; and give all the assistance in their power, in every respect, to aid the committees, and to further this blessed undertaking. Let this be continued from year to year, till the desired end be accomplished." [13]

---

[13] O. Scott, *An Appeal to the Methodist Episcopal Church* (Boston: David H. Ela, 1838), pp. 11, 12.

From 1800 to 1828, a careful examination of the printed minutes does not reveal a single action against slavery. Many of the ministers of the free states became advocates of abolition, and many ministers in the slave states had grave questionings, but if the Church was to remain a unit, it was felt that antislavery agitation would do no good and might do infinite harm. The Church, therefore, turned its attention to active work for the Negroes as a compensation for its timidity on opposition to the slave laws.

William Capers, later elected Bishop, was one of the most zealous of the workers in this great cause. In 1829, he developed a form of organization for serving the slaves which soon swept over the entire South.

Wightman, in his life of Bishop Capers, gives a most interesting account of this form of work for the slaves. Bishop Capers, who was then a Presiding Elder of the Methodist Church was, presumably on his own request, appointed Superintendent of Negro Missions in South Carolina. He immediately organized two such missions. One was on the Ashely River to which Rev. John Honaur was appointed as missionary. Another was on the Santee River to which Rev. J. H. Mossey was appointed as missionary.

So successful was their work of the Methodist Church under Mr. Capers, that soon Hon. Charles C. Pinkney, one of the leading planters of South Carolina, and a very prominent political leader of his day, came to Mr. Capers and asked that a Methodist exhorter be appointed to his plantation, although Pinkney was himself an Episcopalian. The matter was referred by Mr. Capers to the presiding Methodist Bishop and to the Annual Conference and such a missionary was appointed. Before long other Episcopalians made such requests. Among them were Col. Lucius Morris and Mr. Charles Baring of Pon Pon.

After Mr. Capers became Bishop he carried forward work for the slaves in a very aggressive manner. He himself wrote a Catechism for use with the slaves and in Columbia, South Carolina, the Washington Street Methodist Church has a large memorial tablet to Bishop Capers, setting forth something of his extensive work for the religious life of the slaves.[14]

In 1836, when the abolition movement was in full swing, Capers was asked to state the position of the southern section of the Church on the question of abolition. This he did in the following words:

> "We regard the question of the abolition of slavery as a civil one, belonging to the State, and not at all a religious one, or appropriate to the Church. Though we do hold that abuses which may sometimes happen, such as excessive labor, extreme punishment, withholding necessary food and clothing, neglect in sickness or old age, and the like, are immoralities to be prevented or punished by all proper means, both of Church discipline and the civil law, each in its sphere.

> "2. We denounce the principles and opinions of the abolitionists in toto, and do solemnly declare our conviction and belief, that whether they were originated, as some business men have thought, as a money speculation, or, as some politicians think, for party electioneering purposes, or, as we are inclined to believe, in a false philosophy, overreaching and setting aside the Scriptures, through a vain conceit of a higher refinement, they are utterly erroneous and altogether hurtful.

> "3. We believe that the Holy Scriptures, so far from giving any countenance to this delusion, do unequivocally authorize the relation of master and slave: 1. By holding masters and their slaves alike, as believers, brethren beloved.

---

[14] For full account of this work see Wightman's *Life of Bishop Capers*, (Nashville: Southern Methodist Publishing House, 1856), pp. 291-329.

2. By enjoining on each the duties proper to the other. 3. By grounding their obligations for the fulfilment of these duties, as of all others, on their relation to God. Masters could never have had their duties enforced by the consideration, 'your Master who is in heaven,' if barely being a master involved in itself anything immoral.

"Our missionaries inculcate the duties of servants to their masters, as we find those duties stated in the Scriptures. They inculcate the performance of them as indispensably important. We hold that a Christian slave must be submissive, faithful and obedient, for reasons of the same authority with those which oblige husbands, wives, fathers, mothers, brothers, sisters, to fulfil the duties of these relations. We would employ no one in the work who might hesitate to teach thus; nor can such a one be found in the whole number of the preachers of this Conference." [15]

The results of Mr. Capers' work was gratifying for at the time of his death, he had twenty-six missions in South Carolina alone, served by thirty-two missionaries; there were 11,546 colored members and the annual funds subscribed in that State for this colored work was $25,000.[16]

The general influence of such work is summarized by Capers' biographers as follows:

"Beyond all this, several important consequences may be observed. That the religious sentiment of the country should be directed, clearly and strongly, in favor of furnishing the colored population with the means of hearing the gospel of their salvation, and of learning their duty to God and their accountability in a future life, is a very cheering aspect of the whole subject. The history of these missions brings out the fact that the Christian minister has been welcomed on the plantations; that chapels have been built; liberal contributions been furnished by the planters; masters and servant are seen worshipping God together; the spirit of Christian

---

[15] Wightman, *op. cit.*, pp. 295-296.
[16] *Ibid.*, p. 297.

light and love has reacted upon the one, while it has directly benefited the other. How important is a growing public sentiment which shows itself in such aspects as these!" [17]

Mr. Capers used two methods of religious instruction: first, the public preaching service, which was always popular with the Negroes. They dearly loved crowds, they had a sense for oratory, and the eloquent preacher was always a great favorite. The second method was the teaching of the catechism.

Both slave children and the older slaves were taught by the Catechetical method. It was of course all oral teaching as most of the slaves could neither read nor write. But the catechism was so written that it taught not only the simple fundamental truths such as the meaning of God, the person of Jesus, the value of the scriptures, but also the great moral lessons of Christianity, honesty, chastity, obedience, industry, truthfulness, etc. These questions and answers of the Catechism were memorized by the Negroes, old and young, and undoubtedly became a great source of moral and religious inspiration. It was perhaps the best possible method of implanting in ignorant minds the great truths on which the Christian civilization of America rests. [18]

Dr. Capers himself wrote a catechism which was widely used among the Negroes and there were numerous others, the most widely used of which was that of Rev. C. C. Jones, a planter, but also a missionary to the Negroes of Georgia. One edition of this was printed in Savannah as early as 1837, and I find numerous other editions, one being published in Philadelphia in 1852. [19]

Dr. C. C. Jones, a Presbyterian minister, pays tribute

[17] Wightman, *op. cit.*, pp. 297, 298.
[18] *Ibid.*, pp. 300, 301.
[19] See copies of this interesting little book of 154 pages.

to the faithful work of the Methodists in his book written in 1842.

"The Methodist perhaps do not yield in interest and efforts to any denomination. From the commencement of their church in the United States, they have paid attention to the Negroes; of which we have had ample proof in the progress of this Sketch. In the slave States they have, next to the Baptists, the largest number of communicants. The Negroes are brought under the same church regulations as the whites, having class leaders and class meetings and exhorters; and cases of church discipline, are carefully reported and acted upon as the discipline requires. The number of Negro communicants is reported at their conferences, as well as labors in their behalf and where it is necessary traveling preachers are directed to pay attention to them. In the South Carolina Conference the missionary society already referred to has a field of operations among the Negroes along the seaboard, from North Carolina to the southern counties of Georgia. The missionaries of this society labor chiefly on river bottoms, and in districts where the negro population is large and the white population is small; and it is understood, receive most of their support from the planters themselves, whose plantations they serve. We know of no other missionary society in this denomination so fully devoted to this particular field; but there are Methodist missionaries for the negroes in Tennessee, Mississippi, and Alabama, and other of the slaveholding states. Without doubt as the Lord has opened wide the door of usefulness to this denomination, among the negroes, it will not fail to exert itself to the utmost. Bishop J. O. Andrew, whose circuit is in the Southern States, has taken up the subject in good earnest and is prosecuting it with energy and success." [20]

In 1840, the Methodists had 94,532 colored members and Harrison states that $168,458 was contributed to this

---

[20] C. C. Jones, *The Religious Instruction of the Negroes in the United States* (Savannah: Thomas Purse, 1842), pp. 93, 94.

work by Southern Conferences during the last fifteen years before 1844.[21]

That work for the colored people was quite general is shown by reports from the various conferences. Thus the report of the Mississippi Conference for 1838 says:

> "Colored missions were greatly multiplied at this Conference, some of which were supplied by some of the best traveling elders, and others by some of the most talented local preachers. The work among the colored people was not all left to the missionaries, but was still kept up by the circuit pastors wherever it could be continued in connection with the regular pastoral charges." [22]

The same conference met at Natchez 1839, and the minutes say:

> "On motion Resolved: That the preachers in charge of circuits in connection with the junior preachers, be required to take into their regular pastoral care all the colored societies within their bounds as far as practicable, and preach to them, and meet them in class apart from the white congregation, as often as possible." [23]

This Mississippi Conference in 1840 passed the following minutes:

> "A committee of five, consisting of B. M. Drake, B. A. Houghton, R. D. Smith, Thomas Clinton, and J. G. Jones, was appointed to take into consideration the best method of giving religious instruction to the colored people under our pastoral charge. The committee reported the plan of oral catechetical instruction, which was adopted, and William Winans, B. M. Drake, and J. G. Jones were appointed to prepare and publish a suitable catechism for this purpose. In

---

[21] Harrison and Barnes, *The Gospel Among the Slaves* (Nashville: Barbee & Smith, 1893), p. 196.

[22] Jones, *Methodism in Mississippi* (Nashville: Publishing House of M.E. Church, 1908), Vol. II, p. 411.

[23] *Minutes of the Mississippi Conference,* Natchez 1839 (Daily Courier Office, Natchez, 1840).

a few months the catechism was prepared and the first edition published; but before it became necessary to publish a second edition Capers' first and second catechisms for the oral instruction of the Southern colored people were published and at once became connectional in all the Southern Conferences. They were not only used by the pastors of the colored people, but by their Sabbath school teachers and their owners on the plantations. It was becoming common for the planters to have suitable places at home for the assembling of their colored people on the Sabbaths which intervened between the visits of their missionaries to learn an additional lesson from the catechism." [24]

Reference has already been made to the work in South Carolina, and similar reports could be copied from almost every Southern Conference.

The official position of the Church was early against slavery, but due to the fact that there was a large contingent in the South, the rules were gradually modified until the great break came in 1844. In the debate over Bishop Andrews' ownership of slaves, Dr. Durbin pointed out: "That in the earliest years of the Methodist Church there has been the strongest possible opposition to slavery, and that much pressure has been put on all Methodists to emancipate their slaves. However, the Church has recognized the difficult position in which members of this church had found themselves. In some states manumission was prohibited by civil law save in exceptional cases! Therefore Dr. Durbin pointed out the whole church had been lenient with those who held slaves. He felt however the time had come when the Church must take a rigid position against all slave holding, particularly in the part of the ministers of the Church. In the case of Bishop Andrews, he felt sure the

---

[24] Jones, *Methodism in Mississippi*, Vol. II, pp. 442, 443.

Church had no obligation to make further concessions." [25]

In order to maintain the unity of the Church, the subject of slavery had been ignored as far as it was possible to do so. The irenic view of the College of Bishops is proof of their desire to maintain harmony between the sections of the Church.

As early as the General Conference of 1836, the address of the Bishops warned against dragging the slavery issue into the Church in the following language:

"To the Members and Friends of the Methodist Episcopal Church.

"We now approach a subject of no little delicacy and difficulty, and which we cannot but think has contributed its full proportion to the religious declension over which we mourn. It is not unknown to you, dear brethren and friends, that in common with other denominations in our land, as well as our citizens generally, we have been much agitated, in some portions of our work, with the very excitable subject of what is called abolitionism. This subject has been brought before us at the present session—fully, and we humbly trust, impartially discussed, and by almost a unanimous vote highly disapproved of; and while we would tenderly sympathize with those of our brethren who have, as we believe, been led astray by this agitating topic, we feel it our imperative duty to express our decided disapprobation of the measures they have pursued to accomplish their object. It cannot be unknown to you, that the question of slavery in these United States, by the constitutional compact which binds us together as a nation, is left to be regulated by the several state legislatures themselves; and thereby be put beyond the control of the general government, as well as that of all ecclesiastical bodies; it being manifested that in the slaveholding States themselves, the entire responsibility of its existence or non-existence rests with those state legislatures. And such is the aspect of affairs in reference to this question, that whatever

---

[25] Matlock, *The History of American Slavery and Methodism* (N.V., 1849), pp. 35, 36.

else might tend to meliorate the condition of the slave, that these are the least likely to do him good. On the contrary, we have it in the evidence before us, that their inflammatory speeches, and writings, and movements, have tended, in many instances, injuriously to affect his temporal and spiritual condition, by hedging up the way of the missionary who is sent to preach to him Jesus and the resurrection, and by making a more rigid supervision necessary on the part of his overseer, thereby abridging his civil and religious privileges.

"These facts, which are only mentioned here as a reason for the friendly admonition which we wish to give you, constrain us as your pastors, who are called to watch over your souls as they who must give an account, to exhort you to abstain from all abolition movements and associations, and to refrain from patronizing any of their publications; and especially from those of that inflammatory character which denounce in unmeasured terms those of their brethren who take the liberty to dissent from them. Those of you who may have honest scruples as to the lawfulness of slavery, considered as an abstract principle of moral right and wrong, if you must speak your sentiments, would do much better to express yourselves in those terms of respect and affection, which evince a sincere sympathy for those of your brethren who are necessarily, and in some instances, reluctantly associated with slavery in the states where it exists, than to indulge in harsh censures and denunciations, and in those fruitless efforts, which, instead of lightening the burden of the slave, only tend to make his condition the more irksome and distressing.

"From every view of the subject which we have been able to take, and from the most calm and dispassionate survey of the whole ground, we have come to the solemn conviction that the only safe, scriptural, and prudent way for us, both as ministers and people, to take, is wholly to refrain from the agitating subject, which is now convulsing the country, and consequently the Church, from end to end, by calling forth inflammatory speeches, papers and pamphlets. While we cheerfully accord to such, all the sincerity they ask for their belief and motives, we cannot but disapprove of their measures, as alike destructive to the peace of the Church, and to the happiness of the slave himself.

> Robert R. Roberts,
>
> Joshua Soule,
>
> Elijah Hedding,
>
> James O. Andrew" [26]

But the avalanche could not be stayed and the Church split over the issue in 1844.

The acute issue of the split arose over the presiding of Bishop Andrews over sessions of the General Conference. Bishop Andrews' first wife owned slaves and at her death their ownership passed to the Bishop. He was later married a second time, and this second wife had insisted that she be guaranteed against the Bishop's insistence that her slaves be liberated. To this insistence Bishop Andrews yielded and gave to her a deed of trust to that effect. Bishop Andrews of course foresaw that his relation to his slaves would bring unpleasant complications at the General Conference. He therefore proposed to resign from the Bishopric and thus avoid raising the issue. But his fellow churchmen of the South would not hear to such a move. They held that the General Conference of 1840 had specifically legislated that the holding of slaves did not constitute "a legal barrier to the election or ordination of ministers to the various grades of office, known in the ministry of the Methodist Episcopal Church."

The legal argument seemed to be on the side of the southern delegates. But sentiment in the Church had changed. The whole country was in bitter conflict over the issue of slavery, and it was impossible for members

---

[26] Matlock, *American Slavery and Methodism*, pp. 42, 43.

of the Church to hold themselves aloof from the bitter controversy. The Wesleyan secession of antislavery members had genuinely alarmed the Church. Many northern members firmly believed that great numbers would withdraw from the Church, if it temporized with the slavery question.

Here in Bishop Andrews was an acute issue. If they permitted him as a slaveholder to preside, they felt it committed them to the position of condoning slavery. On the other hand, the southern delegates felt that yielding this point would be throwing over once and for all the principle of slavery. The only way out seemed to be a separation of the two groups holding opposing opinions.

The southern delegates to the General Conference promptly called a meeting in Louisville, Kentucky, where the new Church was organized, the name adopted, the discipline of the mother church accepted practically in toto, and plans made for the first General Conference, to be held in Petersburg, Virginia, in 1846.[27]

Four years prior to the great split in the Methodist Church, a smaller group had withdrawn and established the Wesleyan Methodist Connection because of the question of slavery.

At the General Conference of the Methodist Episcopal Church (meeting 1848), there was little or no discussion of slavery except in the committee on Fraternal delegates. This committee reported to the Conference May 5, as follows:

"That they have had under consideration the letter from the Rev. Dr. Pierce, and that they recommend to the General Conference the adoption of the following preamble and

[27] Weatherford and Johnson, *Race Relations* (New York: D. C. Heath, 1935), p. 207.

resolutions: Whereas, a letter from Rev. L. Pierce, D. D., delegate of the Methodist Episcopal Church, South, proposing fraternal relations between the Methodist Church and the Methodist Episcopal Church, South, has been presented to this conference; and whereas, there are serious questions and difficulties existing between the two bodies, therefore: Resolved, That while we tender to the Rev. Dr. Pierce all personal courtesies, and invite him to attend our sessions, this General Conference does not consider it proper at present to enter into fraternal relations with the Methodist Episcopal Church, South." [28]

The Methodist Episcopal Church General Conference for 1852 met in Boston. All memorials from Annual Conferences and districts on individual churches relating to slavery were referred to a committee, which committee reported back on Saturday before the conference adjourned on Tuesday. Since it looked as though no action was going to be taken, Professor Calvin Kingsley moved from the floor the following resolutions:

"1. We declare that we are as much as ever convinced of the great evil of slavery; therefore, no slaveholder shall be eligible to membership in our Church hereafter, where emancipation can be effected without injury to the slave.

"2. There shall be a fund raised, called the Extirpation Fund, to be constituted by annual collections in all our congregations where the people are willing to contribute; which fund shall be under the control of commissioners appointed by the General Conference, and shall be appropriated by them in assisting our brethren who may be connected with slavery to remove their slaves to a free state, if necessary, in order that they may enjoy freedom; and also in purchasing, for the purpose of freeing them, such slaves as it may be necessary to purchase to prevent severing family relations where a portion of the family may be set free by being re-

---

[28] Matlock, *The Antislavery Struggle and Triumph in the Methodist Episcopal Church* (New York: Phillips & Hunt, 1881), pp. 189, 190.

moved to a free state, or otherwise; and, also in rendering such other pecuniary assistance to our brethren, who are desirous of emancipating their slaves as such commissioners, under the direction of the General Conference, may think necessary.

"3. If there be cases where the emancipation of the slaves cannot be effected without manifest injury to the slave himself, our preachers shall prudently enforce upon all our members in such circumstances the necessity of teaching their slaves to read the word of God, and of allowing them time to attend upon the public worship of God on our regular days of divine service." [29]

This resolution was laid on the table for one day and was never allowed to come to the floor.

Following this conference, the next four years were rife with discussion of the question. The *Christian Advocate of New York*, the *Western Christian Advocate of Cincinnati*, and the *Pittsburgh Christian Advocate* were all opposed to slavery, but equally opposed to expelling slaveholders from the Church. On the other hand, *Zion's Herald*, the *Northern Advocate*, and the *Northwestern Advocate* took the more drastic view.[30]

The position of the more conservative papers was represented by Dr. Bond, editor of the *New York Christian Advocate*.

"It is admitted that many of our members who hold slaves cannot make them free, because the laws under which they live do not allow emancipation and residence in the State. To discharge from service, or to renounce ownership, is, therefore, only to turn the slave over to the sheriff to be sold at public auction, with the certainty that the purchaser will be a merciless slavetrader; or, to remove them to a free State, with or without their consent, which may involve the separa-

---

[29] Matlock, *Antislavery Struggle and Triumph in the Methodist Episcopal Church*, pp. 213, 214.

[30] *Ibid.*, p. 217.

tion of husband and wife, parents and children. In vain we plead that both the one and the other would be a violation of the law of God—the golden rule itself. The only answer is, 'Slavery is a sin under all circumstances, and the Church cannot tolerate sin.' But we deny the premises. Sin is a transgression of the law, and therefore a fulfillment of the law cannot be sin. If, then, the premises are false, the conclusion from them is necessarily erroneous. Indeed, if we admit the premises, we accuse the apostles of our Lord of conniving at and tolerating sin: for nothing can be clearer from Scripture than that the emancipation of slaves was not made a condition of membership in the primitive church, simply because it was impracticable under the laws of the Roman Empire—Most of the slave States have copied the slavery code of heathen Rome, and prohibit emancipation, and hence our members who own slaves are placed under similar circumstances with those who professed Christ under the ministry of the apostles; and the practice of the first heralds of salvation shows that slaveholding is not a sin under all circumstances, and therefore circumstances must now, as then, govern the action of the Church in regard to it." [31]

Dr. Hosmer of the *Northern Christian Advocate* represented the more drastic view. He sets it forth as follows:

"No Christian can, by any possibility, either be a slave or a slaveholder, in any proper sense of these words; . . . because no man can serve two masters—that is, two supreme masters. If the slave must obey man, whatever he may command, he cannot obey God; . . . because no Christian can exercise unlimited control over another human being; . . . because slavery is an unholy invasion of another's rights; . . . because a Christian must love the colored man as himself . . . But we go one step further, and affirm that a man cannot be a man, in any proper sense of the word, and be a slave. The same is true of the slaveholder. To be a slave is to sink below the order of humanity into that of brutes. The slaveholder

[31] Matlock, *Antislavery Struggle and Triumph in the Methodist Episcopal Church,* pp. 218, 219.

descends not only below religion, but below all the more honorable principles of humanity." [32]

The General Conference of the Methodist Episcopal Church met in Indianapolis in 1856. Twenty-nine out of thirty-eight Annual Conferences, memorialized the General Conference in favor of Antislavery action, while the Bishops in their Episcopal Address called attention to the fact that the constitutional majority of Annual Conferences had not voted in favor of a change in the rule on slavery. It was, therefore, necessary for this General Conference to submit to the Annual Conferences a change in the rule. This they tried to do by a resolution as follows:

"What shall be done for the extirpation of the evil of slavery?

"Answer 1. We declare we are as much as ever convinced of the great evil of slavery. We believe that all men by nature have an equal right to freedom, and that no man has a moral right to hold a fellow-being as property. Therefore, no slaveholder shall be eligible to membership in our Church hereafter where emancipation can be brought into the legal relations of slaveholders, voluntarily or involuntarily, by purchasing slaves in order to free them; therefore, the merely legal relations shall not be considered of itself sufficient to exclude a person who may thus sustain it from the fellowship of the Church.

"Answer 2. Whenever a member of our Church by any means becomes the owner of a slave, it shall be the duty of the preacher in charge to call together a committee, of at least three members who shall investigate the case, and determine the time in which such slave shall be free, and on his refusal or neglect to abide by the decision of said committee, he shall be dealt with as in case of immorality.

"Answer 3. It shall be the duty of all our members and

[32] *Ibid.*, pp. 219, 220.

probationers who may sustain the legal relation of slave-holder, to teach their servants to read the word of God; to allow them to attend the public worship of God on our regular days of divine service; to protect them in the observance of the duties of the conjugal and parental relations; to give them such compensation for their services as may, under the circumstances, be just and equal; to make such provisions as may be legally practicable to prevent them and their posterity from passing into perpetual slavery, and to treat them in all respects as required by the law of love.

"Answer 4. It shall be the duty of our preachers prudently to enforce the above rules.

"All of which is respectfully submitted.

M. Raymond, Chairman." [33]

The resolution was not carried and the question went over to the next General Conference. The General Conference for 1860 met at Buffalo, New York, and the committee on slavery brought in a report as follows:

"Question. What shall be done for the extirpation of the evil of slavery?

"Answer. We declare that we are as much as ever convinced of the great evil of slavery. We believe that the buying, selling, or holding of human beings as chattels is contrary to the laws of God and nature, and inconsistent with the golden rule, and with that rule in our Discipline which requires all who desire to continue among us to 'do no harm,' and to 'avoid evil of every kind.' We therefore affectionately admonish all our preachers and people to keep themselves pure from this great evil, and to seek its extirpation by all lawful and Christian means." [34]

---

[33] Matlock, *Antislavery Struggle and Triumph in the Methodist Episcopal Church*, pp. 229, 230. For the full discussion of the resolution, see p. 231.

[34] Matlock, *The Antislavery Struggle and Triumph in the Methodist Episcopal Church*, pp. 310, 311.

This resolution lacked four votes having the necessary two-thirds majority. The advocates of anti-slavery, however, put through a motion which adopted the language of the resolution, entered it into the journal, and inserted it into the Pastoral Address, but did not make it a part of the discipline.[35]

This action greatly antagonized the border conferences, and came near splitting the Church again.[36]

Immediately following the war the Methodist Episcopal Church undertook very widespread efforts to help the Negro educationally and spiritually. The work of this group was most effectually carried out through a number of schools and colleges, the most outstanding of which was Menarry Medical College of Nashville, Tennessee.

As we have noted before, the Methodist Episcopal Church, South, was organized in Petersburg, Virginia, 1845. The report for the year 1845-1846 indicates membership as follows: Kentucky whites 1098, colored 481; Missouri Conference whites 23,950, colored 2530; Holston Conference whites 34,446, colored 3975; Tennessee Conference whites 32,749, colored 7356; Virginia Conference whites 26,426, colored 4949; Arkansas Conference whites 7706, colored 1775; Memphis Conference whites 23,134, colored 4303; North Carolina Conference whites 19,639, colored 6390; Mississippi Conference whites 13,494, colored 7799; South Carolina Conference whites 32,306, colored 39,495; Texas Conference whites 1725, colored 501; East Texas Conference whites 3733, colored 644; Georgia Conference whites 38,967, colored 14,687; Florida Conference whites 3827, colored 2345;

---

[35] *Ibid.*, p. 313.
[36] *Ibid.*, pp. 319-321.

Alabama Conference whites 27,466, colored 12,768.[37]

In 1847, the Church reported 124,961 colored members; in 1848 it reported 127,241 colored members. In 1853, it reported 146,949 colored members.[38]

In 1860, the conferences reported the following numbers of colored members: Kentucky Conference, 5069; Louisville Conference, 4150; Missouri Conference, 2006; St. Louis Conference, 1375; Tennessee Conference, 8071; Holston Conference, 4156; Memphis Conference, 7002; Mississippi Conference, 12,684; Louisiana Conference, 5834; Virginia Conference, 7070; West Virginia Conference, 276; North Carolina Conference, 12,043; South Carolina Conference, 42,469; Georgia Conference, 22,339; Alabama Conference, 21,856; Florida Conference, 6589; Rio Grande Mission, 166; Texas Conference, 3196; East Texas Conference, 1993; Arkansas Conference, 1013; Wichita Conference, 2158; Indian Mission Conference, 337; Pacific Conference, 893; making a grand total of 171,857.[39]

It is claimed that the Methodist Episcopal Church spent $1,800,000 on its mission to the slaves between 1844 and 1864.[40]

The Methodist people took great pride in the work among the slaves, perhaps finding some compensation for their feeling of injury over the antislavery agitation. In the report of the Mississippi Conference held at

---

[37] Deems, *Minutes of the Annual Conferences of the Methodist Episcopal Church, South—1845-1846* (T. K. & P. G. Collins, Printers, 1846).

[38] See Deems Register, 1845-1853.

[39] *Minutes of the Annual Conferences of the Methodist Episcopal Church, South,* 1860 (Nashville: Southern Methodist Publishing House, 1861), pp. 195-293.

[40] Harrison and Barnes, *The Gospel Among the Slaves* (Nashville: Barbee & Smith, 1893), p. 298.

Brandon, Mississippi, 1857, one finds the following report on Missions:

The report claimed that the work among colored people was the peculiar pride of the Mississippi Conference. The Conference was almost emotional about the great results they felt had been achieved. It said the whole region between the Yazoo and the Mississippi River was wide open to missionaries. It claimed that many of the finest young men were volunteering and preparing to be missionaries to the Negroes. It speaks of the most liberal contribution of money by the various churches, even though it was a year of financial stress. It speaks of 400 slaves being catechized in one pastor's charge alone, and the baptism of both children and adult slaves were said to be numerous.[41]

Deems, in his *Annals of Southern Methodism for 1857*, speaks as follows:

"The Missions of the Southern Methodist Church to the colored population are often overlooked or forgotten by the Church census-takers and statistic reporters of our benevolent associations. We hesitate not to say that this field, which seems by common consent almost to have been left for our soul occupancy, is one of the most important and promising in the history of missions. At home too often its humility obscures it, while abroad a false philanthropy and rabid ultraism repudiate its claims. But still the fact exists; and whether we look at the large number of faithful, pious, and self-sacrificing missionaries engaged in the work, the wide field of their labors, or the happy hundreds and thousands who have been soundly converted to God through their instrumentality, we can but perceive the propriety and justice of assigning to these missions the prominence we have. Indeed, the subject assumes an importance beyond the conception even of those more directly engaged in this great work, when it is remembered

[41] For full account, see Mississippi Conference Journal, Minutes for 1857, (Daily Vicksburg Whiz—Vicksburg, 1857), pp. 16, 17.

that these missions absolutely number more converts to Christianity, according to statistics given, than all the members of all other missionary societies combined. We have often averted to the importance of this field of labor, and to the high estimate which should be placed on the faithful ministers of Christ who are laboring within its bounds." [42]

How to carry forward this work effectively and economically was ever before the conferences. It was also important that the welfare of masters and slaves should be jointly served. The Mississippi Conference of 1858 held at Woodville was wrestling in a most masterly way with this problem.

The Mississippi Conference Journal of 1858 speaks as if the conference carried the major responsibility of Christianizing the slaves of its territory. Therefore the whole conference gave itself earnestly to considering the most effective means of accomplishing the best results. First of all, they believed the churches for slave worship must be erected. It was plainly said that a barn, a sugar house, or the open floor of a cotton gin were not adequate quarters for slave worship, and that slaves would not respond to religious teaching under such surroundings. It was therefore suggested that two or more planters erect church buildings contiguous to their plantations to serve the slaves of all masters so uniting. It was recommended that the *masters and their wives, their children and the overseers, worship with the slaves in such churches*. It cites examples of such procedure in Louisiana and South Carolina.

It was urged that the planters so participating see to it that these churches become self-sustaining as promptly as possible. It was particularly stressed that the wor-

---

[42] Deems, *Annals of Southern Methodism, 1857* (Nashville: J. B. McFerrin, 1858), p. 137.

shipping of slaves and masters together would have a salutary effect on both, inciting the slaves to greater respect, and the masters to greater sympathy and interest.[43]

During the year 1860, the Methodist Episcopal Church, South, had 335 missionaries at work among the slaves and they spent that year $139,545.22 on this work.[44]

Mississippi and South Carolina were the leaders in this work, but all the States were aggressive in their efforts. Among the antislavery preachers who gave themselves wholeheartedly to this work were Bishop Capers of South Carolina, Bishop James O. Andrew of the same state, Bishop Alticus G. Haygood of Georgia, William Winans of Mississippi, not a Bishop but a great leader, and one of the most active.

When one follows this interesting account, one does not wonder that the Lutheran Church Review, in an article on the Lutheran Church and Negro Evangelization should say: "After all has been said however, it must be admitted that the principle work done during slavery days for the christianizing of the colored race, was done by the Methodist Episcopal Church, South." [45]

---

[43] For a full report of this most interesting movement, see *Mississippi Conference Journal, 1858*, pp. 23, 24.
[44] Harrison and Barnes, *The Gospel Among the Slaves*, p. 323.
[45] *Lutheran Church Review* (1890), Vol. 9, p. 137.

CHAPTER IV

THE ATTITUDE OF THE BAPTIST DENOMINATION TOWARD THE NEGRO DURING SLAVERY

The first Baptist Church in America was founded by Roger Williams in 1639. The denomination grew slowly so that one hundred years later there were only seventeen churches. Bacon says the Baptists were among the earliest dissenters in Virginia and that they established churches there in the early eighteenth century.[1]

Gewehr says there were 10,000 Baptists in Virginia in 1776, and 20,000 in 1790.[2] The Baptist Church had earlier spread to South Carolina, the first church in that state, being established in Charleston in 1690.[3]

"In general the Negroes were followers of the Baptists in Virginia, and after a while, as they permitted colored men to preach, the great majority of them went to hear preachers of their own color, which was attended with many evils." [4]

One of Whitfield's workers, Nicholos Bedgegood, turned Baptist in 1757, and gathered a small group around him.[5]

---

[1] Bacon, *A History of American Christianity* (New York: Charles Scribner's Sons, 1901), p. 53.

[2] Gewehr, William, *The Great Awakening in Virginia* (Duke University Press, 1930), p. 106.

[3] Du Bois, *The Negro Church* (Atlanta University Press, 1903), p. 18.

[4] *Ibid.*, p. 18.

[5] Simms, *The First Colored Baptist Church in America* (Philadelphia: Lippencott, 1888), p. 17.

The earliest Negro Baptist preacher in Georgia was George Liele (sometimes spelled "Lisle" or "Liehle") who is supposed to have been born in Virginia about 1750, but who came into possession of Henry Sharp who moved from Virginia to Georgia sometime around 1770. Mr. Sharp with his slave settled on a plantation near Savannah in Burke County, Georgia. Mr. Sharp was a Baptist and a deacon in the Baptist church of which Rev. Matthew Moore was the pastor. Although the records are none too certain, George Liele seems to have been converted under the preaching of Rev. Moore and was licensed to preach. The church gave Liele liberty to preach and his master gave him the time. Later, Mr. Sharp freed George Liele in order that he might give his entire time to preaching. He preached up and down the Savannah River, crossing over into South Carolina from time to time.

According to Woodson, who quotes Dr. W. H. Brooks, the first Negro Baptist Church in America was founded by Dr. Palmer, at Silver Bluff, South Carolina, sometime between 1773 and 1775. George Galpin, one of the South Carolina planters, was a patron of this church and it is known that George Liele preached there.[6] Both Mr. Sharp and Mr. Galpin were sympathetic with this work and gave it their support. When the British came to Savannah, the Silver Bluff Church seems to have been abandoned, but it was revived after peace came in 1783, under the direction of Rev. Jesse Peter, who as a slave had remained in South Carolina during the period of the Revolution. George Liele preached at Brampton and Yamacraw, and one of the most fruitful results of his labor was the winning of Andrew Bryan

---

[6] Woodson, *History of the Negro Church* (Washington, D. C.: Associated Publishers, 1921), p. 41f.

and three other fellow slaves, one woman named Cate, belonging to Mrs. Eunice Hogg, Andrew, Hannah—Andrew's wife—and Hagor, all three belonging to Mr. Jonathan Bryan.[7] Andrew Bryan soon began preaching, but he and a number of fellow slaves were whipped because of their church activities, there being a fear that gathering together might give rise to insurrection. However, Andrew's master seems to have been wholly sympathetic for he allowed Andrew to use a barn near Brampton as a preaching place, and it was here that Rev. Abraham Marshall (white) and Rev. Jesse Peter (colored) baptized forty converts and organized a church on January 20, 1788, which was probably the first organized Negro church in Georgia. This congregation began building a church in the suburbs of Savannah in 1792, and it is probably this fact that has caused some church historians to give the date of the first Negro Baptist Church as of this date (1792).[8] George Liele had removed to Jamaica where he was instrumental in establishing Baptist churches.

As early as 1790, there is a report from a preacher on the Pee Dee River in South Carolina, saying, "There is in Georgia a Baptist Church composed wholly of blacks"[9] which we assume referred to this church in Savannah. The report goes on to say, "There are a great number of Negroes in other churches in that state, in this (namely, South Carolina) and in North Carolina, and Virginia. God hath done great things for them, and their owners begin to discover that their slaves are of in-

---

[7] Love, *History of the First African Baptist Church* (Savannah: Morning News Print, 1888), p. 1.

[8] *Ibid.*, p. 1f.

[9] Rippon, *Annual Register*, 1790, 1791, 1792, and parts of 1793, p. 105.

creasing value to them when they become religious. I
am very fond of teaching them; have preached to 300
of them at a time and not one white present but myself.
They sing delightfully, and those who are truly religious, in general far exceed the whites in love to each
other and in most other duties. Many of them can read
and are remarkably fond of hymns. We have several in
our church who go to the plantations and preach to
their own color on Lord's-day evenings, and at other
times when we have no service in the meeting house." [10]
        Probably a little later than this (date not given),
George Liele wrote a letter to London in which he says:
"The last accounts I had from Savannah were that the
Gospel had taken very great effect both there and in
South Carolina. Brother Andrew Bryan, a black minister
at Savannah, had two hundred members in full fellowship and had certificates from their owners from one
hundred more who had given in their experiences and
were ready to be baptized." [11] David George was the
Slave of George Galpin of the Silver Bluff Church.
When the British soldiers came to that section in 1778,
George Galpin became a refugee and David George
and fifty other slaves went over to the British.[12]
Of this same David George, George Liele's letter
cited above says: "Also I received accounts from
Nova Scotia of a black Baptist preacher, Brother
David George (he had gone to Nova Scotia, 1782),
who was a member of the church at Savannah.
He had the permission of the governor to preach in three
provinces; his members in full communion were then
sixty, white and black, the Gospel spreading. Brother

[10] Rippon, *op. cit.*, p. 105.
[11] *Ibid.*, p. 335.
[12] Woodson, *op. cit.*, p. 42.

Amos (presumably also from Savannah) is at Providence, he writes me that the gospel has taken good effect and is spreading greatly, he has about three hundred members. Brother Jesse Gausling, another black minister, preaches near Savannah in South Carolina, at a place where I used to preach. He was a member of the church at Savannah and has sixty members, and a great work is going on there." [13]

Speaking of Andrew Bryan, Jonathan Clark wrote a letter to Rippon's Register in 1790, saying, "Edward Davis, Esq., indulged him and his hearers to erect a rough building at Yamacrow, in the suburbs of Savannah. . . . In this their beginning of worship they had frequent interruptions from the whites, as it was at that time that many of the blacks had absconded and some had been taken away by the British. This was a plausible excuse for their wickedness in the interruptions. The whites grew more and more inveterate, taking numbers of them before the magistrates, they were imprisoned and whipped. Sampson, brother of Andrew, belonging to the same master, was converted about a year after him and continued with them in all their persecutions, and does until now. These with many others were twice imprisoned; and about fifty were severely whipped, particularly Andrew, who was cut and bled abundantly. While he was under their lashes, Brother Hambleton says he held up his hands and told his persecutors that he rejoiced not only to be whipped, but would freely suffer death for the cause of Jesus Christ. The Chief Justice, Henry Osborn, Esq., James Habersham, Esq., and David Montague, Esq., were their examinants and released them. Their kind master also interceded for

---

[13] Rippon, *op. cit.*, p. 336.

them, and was much affected and grieved by their punishment. Brother Hambleton was also an advocate for them, and further says that one of their examinants, George Wolton, Esq., spoke freely in favor of the sufferers, saying that such treatment would be condemned even among Barbarians." [14]

This same letter from Savannah gives the exact wording of two certificates from Brother Abraham Marshall when he organized the church at Brampton in 1788. The first certificate refers to the establishment of the church and reads as follows:

> "This is to certify that upon examination into the experiences and characters of a number of the Ethiopians at and adjacent to Savannah, it appears that God has brought them out of Darkness into the light of the Gospel, and given them fellowship one with the other; believing that it is the will of Christ, we have constituted them a Church of Jesus Christ, to keep His worship and ordinances. January 19, 1788.
> A. Marshall, V.D.M." [15]

The other certificate refers to the ordination of Andrew Bryan, and reads as follows:

> "This is to certify that the Ethiopian Church of Jesus Christ at Savannah, have called their beloved Brother Andrew Bryan to the work of the ministry. We have examined into his qualifications, and believing it to be the will of the great head of the Church, we have appointed him to preach the Gospel, and administer the ordinances as God, in his providence may call. January 20, 1788.
>
> A. Marshall, V.D.M." [16]

"On the death of Jonathan Bryan, his son, Dr. William Bryan, generously continued them (the church)

---

[14] Rippon, *op. cit.*, pp. 339-343, passim.
[15] *Ibid.*
[16] *Ibid.*

the use of the barn for worship until the estate was divided by the family." [17]

The writer of these quotations thinks the number of members at this time was five hundred and seventy-five. This brief account of the early Negro Baptists in Georgia and South Carolina points clearly to two facts. First, the Negroes themselves showed great devotion and aptitude in the Christian religion, and it also indicates that there were many generous and Christian planters who were eager to give the Negroes every possible opportunity both for growing in the Christian faith and for full freedom and independence in worship.

In 1793, we find a reference to a Negro Baptist Church in Williamsburg, Virginia, which was "composed wholly of black people, or rather people of color, was admitted into the association." [18] On November 12, 1793, as American correspondent from Baltimore, Maryland, wrote Rippon's Register: "The only piece of good news I can inform you of at present is that an acquaintance of mine living near Little Rock in Virginia, mentions a gracious and wonderful revival of religion among the poor Ethiopians in his neighborhood—and that forty Negroes were baptized in one day and that the work went on astonishingly." [19]

The fine relationship which existed between whites and blacks at this time is shown by the fact that the white Baptist Church in Portsmouth, Virginia, upon the death of their minister appointed a Negro minister, Josiah Bishop, to preach for them." [20] The Gloucester,

---

[17] Ibid.

[18] Semple, A History of the Rise and Progress of the Baptists in Virginia, p. 126.

[19] Rippon's Register, 1794-1797, p. 75.

[20] Journal of Negro History (quoting from Semple's history of the Baptists in Virginia, p. 355), Vol. VII, p. 12.

Virginia church also called a colored pastor, William Lemon.[21] Joseph Willis, a Negro minister licensed in 1798, became the organizer of the white and colored Baptist Association in Louisiana in 1818.[22]

The question of slavery early began to trouble the Baptist Church. In 1798, the Mill's Creek Church sent up to the Kentucky Baptist Association the query: "Has a black slave a right to a seat in the Association?" The prompt answer sent back was, "Yes, provided he be sent as a messenger from a church." [23] The Lick Creek Church was in 1795 split presumably over the slavery question and was suspended until they could get together. "A disaffection existing in the Rolling Fork Church, on account of slavery, the whole church except three withdrew from the Association." [24] After the Revolutionary War the freedom of the slaves to preach and carry on their own religious activities, began to be limited somewhat, possibly due to a fear that groups gathering together might discuss freedom and insurrection since the colonies had but recently gained their own political freedom, and hence it was in the air. These restrictions not only caused disturbance in the Church itself, but evidently made many Negro preachers, who before had had large liberty, rather restless. Woodson records several such cases, though he gives no reference to the authority for these records: A slave of Thomas Jones in Baltimore County ran away in 1793. Accounting for his flight, his master said: "He was raised in the family of religious persons commonly called Methodists and has lived with some of them for years past on

[21] *Journal of Negro History*, Vol. VII, p. 12.
[22] *Ibid.*, p. 13.
[23] Clarke, *Annals of the Salem* (Kentucky) *Association*, p. 6.
[24] *Ibid.*

terms of perfect equality; the refusal to continue him
on these terms gave him offense and he therefore absconded. He had been accustomed to instruct and exhort his fellow creatures *of all colors* in matter of
religious duty." [25] Woodson tells also of a Negro Jacob
who ran away from Thomas Gibbs of Maryland, "hoping to enlarge his liberty as a Methodist minister."
Another Negro preacher named Richard ran away from
Hugh Drummond, and still another called Samboe ran
away from Henry Lockey at New Bern, North Carolina.[26] Hundreds of such incidents could be related to
illustrate the growing desire for freedom on the part of
the Negro, and hence the growing watchfulness of the
owners, which made them more and more reluctant to
allow freedom of assembly for religious purposes, without careful white supervision. This drew the Church
into the controversy as we shall see.

Andrew Bryan was still allowed full liberty of his
ministry as is set forth in a letter he wrote to Dr.
Rippon in 1800:

> "We enjoy the rights of conscience to a valuable extent,"
> he writes, "worshipping in our families, and preaching three
> times every Lord's Day, baptizing frequently from ten to
> twenty at a time in the Savannah, and administering the sacred
> supper, not only without molestation, but in the presence,
> and with the approbation and encouragement of many of the
> white people. We are now about 700 in number, and the work
> of the Lord goes on prosperously. . . . Henry Frances lately
> a slave to the widow of the late Col. Leray Hammond, of
> Augusta, has been purchased by a few humane gentlemen
> of this place, and liberated him to exercise the handsome
> ministerial gifts he possesses among us, and to teach our youth
> to read and write. He is a strong man, about 49 years of age,
> whose mother was white and whose father was an Indian.

---

[25] Woodson, *op. cit.,* p. 72.
[26] *Ibid.*

His wife and only son are slaves. Brother Frances has been in the ministry fifteen years and will soon receive ordination, and will probably become the pastor of a branch of my large church, which is getting too unwieldy for one body; should this event take place, and his charge receive constitution, it will take the rank and title of the 3rd Baptist Church in Savannah." [27]

That it was not purely a matter of prejudice, nor a matter of fear of insurrection that caused the liberty of the Negro in the Church to be somewhat limited is clearly brought out in a report of the Dover Baptist Association in Virginia, in the year 1802. Here it was said that some churches admitted to their church meetings all male members *whether slave or free*.

"By experience this plan was found vastly inconvenient. The degraded state of the minds of the slaves, rendered them totally incompetent to the task of judging correctly respecting the business of the church, and in many churches there was a majority of slaves; in consequence of which great confusion often arose. The circular letter argued and advised, that although all members were entitled to the privilege, yet that none but free male members should exercise any authority in the church. The Association after some debate, sanctioned the plan by a large majority." [28]

It is reported in 1809 that the church in Williamsburg, Virginia, was almost, if not altogether, composed of people of color, but that Moses, a black preacher, was often whipped for holding meetings. "It seems the Association had advised that no person of color should be allowed to preach, on the pain of excommunication; against this regulation many of the blacks were rebellious and continued to hold meetings." [29]

---

[27] Rippon, *Baptist Annual Register*, 1798-1801, p. 366.
[28] Semple, *A History of the Rise and Progress of the Baptists in Virginia*, p. 130.
[29] *Ibid.*, p. 148.

An African Mission was formed in Richmond, Virginia, in 1816, and this was approved by the General Baptist Convention held in Philadelphia in 1817. The minutes read as follows: "In April last, a Baptist African Society was formed in Richmond, Virginia, with a special view of commencing a course of contributions which, should the Lord of His infinite goodness succeed, may prove the means of spreading through the land of Ham the knowledge of the Redeemer. Among the mysterious movements of Divine Providence, by which good is educed from evil, it will perhaps be found that one design intended to be accomplished, by permitting unoffending Africans to be brought as slaves to our shores, is that they may here learn the way of salvation, and return to Africa bearing the glorious tidings. It is earnestly hoped by the convention that the example set in Richmond, and which has already been copied by the first African Baptist Church in Philadelphia, will excite the people of color, throughout the whole Union, to make one vigorous and continued effort. Funds for the African Mission, when collected, will be carefully reserved for the single purpose. The measure so desirable in itself, so easy of accomplishment, and so consonant with the spirit of missions which the Lord hath sent forth, will surely engage the attention of thousands." [30]

Lott Cary, a slave, and an exhorter in the First African Baptist Church of Richmond, was very influential in organizing this society. The society was composed of the Negro members of the church; it held annual meetings and in the first four years of its existence is said to have accumulated $700 in cash. As no one else seemed interested in going to Africa, Cary himself determined

---

[30] *Proceedings of the General Baptist Convention* (Philadelphia, 1817), From a Report of the Baptist Board of Foreign Missions, p. 180.

to go. He became a very powerful factor in developing that struggling colony.[31] The Baptist General Convention meeting in New York 1826, passed resolutions approving the American Colonization Society, and recommending that all churches take collections for this society on the 4th of July or other proper sessions.[32]

The Sunbury Association in Georgia in 1830 called attention to the fact "that colored brethren and even slaves who sustain a pious character are received and treated with a cordiality and kindness which can rarely be found betwixt white and colored professors of religion, where there are no slaves. True religion makes good masters and good slaves." [33]

Certain unhappy events in the South, such as the Vesey Plot in Charleston, 1822, and the Nat Turner Rebellion in Southampton County, Virginia, in 1831, caused many of the legislatures of southern states to pass drastic laws against free assembly of Negroes, even for religious purposes. Most of the churches were opposed to such regulations as they felt religion made slaves better men, hence better workers, and more loyal rather than the reverse.

The Charleston Baptist Association in 1835:

"Resolved, that as Christians we feel a responsibility in regard to the religious instruction of this class of people (referring to Negroes): that we hereby affectionately call upon the churches in this connection to use every consistent method, in accordance with the laws of the land, to give them the knowledge of salvation (through oral teaching—since it was unlawful to teach them to read) through Jesus Christ,

---

[31] Woodson, op. cit., p. 137f.

[32] See Proceedings of the Baptist General Convention, New York, 1826, passim. Also Proceedings of the Baptist General Convention, 1826, pp. 21-22.

[33] Christian Index, 1830, p. 115.

and that in the discharge of their whole duties with respect to them, our brethren be urged to act, not as taunted and insulted by fanatics, but as ever remembering that they also have a master in Heaven.

"We moreover urge on the members of our state legislature, not to curtail or restrict the religious privileges of these people, except in cases where necessity, either as to some existing abuse or obvious danger, shall clearly require their interposition, and that they be not induced to adopt any measures with respect to the colored people, which may seem to have been dictated, either by retaliation on the innocent, or by suspicion or dread. We are well assured, that no wise Legislature has anything to fear, from the Christian religion, disseminated among any class of its population, but that they will find it the surest safeguard of every interest they could desire to protect.

"Resolved that the Moderator draw up a memorial embracing the above resolutions, (both this one and the one on abolitionists) to be forwarded to the Legislature at its next session." [34]

In 1836, it was reported that Georgia had six Baptist churches with colored members only, having a total membership of 6,038. The largest of these churches was the First Africa Church at Savannah, with 2,795 members.[35] Two Baptist churches were reported in Alabama with exclusive colored membership in this same year. One of these was at Huntsville, and the other at Cottonport. Their aggregate membership was 339. One Baptist church at Mobile—not reported as exclusively colored— had 150 colored members.[36]

Very active work for the Negroes was under way in St. Louis, Missouri, as early as 1818, and in 1822, a

---

[34] *Minutes of the Charleston* (S. C.) *Baptist Association, 1835*, pp. 6, 7.

[35] Allen, *Triennial Baptist Register, No. 2*, 1836, p. 203.

[36] *Ibid.*, pp. 210, 211.

separate church was organized for colored people, but still under the supervision of white brethren. Rev. J. M. Peck was for years the white representative who regularly visited and gave guidance to this church. This church built a new brick edifice and became an independent organization in 1827. Rev. John Berry Meacham, "a free man of color" who had attained his freedom by industry, was their pastor. Meacham's father, a Baptist preacher and a slave in Virginia, was purchased by this congregation. This preacher, Meacham, was reported to have been instrumental in purchasing twenty slaves and giving them freedom.[37]

Dr. J. M. Carroll gives a very interesting story of the introduction of the Baptist Church into Texas in 1840, just four years after the new republic of Texas came into existence. A group of Baptists at Washington, Texas, wrote the Baptist Board of Foreign Missions in 1837, asking that they send a missionary to Texas. They wrote to the Foreign Board because Texas was not a part of the United States and hence was foreign territory. This letter finally came to the Home Mission Board of the Baptist Church, and as a result, James Huckins, a graduate of Brown University, and a student at Andover Seminary, was sent out. He passed through New Orleans, and found no Baptist Church there. When he arrived at Galveston, Texas, he discovered several Baptists but no church, so he stayed there a short period to organize such a church on February 3, 1840. On the following Sunday his diary says he added five members to the church, all persons of color. Many people came to hear the examination of these colored members, among whom was old Reuben,

[37] Allen, *op. cit.*, pp. 278-279.

whose narrative was "so clear, so graphic, so full of feeling that many hearts were melted and all were forced to admit that Reuben had been taught of God." [88]

Dr. Carroll, in his *History of Texas Baptists*, devotes a chapter to "Baptist Work Among the Negroes Prior to the Civil War." One can summarize it very briefly. Immediately following the arrival of James Huckins as a missionary worker in 1840, others began work, notably Rev. M. W. Fryon and Brother Baylor. In 1848, the first state Baptist Convention met and Elder Noah Hill reported on the "Religious Condition of the Colored People." This report justified slavery from the Bible, as he thought, but pled earnestly and sincerely for aggressive work to evangelize the slaves. In the report to the 1850 state convention, special attention is called to the numbers of colored members in the Baptist churches of Galveston and Houston. In the Convention report of 1851 it is stated that "All Baptist pastors, except three or four give special attention to the colored people." It also says that in some cases masters gather their slaves on Sabbath morning and read them the Scriptures and give oral instruction to the children. In 1852, Rev. Noah Hill was employed jointly by the State Convention and the Southern Baptist Convention to serve as missionary to the Negroes. The Convention of 1856 declared that the design of God in introducing slaves into America was to Christianize them, and accordingly they urged the employment of three missionaries for this work. The 1857 Convention calls attention to the fact that while in some cases colored people have separate Baptist churches, in most cases they are members of the same churches as their masters. It points out that in some churches *there*

---

[88] Carroll, *A History of Texas Baptists* (Baptist Standard Publishing Company, 1923), p. 137f.

are more black members than white. One church is mentioned—Wharton—where there were nearly four blacks to one white—namely, 94 blacks and 24 whites. One church, with all colored members, was in 1854 received into the Convention. But in 1855, another church was not accepted because the Committee thought independent Negro churches were inconsistent with the condition of the blacks as servants. The summary of the chapter points out the keen sense of responsibility of the Baptists for the religious instruction of the slaves, and commends highly the piety of the slaves.[39]

We must now turn our attention back to an earlier period, when the Boston Board of the Triennial Convention was organized in 1814. This Board charged with the responsibility of carrying on the missionary activities of the Baptist denomination, by its constitution, made slaveholders and non-slaveholders, of equal social and moral equality, and gave to them equal rights in all the activities of the Board.[40]

Richard Furman of South Carolina, a slaveholder, was the first president of this Board, holding office until 1820. His successor was Robert B. Semple of Virginia, also a slaveholder, who remained in office from 1820 to 1832. Spencer Cone, of New York, was the next president, being a nonslaveholder and holding office from 1832 to 1841. Cone was succeeded by William B. Johnson, another South Carolinian, and a slaveholder. Johnson held office until 1844, and was succeeded by Frances Wayland, a nonslaveholder. The Society was disbanded over the slave question in 1845.[41]

---

[39] Carroll, *op. cit.*, Chapter XXXV.
[40] Foss and Mathews, *Facts for Baptist Churches* (American Baptist Free Missionary Society, 1850), p. 14.
[41] *Ibid.*, p. 15.

In 1833, a Board of Baptist ministers, in and near London, England, addressed a communication to the American Baptist Board of Foreign Missions, in which these British Christians expressed their deep affection for the American Christians and then made an earnest plea that the American Baptist Church would align itself against slavery in an unequivocal fashion. They wrote, "We indulge the hope that you will seriously inquire whether, as the Disciples of Christ, it is not your imperative duty, without delay, to raise your voice against the cruel and degrading bondage in which our African brethren and their descendants are held in various parts of your land." [42]

Nine months passed before this letter from the English Church was answered. On September 1, 1834, the Baptist Board of Foreign Missions, acting on behalf of the Triennial Convention, wrote reminding the English churchmen, that the English nation had introduced many of these slaves, long before the American colonies had declared their independence, and that many efforts of these colonies to rid themselves of slaves, had been nullified by the Kings of England. The Committee appointed to answer the letter "were of the opinion that as a Board and as members of the General Convention association for the exclusive purpose of sending the Gospel to the heathen, and to other benighted men not belonging to our country, we are precluded by our constitution from taking any part in the discussion of the subject proposed in your communication." [43]

The English Christians wrote another letter of similar import and in 1835, sent Elders Cox and Hoby to America to plead their cause. It was claimed by anti-

[42] Foss and Mathews, *op. cit.*, pp. 17-19.
[43] *Ibid.*, p. 20.

slavery leaders of the Baptist Church, "That the influence of the Triennial Convention was employed to keep them as silent as possible in regard to the enormous sin of American slavery." [44] The attitude of the English Baptist Christians grew more and more insistent until in 1836, they declared they must receive with great suspicion reports of religious revivals in America.[45] They even went to the length of refusing to extend the hand of fellowship to those Baptists in America who continued to hold slaves.

A persistent effort was made by the American Baptist Board of Foreign Missions to maintain the position that their constitution was specific in setting up missions as their one object, and they held that this precluded their raising the question of slavery or antislavery.

In 1832, the American Board of Home Missions Society was organized at Philadelphia, the basis of membership being made, membership in a Baptist Church, and the contribution of specific sums of money to the Society. This of course took no notice of whether a member was a slaveholder or a nonslaveholder. Soon the controversy raged around this Society. Should the Society accept members who were slaveholders, and the more acute issue—should the Society commission workers who were slaveholders, should such apply? These were the acute issues. By 1844, it was reported that the Home Missionary Society had appointed twenty-six missionaries who were slaveholders. When these charges were brought to the attention of the Executive Committee of the Home Mission Society their reply was: "They found in their appropriate work, enough to task their utmost strength, without allowing them either the

[44] *Ibid.*, p. 29.
[45] *Ibid.*, p. 36.

time or the inclination to diverge to other objects." [46] However, the Society was not permitted to rest content behind this convenient smoke screen. Representatives from the southern states were very influential in the Society, since it was reported with some degree of disapproval that they paid more money into the treasure than members from other sections.[47] It was to be expected therefore that they would allow no uncertainty as to whether they held equal status with others in membership, but also as to whether they had full representation in commissioned workers. Indeed, the fact that they contributed more liberally than others indicated they wanted the Society to carry on an aggressive work among their slaves. To make absolutely sure of this status, the Alabama State Baptist Convention on November 25, 1844, addressed certain resolutions to the Baptist Board of Home Missions in which they specifically set forth: first, that parties to a voluntary cooperation must be of equal standing and influence (referring to slaveholders and nonslaveholders); second, that the issue must be faced squarely and a forthright answer given as to whether slaveholders were considered equal; third, that the local church alone had authority to pass on the Christian character of any applicant for mission service; fourth, that all funds designated for mission purposes would be withheld until a satisfactory answer was given; and lastly, that all other Baptist State Conventions should be informed as to their action.[48]

This put the question of slaveholding as a disqualification for missionary service squarely up to the Society. The Board answered on December 17, 1844, saying that

[46] Foss and Mathews, *op. cit.*, p. 67.
[47] *Ibid.*, p. 90.
[48] Foss and Mathews, *op. cit.*, pp. 104, 105.

in thirty years in which the Board had existed, no slave-holder had applied for appointment. "If however anyone should offer himself as a missionary having slaves, and should insist on retaining them as his property we could not appoint him. One thing is certain, we can never be a party to any arrangement which would imply approbation of slavery." [49]

This letter raised a storm of protest both North and South. There were many northern members who were nonslaveholders, but who protested the Board had exceeded its authority; that it had only one business, and that was to carry forward home mission work, and that the donors of money, whether slaveholders or nonslaveholders, had a right to determine how that money should be spent.

The Alabama Board, on receipt of the reply of the Board of Foreign Missions, representing the Triennial Convention, immediately passed the following resolutions: "Resolved, that with much reluctance and grief we are compelled to consider the communication received from the Acting Board of the Baptist General Convention to be a full and candid avowal, that they 'are not willing to acknowledge our entire social equality as to all the privileges and benefits of the Union' and therefore in the opinion of both parties, our united efforts cease to be agreeable, useful, or proper." [50]

The Board representing the Virginia State Convention promptly sent out a letter to all churches in the State saying "that all farther connection with the Board (of the General Convention) on the part of members (of Virginia State Convention) is inexpedient and im-

---

[49] *Ibid.*, p. 106.
[50] Foss and Mathews, *op. cit.*, p. 112.

proper." [51] This board further resolved, first, that the decision of the Boston Board was unconstitutional; second, that their treasurer deposit all sums coming into his hands in a bank, subject to the action of the Virginia State Convention (instead of sending it on to the Boston Board); third, calling a convention of those likeminded with themselves, to determine what steps should be taken to continue their mission work; fourth, asking all churches to appoint delegates to this convention; and lastly, asking that their actions be published abroad.[52]

The Executive Committee of the Georgia Baptist Convention promptly passed resolutions approving the action of the Virginia group.[53] The Tennessee Baptist Foreign Mission Society met April 2, 1845, and after stating that the Baptist Triennial Convention was organized to represent the whole church, and had definitely committed itself to noninterference with the question of slavery, therefore, they believed the Acting Board had disobeyed the instructions of the Triennial Convention, in its answer to the Alabama Board, and had thus rendered themselves obnoxious to the whole Church; they repudiated such action by the Boston Board, and refused to sanction the dissolution of the 'Foreign Mission Union'; they declared they would continue to send their funds to the Boston Board; and declared they did not believe the Triennial Convention would sustain the action of the Boston Board.[54]

In the discussion which followed it was often stated that the separation should be made without ill feeling, and that even if slavery were not involved, there would

---

[51] *Ibid.*, p. 112.
[52] Foss and Mathews, *op. cit.*, p. 112.
[53] *Ibid.*, p. 112.
[54] *Ibid.*, p. 113.

be ample reason for the division. Elder Wayland, of the Foreign Mission Board wrote Elder Jeter of Richmond: "We have shown how Christians ought not to act, it remains for you to show how they ought to act." [55] One must pass over a great volume of discussion in which the issues were thoroughly confused, and no section was completely united in its opinion. However, the Southern Convention did meet in Augusta, Georgia, on May 8, 1845, with some three hundred delegates, representing the states of Maryland, Virginia, North Carolina, South Carolina, Alabama, Louisiana, Kentucky, and the District of Columbia. The states of Mississippi, Tennessee, Arkansas, and Florida were represented by letter.[56] There were representatives of Georgia present though the account we have consulted did not mention them.

A constitution was adopted and the first regular meeting of the Convention was set for May and convened at Nashville, Tennessee.

The history of the Baptist Home Mission Board and that of the American and Foreign Bible Society, followed closely the pattern of the Foreign Mission Board; namely, a struggle to confine their activities to their specific task, without taking any stand on slavery, but finally forced to face the issue and split over the same.[57]

While this controversy was raging, be it said to the credit of Baptist churches, there seemed to be no lag in their interest in the religious instruction of the slaves, whether such were located in the North or the South. The Southern Baptist Convention met in Richmond, Virginia, in 1846, and received a very elaborate report on missions in Africa, but the report of the Committee

---

[55] *Ibid.*, p. 134.
[56] Foss and Mathews, *op. cit.*, pp. 165, 166.
[57] *Ibid.*, p. 320f.

on the Instruction of Colored People, was even more full. The report said interest had been steadily growing for several years; that in many churches the pastor preached a sermon each Sunday specifically for colored people; that colored deacons were appointed to have oversight over moral character; that Sunday Schools were organized for young people and children; and that pious masters were being encouraged to have their slaves present at family worship. The report went so far as to say that the slaves were as much of a moral charge on their masters, *as were their own children.* There was a caution sounded about having highly emotional meetings, and a plea that religious work should be more to inform the Negroes than to affect them.[58]

As we have seen, the Alabama Baptist Convention in 1844 focused the issue which brought about the separation between northern and southern Baptists. In their State Convention of 1848, Rev. B. Manly, then President of the State College (State University) at Tuscaloosa, who was also Chairman of the Committee on Religious Instruction of Colored People, made a report on this religious instruction. "We rejoice in the abundant evidence that the subject is receiving continually deeper and wider attention. One most cheering fact is that such has been the success everywhere met with, that no effort once begun has been abandoned, but there has been a continual progress. . . . A huge majority, it is believed, of all the ministers connected with this body, have separate exercises for the colored people, in addition to the regular services of the churches, which as usual, they also attend in considerable numbers." [59]

---

[58] *Minutes of the Southern Baptist Convention, 1846,* p. 16.
[59] Reported in the *Thirteenth Annual Report of the Association for the Religious Instruction of Negroes in Liberty County, Georgia,* 1848, pp. 25-32.

One could quote similar statements from all the State Conventions of the South, showing a real zeal for evangelization. From time to time there appeared the names of individual colored churches with reports of their activity. Thus the African Church of Mobile, the First Colored Church of Louisville, the Union and Zion Churches of Cincinnati, et al. As early as 1780, a Baptist church had been organized in Richmond, Virginia, and prominent names like Broadus, Keeling, Taylor, Ryland, Jennett, Winfru, Curry, Tupper, and Jeter were from time to time connected with it.[60] This Church erected a new edifice in 1841, and the old edifice was turned over to the colored members who were organized under the name of the First African Baptist Church, with Dr. Ryland, then President of Richmond College, acting as pastor.[61] It was reported that the colored members numbered seventeen hundred and eight.

In the Southern Baptist Convention of 1849, meeting in Charleston, it was reported that the colored members themselves were contributing liberally to the cause of missions.[62] The Baptist denomination was very liberal in giving the Negroes a large share in the control of their churches, which probably accounts for the extraordinary hold that denomination secured and continues to exercise in the life of the Negroes of the South.

In 1857, Carroll reports that "in Texas there are a few places within our state where the colored brethren have separate organizations presided over by white ministers, in other places they have their own colored ministers." [63]

---

[60] *First Century, First Baptist Church, Richmond* (Culter & McCarthy, 1880).

[61] *Ibid.*, p. 85.

[62] *Southern Baptist Missionary Journal*, July 1849, p. 26.

[63] Carroll, *A History of Texas Baptists*, p. 257.

Du Bois states that there were 175,000 Negro Baptists in 1859.[64] Many of these Baptists were in separate colored churches, some of which had been organized as missions, some of which had arisen when the membership became too large for the buildings and the whites built a new edifice, leaving the old building to the colored members, and sometimes these colored churches arose as a protest against discrimination which the Negroes found in the mixed churches.

The Baptist churches continued very active in work for the Negroes all during the Civil War. Every state convention received reports on the "Instruction of the Colored Population" and one cannot read these reports without being impressed with the zeal and earnestness of these Civil War churches. Nor did they cease their efforts when the Civil War was over and the slaves were emancipated. The Southern Baptist Convention meeting in Russelville, Kentucky, 1866, passed the following resolutions submitted by the Committee on Religious Instruction of Colored People:

"Resolved, that in our changed relations with the colored people, we recognize as heretofore, our solemn obligations to give religious instructions to them, by all those means which God has ordained for the salvation of men.

"Resolved, that we earnestly recommend to our brethren to increase the work of Sabbath School instruction among them, and that when practicable, a Sunday School be established for them in every church.

"Resolved, that we suggest to the pastors of our churches, the duty of giving theological and other instruction to such colored brethren as are now preaching, and to such as, in the judgment of the churches, may be called to this work.

---

[64] Du Bois, *The Negro Church*, p. 29.

"Resolved, that we recommend to our people to encourage the Negroes to establish day schools for the instruction of their children, and also to encourage our young men and young women to engage in the work of teaching them.

"Resolved, that while we are not opposed to any right-minded man aiding in this important work, it is our decided conviction from our knowledge of the character of the people, and of the feelings of our citizens, that this work must be done mainly by ourselves." [65]

Thus, it will appear that after the Civil War the white Baptists were still deeply interested in the religious instruction of the Negroes, that they wanted to give them Sunday Schools, that they wanted them to have day schools, and that they urged southern white men and women to teach in these schools.

The Northern Baptist Convention continued its services to the Negroes through sending missionaries, but more largely through establishing colleges, among the best known being Shaw University in Raleigh, North Carolina; Roger Williams, founded at Nashville, but later removed to Memphis; Morehouse in Atlanta; Leland in New Orleans; and Benedict in Columbia, South Carolina.

---

[65] *Proceedings of the Southern Baptist Convention, 1866,* pp. 85, 86.

CHAPTER V

THE ATTITUDE OF THE LUTHERAN CHURCH TOWARD THE NEGRO DURING SLAVERY

Among the earliest settlers of New Amsterdam were Lutherans, mainly from Holland. The first Lutheran minister is said to have been Jonas Michaelius who came over about 1628.[1]

These early Lutherans were persecuted, but the historian reminds us that such persecution was not due to social or political ideas, but to religious convictions. "They never figured as political agitators and the little band on Manhattan Island sought only the enjoyment of their spiritual rights under their own vine and fig tree."[2]

Dr. Robert Fortenbaugh, referring to the whole attitude of the Lutheran Church, says: "They particularly emphasized the confessional idea and considered that the interest of an ecclesiastical body should embrace only the strictest of ecclesiastical matters. Obviously no place was found in their deliberations for consideration of reform movements, laudable as these might be as social and political desiderata and which as private citizens they might wish to consider."[3]

---

[1] Wolf, *The Lutherans in America* (New York: J. A. Hill & Co., 1889), p. 112.

[2] *Ibid.*, p. 114.

[3] Robert Fortenbaugh, "American Lutheran Synods and Slavery 1830-1860"—*The Journal of Religion*, January 1933, p. 73.

On this same point Heathcote remarks: "The Lutheran Church in America conceiving the true mission of the church to be the spread of the gospel and the saving of men's souls, and believing that political and social issues are the province of citizens in their civil capacities, and not in their ecclesiastical organizations, has persistently refused to permit itself to be drawn either as a champion or as an opponent, into the arena of the affairs of state, whether they be political or so-called 'social reform' just as with equal steadfastness, it has resisted any attempted exercise of state domination or control in purely religious matters."

"So conservative was the Lutheran Church that it was not until the Civil War was well begun in 1862 that its southern churches severed their connection with the old general synod and organized a separate general body on confederate territory." [4]

During the last quarter of the seventeenth century a company of Dutch Lutherans withdrew from New York and settled on the Ashely River in South Carolina. Swedish Lutherans also had settled early in Delaware, and in 1734, the Salzburgers, a company of persecuted German Lutherans settled in Georgia, at Ebenezer. John Martin Boltzius was their pastor. These early Salzburgers were on principle opposed to slavery, but the pressure of their situation led them to a compromise on this principle.

"In the South, Boltzius, the leading pastor of the Salzburgers, resisted and protested against slavery, as introducing a heathenism more to be dreaded than that of the Indians, and as a great injustice to white labor. But he soon found it necessary to purchase slaves in order

---

[4] Heathcote, *The Lutheran Church and the Civil War*, pp. 8, 9.

that the work of the colony be done, and sought in every way to ameliorate their condition and provide for their religious training. The vicious principle of the system which regards the slave as a thing, and not as a person, thus disappeared. He appealed to friends in Germany to provide him with money to purchase children directly from the slave-ships, in order to train them as Christians, and save their souls. At the death bed of a slave child, one of these Georgia pastors exhorted its owner, a lady, to 'become as this child.' The venerable Madison County (Virginia) congregation owned slaves, as a part of its endowment, having a precedent for this, however in Gloria Dei Church, Philadelphia, where the pastor 'hired out the negroes that had been purchased.' "

The general influence of the Lutherans of the South was in harmony with the example of the first Georgia pastors. The most prominent Lutheran clergyman in the South of this century, Dr. John Bachman, ministered faithfully to a large number of slaves belonging to his congregation in Charleston, S. C.[5]

"When Pastor Boltzius yielded his objections of this measure, the ground which he assumed, as far as we can learn from his letters was as follows: He admitted that there was wrong, in the abstract, to place our fellow men in a state of bondage; yet if by removing the African from the heathenism of his native land to a country where his mind would be enlightened by the gospel, and provision made for the salvation of his soul, the evils of slavery might be endured in the consideration of the moral and spiritual advantages which it bestows upon its unfortunate victims. By this mode of reasoning, and by means of an essay from the pen of James Haber-

[5] Jacobs & Haas, *The Lutheran Cyclopedia* (Charles Scribner's Sons, New York, 1899), p. 448.

sham, Esq., the Salzburgers, including their pastors, after considerable hesitation, consented to have slaves brought into the colony. They did not do so, however, until after they had freely conferred with their Christian friends in Germany. The Rev. S. Urlsperger, in advising them upon this subject, says: 'If you take slaves in faith, and with the intent of conducting them to Christ, the action will not be a sin, but may prove a benediction.' This advice determined their future course in reference to this important question. The discussion of this subject had, however, produced great excitement in the Colony. In the language of another, 'The whole province dwelt, as it were on the brink of a volcano, whose intestine fires raged higher and higher, threatening at no distant period a desolating eruption.' It was under these circumstances, and when the community seemed to be on the brink of a civil war, that Mr. Boltzius wrote to the Trustees, withdrawing, on behalf of himself and the Salzburgers, their objection to the repeal of the law." [6]

The Norwegian Lutherans early took a strong position on the question of slavery.

"The 'Old Constitution.' Church Constitution For The Evangelical Lutheran Church At Jefferson Prairie, Etc., In North America.

(Article 14)

"We united ones repudiate altogether the fearful sin of giving our consent to the slave traffic; but rather use all possible diligence in bringing about, and supporting, opposition to it, to the freeing of the negroes, since Jesus said, 'All things therefore whatsoever ye would that men should do unto you, even so do ye also unto them; for this is the law and the prophets' (Matt. VII:12). They are also redeemed with the same blood and intended to inherit the same bliss, as other

---

[6] P. A. Strobel, *The Salzburgers and Their Descendants* (Baltimore: T. Newton Kurtz, 1855), pp. 104, 105.

races. We advise that each one give this matter close consideration." [7]

As early as 1809, the Lutherans of North Carolina "Resolved, that pastors have permission, on the wish and pledge of their Christian masters, to baptize their slaves." [8]

At the Annual Meeting of 1810 it was resolved: "It shall be permitted to every preacher to baptize the children of slaves of all Christian masters if they, the masters and mistresses, bind themselves to care for the Christian education of such children." [9]

The Synod of 1814 declared: "Resolved: It is our duty to preach the gospel to the negroes, and after proper instruction to admit them to all the means of Grace of the Church, and for this purpose to make room for them in the churches. That masters are, in love, requested to grant liberty to their slaves for this purpose, and herewith it is placed on record that it is the duty of the master to have them instructed in Christianity." [10]

"The Swedish Congregation in Christiania, on the arrival of Rev. S. Hisselius in 1719, decided to sell a part of their church land, using the proceeds to support the minister. Accordingly, fifty acres were sold for forty pounds, which instead of being put to interest, was used to purchase negroes for service in the parsonage." [11]

---

[7] Rohne, *Norwegian American Lutheranism Up to 1872* (New York: MacMillan Co., 1926), p. 109.

[8] *Minutes of the Evangelical Lutheran Synod of North Carolina, Seventh Convention at Guilford County*, Translated from the German Protocol-Peschau, (Newberry, S. C.: Aull & Houseal, 1894).

[9] *Kurzer Bericht von den Conferenzen, 1810* (New Market, 1811), p. 16.

[10] *Minutes of the Evangelical Lutheran Synod of North Carolina 1813-1826*. Translated by F. W. E. Peschau (Newberry, 1894).

[11] Unpublished Manuscript of Dr. Robert Fortenbaugh, p. 16.

In the venerable Madison County, Virginia, parish, the first Lutheran Church in Virginia, 1734, the first pastor, John Casper Stoever, and two lay members went to Germany and Holland soliciting for support of the parish. They collected $10,000. "The money was used to build a church, to purchase a farm and home for the pastor, and to purchase slaves to work the farm." [12]

The Synod of South Carolina took numerous actions on the question of slavery and on religious care of the slaves. The first of these seems to have been taken at the twelfth meeting convening at Barnwell, November 17, 18, and 19, 1835. It is in the form of a committee report.

"Report No. 1.

"5. In common with our fellow citizens of the South, your committee could not fail to partake of the excitement which has prevailed in our country on the crusade commenced and carried on by individuals of the North, against the liberty and peace of our Southern country, calling themselves Abolitionists. The committee recommend the adoption of the following preamble and resolutions, in accordance with the views contained in the Address of the President of the Synod.

"PREAMBLE

"Whereas individuals and Societies of the North, calling themselves Abolitionists, under the pretense of ameliorating the condition of our servants, sever the bonds of attachment which exist between the master and the slave; and whereas this unjustifiable interference with our domestic institutions is opposed to the Constitution of our common country, is subversive of our liberties as men and contrary to the precepts of our Blessed Savior who commanded servants to be obedient to their masters, and the example of the Holy Apostle Paul, who restored to his lawful owner a runaway slave; wherefore:

---

[12] Cassell, C. W., Finch, W. J. and Henkel, E. O., *History of the Lutheran Church in Virginia and East Tennessee* (Strossburg, Virginia, 1930), p. 180.

"1. Resolved: unanimously, that this Synod express their strongest disapprobation of the conduct of the Northern Abolitionists and that we look upon them as the enemies of our beloved country, whose mistaken zeal is calculated to injure the cause of morals and religion.

"2. Resolved: That we hold no correspondence with the Northern Abolitionists, and that should they send to us any of their incendiary publications, we will immediately return them.

"3. Resolved: That whilst we learn with heartfelt pleasure, that none of the ministers in our connection in the United States, have adopted the sentiments of the Abolitionists, the members of this Synod pledge themselves, in behalf of their churches in connection with them that they never will countenance such doctrines.

"In conclusion, your committee recommend that the address of the President be printed and appended to our minutes (See Appendix A)." [13]

The following year the same synod passed rather bitter resolutions on the subject of abolition activities as follows:

"It having been stated that some person or persons in all probability of our own creed, living, perhaps, in the distant North, had made violent and unchristian attacks upon some of the clerical members of this Body by name, in some of the Northern prints, for holding property in the person of slaves, some expression of the opinion of this Body ensued, relative to the manner in which all such attacks should be treated, and the impropriety and injustice of the interference or intermeddling of any religious and deliberative Body with the subject of Slavery and Slaveholding, emancipation or abolitionism, as agitated by the affected patriots and self-interested, and more than rotten hearted benefactors of this much com-

---

[13] South Carolina Synod 1824-1856. Extracts from the *Minutes of the Twelfth Meeting of the Evangelical Lutheran Synod and Ministerium of S. C. and Adjacent States* (Columbia, S. C.: Branthwaite, 1835), p. 8.

miserated race. As a full expression of the firm and unchanging determination of this Body, therefore:

"XVI. Resolved: That this Synod will not at any time, enter into a discussion of Slavery, as agitated by the Abolitionists of the day, with such an entire absence of principle, and which had already produced such painful results in the deliberative councils and churches, in some branches of christendom." [14]

Stephen A. Mealy, president of the fourteenth Synod meeting at St. John's Church, Charleston, November 11-16, 1837, in his annual report says:

"As I may not again have an opportunity to address you in my present relation to this Body, I would seize the passing occasion to recommend to the Synod, that some provision should be made for the religious instruction of that portion of our colored population within our bounds, who are disconnected with any Christian church. What should be had upon this important subject, I must leave to the united wisdom of this Synod to determine. In the Lutheran congregation in this city, the instruction of the colored people long since received that attention which its importance demands, and perhaps in no other congregation in our country do the colored members possess greater advantages for obtaining the essential elements of religious knowledge. The great majority of denominations in our land have given this subject their prayerful consideration and since God, in His inscrutable providence, has thrown this class of our race among us, it becomes our imperative duty to provide as well for their spiritual as for their temporal wants, and to use our best endeavors that they do not suffer for lack of that knowledge, which maketh wise unto salvation. It is my deliberate impression that there are hundreds of this sadly neglected people,

---

[14] Extracts from the *Minutes of the Thirteenth Meeting of the Evangelical Lutheran Synod and Ministerium of S. C. and Adjacent States*, convened at St. John's Church, Lexington District, S. C., November 1836, (Columbia, S. C.: I. C. Morgan, 1836), p. 20.

who, if rightly approached would *become worthy members of our communion.* (italics mine)

(Stephen A. Mealy, President of Synod)." [15]

The subject seems not to have been up again for several years, for the minutes make no mention of it.

The Twenty-Third Synod of South Carolina met in St. John's Church in Charleston again in 1846, and the matter of religious instruction of slaves was again raised. It comes in the form of a committee's report:

"In the President's address, there are several items of importance, that should claim the careful consideration of this body.

"1. In regard to that item referring to the management and religious instruction of the slave population under the ministry of the Lutheran Church, and other Christian denominations, your Committee is decidedly of the opinion, that it is the best mode that could be adopted to promote the best interest of both master and servant in preserving and strengthening those bonds of confidence and Christian love which the Apostles so warmly recommends to those who stand in this relation in society. We furthermore believe that if this plan should be adopted by all in our Christian community and managed in the spirit of the religion that we all profess to believe, that many of the difficulties, produced by imprudent and officious persons so detrimental to the religious interest of the slave population, would be entirely removed.

"In submitting this report, we would recommend the adoption of the following resolutions.

"1. Resolved: That in the opinion of this body, the plan proposed by the President, relative to the religious instruction and interest of the slave population, is one that would be attended with the happiest results, if prudently managed. We

---

[15] Extracts of *Minutes of the Fourteenth Lutheran Synod and Ministerium of S. C. and Adjacent States* (Charleston, 1837), pp. 37, 38.

therefore recommend to all our pastors, to exert their influence to introduce it into their congregations." [16]

At the same Synod, the President's Annual Address carries the following statement:

"Lutherans, having slaves, should exercise their right as masters to bring them to attend Divine Worship in the churches, where they hold their membership; and if such slaves desire to enter into church relations, let them be advised to unite with the churches where their owners enkindle their devotions at the alters of God. We advise that the members of the Presbyterian, Methodist and Baptist Churches, as well as of others, pursue the same course; that in the event a Lutheran should sell a slave that is a member of the Lutheran Church, to a professor of some other church, then advise said Christian slave to transfer his membership to like church where his master worships. And if another denomination, then likewise advise the slave to bring his membership to the church of his rightful owner. But, in the operation of this system, no compulsory means should be used, no other power, but that of moral suasion and spiritual right, such as rests in the persons of the masters, commanded to train up the subordinated members of their families "in the nurture and admonition of the Lord." It is singular, that in this effort to attend to our own, we have met with some opposition by those who compose not our communion, but we know our right and our duty, and we must stay by our position." [17]

Again in the President's Annual Address at the Synod meeting at St. Mark's Church, Edgefield, 1852, there is exhortation for further work among the slaves.

"We trust the following suggestions will be received in the same spirit of kindness in which they were conceived. It is with some hesitation that we have ventured to present any-

[16] *Minutes of the Twenty-Third Meeting of the Evangelical Lutheran Synod and Ministerium of S. C. and Adjacent States*, November 14-18, 1846 (Charleston: Burges and Jones, 1846), pp. 22, 23.
   [17] *Ibid.*, pp. 6, 7.

thing under this head, but presuming upon your forbearance, we venture the following.

"1. We will present, or rather re-recommend a suggestion, that we find in the President's address for 1843, viz: the religious instruction of the slaves of our own members. True, something had been done to better their moral and spiritual condition by us, but much, very much, yes, remains to be done. In many churches, the room designed for the accommodation of our colored population is not sufficiently large, that when they come to church they can gain a place within, to hear the word. Church councils or vestries should feel themselves especially entrusted with this matter, and, in common with all the lay members of the church, should see to it, that ample and comfortable provision be made for the accommodation of all their servants. And, having made said provision, we should not satisfy ourselves that all is done that can be done, We should then proceed to induce our servants to attend upon our regular ministry. To our brethren of the clergy, we would suggest the propriety, when they can command the time, as an inducement to get our slaves to church, to meet them occasionally apart from the whites, with only the elders or a few citizens present, and preach to, or exhort them, in a plain and simple manner. It will, no doubt, likewise, where we have sufficient time to do so, be of great service, to give oral catechetical instruction to all, both old and young, that we can induce to attend. For this purpose you will find Dr. Jones' Catechism well suited to your wants." [18]

Another reference in the S. C. Synod Minutes before the Civil War was in the President's annual message of 1858.

"While the colored population in our community enjoy the privilege of attending upon the means of grace in connection with their owners, would it not be more encouraging to them, if their respective pastors would, as often as

---

[18] *Minutes of the Twenty-Ninth Meeting of the Evangelical Lutheran Synod and Ministerium of S. C. and Adjacent States,* Convened at St. Mark's Church, Edgefield, S. C. (Charleston: Steam-Power Press of Walker and James, 1852), pp. 9, 10.

time and other circumstances would admit, hold special services for them, and adapt their language and discourses to their capacities; and in addition thereto, give oral catechetical instruction to their children? In my opinion, such a course would be attended with the most happy results." [19]

The same Synod urged catechetical instruction of the slaves in the following language.

"Resolved: That it is the duty of the Clergy of this body to pay a more special attention to the colored population, holding separate religious exercises for their especial benefit, and where it can be done, to give them oral catechetical instruction; and we earnestly recommend to the owners of slaves to give their hearty cooperation to the ministry.

"Resolved: That similar Committees to the one already in existence for the Seminary fund, be annually appointed to confer and advise with the Treasurers of the Synodical and Widow's Funds." [20]

The Synod of 1859 twice refers to this matter of instructing the slaves.

"The committee on minutes of last meeting report the following items of business requiring the action of the Synod:

"On page 15, is a resolution making it the duty of the clergy in our connection to hold special services for the colored population, and give them oral catechetical instruction. Your committee ask if this duty has been performed. Respectfully submitted,

N. Aldrich,
W. Berly.

"In reply to the above the roll was called, and each pastor gave a brief statement of what he had done. It was gratifying

[19] *Minutes of the Thirty-Fifth Meeting of the Evangelical Lutheran Synod and Ministerium of S. C. and Adjacent States,* Convened at Pine Grove Church, Orangeburg District, Oct. 28 to Nov. 1, 1858 (Charleston: Steam-Power Press, Walker and Evans, 1858), p. 8.
[20] *Minutes of the Thirty-Fifth Meeting of the Evangelical Lutheran Synod and Ministerium of S. C. and Adjacent States,* p. 15.

to learn that nearly all had given the subject proper attention, and that our colored brethren had every necessary attention and instruction.

"Bro. A. J. Kern offered the following:

"Resolved: That a committee of three be appointed, to report at next meeting of the Synod, the views of this body on the marriage relation existing between slaves." [21]

The Secretary's report to the same Synod speaks as follows:

"Twenty-four white and twenty colored members have been received, and others are prepared for taking this step as soon as an opportunity is afforded. But while your Missionary had been so signally blessed in his labors, he informs us that the field is too large for a single laborer to occupy to advantage, and urges us to send at least one more laborer into this inviting field. We trust we may be able, at this meeting, to attain this desirable object." [22]

As proof of the activity of the South Carolina Lutheran interest in religious effort for the slaves, the three following tables of Negro Communicants is most significant:

[21] *Minutes of the Evangelical Lutheran Synod and Ministerium of S. C. and Adjacent States,* Convened at Beth-Eden, S. C., Oct. 1859 (Charleston: Steam-Power Press, Walker and Evans, 1859), p. 30.
[22] *Ibid.,* p. 37.

"Minutes of the Thirty-Fourth Meeting, p. 13.

PAROCHIAL REPORTS—(1857)

MINISTERS REPORTING	No. of Congregations	BAPTISMS				MEMBERS RECEIVED		COMMUNICANTS		Burials	SUNDAY SCHOOLS			Benevolent Societies
		White		Colored		White	Colored	White	Colored		Schools	Teachers	Scholars	
		Adult	Infant	Adult	Infant									
TOTAL	51	69	451	112	181	331	249	4138	851	209	32	207	1211	21

"Minutes of the Thirty-Fifth Meeting, p. 9.

PAROCHIAL REPORTS — (1858)

MINISTERS REPORTING	No. of Congregations	BAPTISMS				MEMBERS RECEIVED		COMMUN-ICANTS		Burials	SUNDAY SCHOOLS			Benevolent Societies
		White		Colored										
		Adult	Infant	Adult	Infant	White	Colored	White	Colored		Schools	Teachers	Scholars	
TOTAL	43	74	313	63	176	363	150	3838	832	132	34	187	1139	23

"Minutes of the Thirty-Seventh Meeting, p. 11.

PAROCHIAL REPORTS — (1860)

MINISTERS REPORTING	No. of Congregations	BAPTISMS				MEMBERS RECEIVED		COMMUN-ICANTS		Burials	SUNDAY SCHOOLS			Benevolent Societies
		White		Colored										
		Adult	Infant	Adult	Infant	White	Colored	White	Colored		Schools	Teachers	Scholars	
TOTAL	48	49	417	52	146	337	118	4056	959	198	39	283	1308	23

"Dr. J. Bachman has 'a colored Sabbath School, with 32 teachers, and 150 pupils. There are also religious societies connected with the congregation.' " [23]

The North Carolina Synod urged the churches to provide for the religious care of the slaves in the following language.

"Resolved: That it be recommended by this Synod, that the clergy belonging to the same, use their respective influences in their congregations to have some place provided in each church for the colored people within the bounds of the same, and that a part of their sermons be particularly addressed to them." [24]

Fortenbaugh says that the Pennsylvania and New York Ministeriums did not officially consider slavery, and that the Synods of Ohio and Tennessee likewise refused to speak officially on the subject. [25]

The Hartwich Synod of Albany, New York, and westward, withdrew from the New York Synod because of dissatisfaction with that Synod's attitude. This Synod, organized in 1830, voted mild resolutions in 1836. Because this Hartwich Synod was not radical enough, a group drew off from it in 1837 and formed the Franckean Synod, which was the most aggressive and outspoken of all the Synods against slavery. [26]

When the Franckean Synod drew up its constitution, articles 7 and 8 were specifically aimed at slavery.

---

[23] Copied from the *Minutes of Synod of S. C.,* 1857, 1858, 1860.

[24] *Minutes of the Evangelical Lutheran Synod and Ministerium of N. C., and Adjacent Parts,* Convened at St. John's Church, Cabarrus Co., N. C., May 1837, (Salisbury: Western Carolinian Office, 1837), p. 12.

[25] *Journal of Religion,* January 1933, p. 74.

[26] *Journal of Religion,* January 1933, pp. 74, 75.

"Constitution Article VII:—Of Delegates.

"Section 3. No person shall be entitled to a seat in this Synod as delegate or commissioner who has not attained the age of twenty-one years, and who is not a regular communicant member of the church. Neither shall he be a slaveholder, nor engaged directly or indirectly in the manufacture and traffic of intoxicating liquors to be used as a beverage.

"Article VIII:—Of Ordained Ministers.

"Section 6. No minister of this gospel shall be a member of this Synod who shall not sign the pledge of total abstinence from intoxicating liquors as a beverage; or who is a slaveholder, or traffics in human beings, or advocates the system of slavery as it exists in these United States." [27]

The same convention passed the following resolution:

"Bro. John Uline introduced the following resolutions on the subject of American slavery, which were discussed and unanimously adopted:

"1. Resolved: That slavery as it exists in the United States, the holding in bondage and buying and selling human beings, is a sin in the sight of God, opposed to the spirit of the gospel and a violation of the inalienable rights of man.

"2. Resolved: That we do not deem it inexpedient for ecclesiastical bodies to interfere with the abolition of slavery; but that it is the duty of all such bodies of every evangelical denomination, to bear their decided testimony against the SIN of slavery.

"3. Resolved: That we have abundant cause for deep humiliation before God, that as a denomination, we are so deeply involved in the Sin of Slavery, and that so many of our

---

[27] *Proceedings of a Convention of Ministers and Delegates from Evangelical Lutheran Churches, in the State of N. Y., Fordsbush, Montgomery Co.* (Albany: Hoffman and White), May 24, 1837, pp. 8, 9.

ministers practice the crime, and that so many others justify them in their iniquity.

"4. Resolved: That we view the traffic in human beings as carried on in this country, and between ministers of the gospel and members of churches, as revolting to humanity and as repugnant to the laws of Christ, as ever was the foreign slave trade." [28]

This Synod was so outspoken that the General Synod rebuked them in 1839, and we find the Virginia Synod repudiating the interference of the Franckean Synod as follows:

"On motion of Bro. Stork,

"1. Resolved: That this body disclaims the ecclesiastical censorship of any particular Synod.

"2. Resolved: That the pretensions of this description assumed by the Franckean Synod in regard to other ecclesiastical bodies meet with our decided disapprobation, and that we totally discard any such arrogant assumption of spiritual censorship.

"3. Resolved: That we will not encourage the circulation of the 'Lutheran Herald' published under the auspices of that body, among our members; and that we warmly recommend the 'Lutheran Observer' to all who desire a religious paper, as most admirably adapted to every section of our country, as breathing a spirit of enlarged and comprehensive liberality, calculated to produce unanimity of sentiment and concert of action throughout the church." [29]

The Franckean Synod sent out to all other Synods a Fraternal Appeal on slavery which drew some rather cold response. The Maryland Synod responded.

---

[28] *Proceedings of a Convention of Ministers and Delegates from Evangelical Lutheran Churches, in the State of N. Y., Fordsbush, Montgomery Co.,* May 24, 1837, p. 18.

[29] *Proceedings of the Evangelical Lutheran Synod of Va., Zion's Church, Roanoke Co.,* May 1839 (Printed in the Va. office, Winchester, 1839), p. 11.

"Your committee reports that the second document handed to them is a memorial on the subject of slavery from the Evangelical Lutheran Franckean Synod. Your committee would recommend that as this Synod cannot entertain any subject not immediately connected with our Synodical business, the memorial be laid on the table." [30]

The Synod of the West answered:

"Resolved: That we feel grateful to the Franckean Synod for their well meant attempt to enlighten us on the subject of American Slavery, and that our minds being always open to conviction on any subject, so soon as conviction has done its work, we will act; at the same time recommend to them the propriety of considering well the measures of abolitionists in the present day before they act." [31]

In 1844, the Franckean Synod took the following action:

"On motion, the regular order of business was suspended in order to take up the antislavery question.

"On motion of Bro. D. Ottman, and seconded by Bro. H. L. Dox,

"Resolved: That the vote on the preamble and resolution on slavery be reconsidered.

"After being altered by inserting the 'greater portion' and read churches for 'church' the motion made for adoption, and it being put by the President, it was carried unanimously, by a rising vote.

"The preamble and resolution were as follows:

"Whereas, slavery is manifestly a sin against God, a violation of the laws of nature, the claims of justice, and the doctrines of divine revelation, depriving those who were created in God's own image, and for whom Christ died, of social rights and domestic privileges and the means of reli-

---

[30] *Minutes of the Maryland Synod,* 1842, p. 23.
[31] *Journal of the Synod of the West,* 1842, p. 15.

gious improvement; and whereas we deeply regret that it prevails to such an alarming extent throughout the churches of our land, and is also countenanced and sustained by the greater portion of the Lutheran churches and synods in the United States; therefore

"Resolved: That as this Synod has frequently expressed its entire and decided disapprobation of this unrighteous system, we are called upon to rebuke those who are known to the world as professed followers of Christ, and our duty demands that we dissolve all Christian connection with slave traffickers and slaveholders on the same ground and for the same reasons that we do persons guilty of other sins and immoralities." [32]

In 1846, the Franckean Synod had a committee report on Slavery as follows:

"American Slavery

"The Committee to whom was referred the subject of American Slavery, feeling the importance of progressing in the work of reform, and from time to time planting our standard on higher ground, would as expressive of the sense of this body, report the following, viz:

"Whereas, We have from time to time, at the annual sessions of our Synod, expressed our unqualified disapprobation of the system of American Slavery, as well as our decided condemnation of such professed Christians as are implicated in its perpetuity, either by holding slaves, apologizing for the system, or countenancing it by their silence and 'masterly inactivity' in relation thereto: and

"Whereas, the slave power is becoming more and more daring in the exercise of its influence in the political and religious world; now goading the one to deeds of desperation, to defend its private citadel against the attacks of those who seek its destruction; and now convulsing and separating ec-

---

[32] *Journal of Franckean Synod,* June 1844 (West Sandlake: Herald Office, 1844), pp. 18, 19.

clesiastical associations, who on this subject are like 'a house divided against itself'; therefore,

"Resolved: That our conviction of the hatefulness, the rottenness, and the guilt of American Slavery, grows stronger with every new effort which the advocates put forth to fortify and thus secure its continuance; and that we feel solemnly bound, as we love God, and respect the common principles of humanity, to be vigilant and active, to thrust the sword of truth through the monster's heart that he die.

"Resolved: That as this Synod, since its organization has stood pledged to make use of every energy for the suppression of the sin of slavery, it involves such members of this body, who have withholden their earnest opposition to an inconsistency, and that out of respect to themselves and a due regard to the publicly avowed character of the Synod with which they stand connected, they should forwith identify themselves heartily and practically with the friends of freedom.

"Resolved: That a Special Committee be appointed, to correspond with other Synodical bodies who have taken action on the subject of American Slavery, in order to induce them to appoint a committee to draft a protest, jointly, against slavery, and secure the signatures of as many of the clergy of the Lutheran denomination as possible.

S. Ottman,

N. Van Alstine,

A. Beekman.

The report elicited some remarks, and was unanimously adopted." [33]

In 1847, the Franckean Synod sent out a vigorous protest against slavery, and in 1851, it attacked the Fugitive Slave Law.

"Resolved: That the late Fugitive Slave Bill, passed in

---

[33] *Journal of Franckean Synod*, June 1846, p. 16.

Congress, is the ill-shaped and hydra-headed offspring of bold usurpation and unmitigated cruelty; that it has no safeguard in the natural and social rights of man, nor can it find any sanctions in the clear-pealing thunders of Sinai, its blazing fires and the voice of God, or in the teachings of Calvary, sending its mellowing notes of love and pity upon a despairing world; therefore the Church of God, its altars, its worship and its solemn notes of praise, should afford no retreat of protection; nay, not even the smile which the harlot of slavery, might, as a cordial approval or willing acquiescence to its foul conspiracy against justice, and the inherent rights of co-equal man.

"Resolved: That the only obedience we can conscientiously render to this bill, and to all others of the same affinity, is obedience in suffering its equally unjust penalty as martyrs to truth and conscience, in the spirit of those divine precepts and examples that 'it is better to suffer wrong, than to do wrong,' 'we should obey God rather than man.' " [34]

The Synods of 1855 and 1856 each had a full committee report condemning slavery. We quote only the report of 1855.

"Your Committee, on the subject of Slavery, would respectfully report:

"That although the subject of Slavery, and many of its wrongs, have by their constant agitation become familiar with every school boy; and every body has heard the sad tales and looked upon the horrid pictures of woe connected with the system; so much so, that many hearts have become sick of hearing, and many eyes have grown dim with seeing; and yet Slavery is unchanged. Slavery is Slavery still. Although thousands, noble and true to the cause of God and philanthropy, have lifted up their voices like trumpets, have cried aloud and spared not, and have shown the sin and evil of this system, we still do hear the clanking chains of human chattels, and the fatal strokes of the auctioneer's hammer,

---

[34] *Journal of Franckean Synod,* June 1851, p. 16.

disposing of God's poor, robbed of their manhood and deprived of the possession of their own souls. We still hear the shrieks of children wrested from their parents and see the wailing tear scalding the parental cheek. . . .

"Resolved: That notwithstanding the many efforts that have been put forth, and the long conflict maintained against Slavery and its concomitant evils, it becomes all true philanthropists and lovers of human liberty to continue unceasingly active, in vigorously pressing their cause in final triumph.

"Resolved: That Slavery, as it exists in the United States, is unchanged in its character; that it cannot appropriately receive any more christian epithet than the 'sum of all villainies'; that it is a system of unsoundness and vileness from the crown of its head to the sole of its foot, and a heinous sin against Almighty God. Therefore,

"Resolved: That it illy becomes a christian people to connive at the evil; but places the followers of a meek and lovely Saviour under solemn and binding obligations to labor to the utmost of their abilities for its entire annihilation.

G. W. Hemperley,
N. Van Alstine,
J. Welch." [35]

The Pittsburg Synod refused to unite with the General Synod in 1851 and gave as its reasons the following:

"Reasons for not uniting with the General Synod.

"Your committee, upon whom was imposed the difficult and important task of setting forth the reasons which led to the rejection of the resolution to unite itself with the General Synod, would respectfully and briefly report as follows:

"1. The objection on the ground of the General Synod's doctrinal basis was waived by those who had previously objected on this account, etc. . . .

---

[35] *Journal of Franckean Synod*, June 1855, pp. 14, 15. (See also report for 1856, pp. 13-15.)

"2. It was urged that it would cause distractions and divisions in some of our churches, and it would likewise shut us out to a great extent, from exerting an influence on a large class of our population, and on a portion of the church which it is our duty and desire to bless.

"3. The objection, however, mainly urged, was that the General Synod was identified with slavery; that delegates being slaveholders are admitted as members, and that we by uniting become implicated in the sin of slavery. This position, though strenuously opposed, even to the last, finally having excited the minds of some, influenced them to cast their votes against the union, hence the resolution for the union was lost." [36]

The Lutheran Observer, which claimed to be national in scope was started in Baltimore in 1831. It attempted to be neutral on Slavery, but it was evidently anti-abolitionist. In its issue of March 11, 1836, it is betrayed into a discussion of abolition.

"A few days ago we received a somewhat ranting communication over the signature of 'A Lutheran Abolitionist,' without name or date, or any other evidence to indicate where, when or by whom it was written except the postmark, which is 'Palatine Bridge, (N.Y.) Feb., 22.' The writer declaims in unmeasured terms against slavery; informs us that this subject 'is occupying the attention of the christians of the Lutheran Church in N.Y.,' asks us to insert in our paper an advertisement extracted from the National Intelligencer for the purchase of slaves; and adds 'Lutheran here, will do their duty ere long on this subject and we wish to be heard.'

"We should not have stopped to notice this ebulition of feeling, if the anonymous author had not subjected us to the payment of the postage; but with all his zeal for the rights of slaves, he did not scruple to tax us at 25 cents, and thus set at naught our rights and overlooked the common principles of justice between man and man. And now since we have our pen in hand, we would ask this 'Abolitionist' in

---

[36] *Minutes of Pittsburgh Synod,* June 1851, p. 18.

reference to his communication, Cui bono? were you not previously aware that it is contrary to our established regulations to publish such articles without a responsible signature? Moreover, did you not know from explicit declarations made by us in the Observer, as also from the uniform course we have thus far pursued, that we do not meddle with the 'next question' of slavery, and that your request therefore could not have been complied with even though accompanied by your proper name? . . . But if you are so anxious and decided in your views concerning slavery, why shelter yourself behind a fictitious signature and aim your javelins over our shoulders? If you have taken your position under the banner of abolitionism and are panting to be in the heat of battle, then down with your visor and stand forth a la mode Garrison and Thompson in your own proper name and person; . . ." [37]

In July, 1844, a lengthy article appeared in the Observer commenting on the split in the Methodist Church over Slavery.

On August 23, 1850, the Observer again shows a sympathetic attitude toward the South in an article on the treatment of slaves.

"We often hear and read of the cruelties said to be practiced on the slaves of the South, and without wishing to say anything in defence or extenuation of cruelty, we must maintain, that a vast amount of falsehood and slander has been put into circulation on this subject, while in many cases the truth is suppressed. For instance, how seldom do we hear of the religious and other advantages enjoyed by the slaves, not merely by the permission or connivance of their humane masters, but through their positive efforts to procure them. We feel assured our Christian readers will rejoice to learn, that many masters not only allow, but actually take pains to obtain for them, means of intellectual and moral improvement. In the State of Maryland, and elsewhere, many of them are taught to read and write. Still farther South, more and more attention is paid to their religious instruction on the

---

[37] *Lutheran Observer*, Vol. III, No. 29, March 11, 1836, p. 115.

plantations. The Bible is beginning to be extensively distributed among them. Missionaries are employed in the State of Georgia, for example, to labor for their special benefit. Thousands of them have been hopefully converted within the last few years. A large number of churches and congregations have been organized, consisting exclusively of colored people, and they have a considerable number of very respectable colored preachers. Not a few are members of the same churches with their masters and mistresses, and a great many pastors are devoting an unusual share of their time to the instruction of the slaves on the plantations around them." [38]

The Observer for Oct., 1854, carries a full article on the evangelization of the Negroes in Georgia.

"But I wish to direct a few thoughts to another subject, and that is, that a portion of the members received into the church during our meetings were from the colored population of our country. I would here state, for the information of our northern brethren, that I preach to the colored people of my charge; a portion of the church is assigned to them, where they can hear preaching every Sabbath, if so disposed. The churches generally in this country have made provision for the colored people to hear preaching, and in many places men are employed to preach exclusively to them. You no doubt would be astonished if you could be present in some of our colored congregations and hear them carry on the various parts of music, pray, and exhort. There is more intelligence among them than many people imagine. They are not that oppressed, bornedown, trampled-under-foot people that many represent them to be . . .

"These remarks have not been made from any improper motives, but simply to set forth things in part in their proper light, and to let our people know elsewhere what we are doing in this country for our colored population. I hope these remarks will be received with all kindness by those that may still differ with us in sentiment; ever keeping in mind that we are brethren engaged in one common cause, and that we

---

[38] *Lutheran Observer*, Vol. 18, No. 34, August 23, 1850, p. 339.

should not fall out by the way. May God add his blessing, pardon error, and save us in his kingdom, Amen.

L. Bedenbaugh.

Haralson, Ga., Sept. 20, 1854." [39]

The Missionary, with Passavant as Editor was started in 1848 because the Observer seemed too neutral.

This paper carried a full article by John Bachman, the pastor of St. John's Church in Charleston and one of the most influential ministers of the Lutheran Church of his time. Because of his deep interest in the Negro and because of his wide leadership, we quote it almost complete.

"Strictures on Resolutions of the Middle Conference.

"Charleston, Nov., 24th, 1857.

"Dear Brother Passavant:

"In your valuable paper, The Missionary, of the 1st of October last, there appeared a report and resolutions, in which your brethren of the South, holding the same Christian faith with you, felt themselves aggrieved. Although at the recent meeting of the Synod of South Carolina, it was not deemed advisable to notice these transactions, inasmuch as they did not emanate from a Synod, yet as a general wish was expressed that something should be written, in reply, by the individual who sends you this communication, he accordingly requests the favor of you to insert in your columns the following defence. He does this very reluctantly. He feels convinced that these discussions are rather calculated to irritate than to convince; he believes that they are better adapted to the columns of a secular than a religious paper, and if he is drawn out on this occasion to infringe on a rule which he has heretofore uniformly observed, perhaps the occasion may offer an excuse. Under any circumstances, he will not prolong

---

[39] *Lutheran Observer*, Vol. 22, No. 42, October 13, 1854, p. 116.

the controversy by writing a single line in answer to any reply to this communication.

"................

"The Abolitionists of the North have long made it a standing charge against the South that slaves are prohibited from reading the Word of God. When, some years ago, incendiary tracts, advising the Southern Slaves to insurrection, were scattered throughout the Southern country, at first through the mails, and then by private agents, and when in a few cases insurrections were thus instigated, some of the states passed laws to prevent the teaching of slaves to read and write. These laws soon became a dead letter. The Word of God was never denied them. On a vast number of our Southern Plantations, missionaries, in addition to the regular services on the Sabbath, visit each plantation on some day in the week, to instruct the children from the Catechism and the Bible. The churches of every denomination are all open to them, in some, the colored attendants are more numerous than the whites. When the heads of families retire from the holy communion table, the servants come forward and surround the same altar. Many servants are taught to read by the younger portion of the white members of the family, and the Bible is found in thousands of families of the colored population. In our churches, the ministers appoint the intelligent, best educated and most pious among the slaves to the superintendence and instruction of their fellow servants, under the name of leaders. These read and expound to them the Bible, and visit them in sickness and in trouble. It is by all these instrumentalities that the slaves of the South are preserved from these temptations to vice, which render the same race in the North less submissive to the laws and less inclined to religious influences. . . .

"................

"In conclusion, allow us to present the following as a summary of our views on this subject.

"1. Whilst we freely accord to all our brethren of the nonslaveholding states the right of entertaining their own opinions on the subject of slavery, and of framing the laws of their states in accordance with their views, we regret that even a small number should have undesignedly misrepresented the institutions and people of the South, with which they appear wholly unacquainted, and in language so unkind and uncharitable.

"....................

"4. Inasmuch as our secular presses are best adapted to discuss the subject of slavery, and as these may be read every day in the week, we possess the means of being fully informed on these subjects; on the other hand, as our religious papers are intended to cultivate piety and exercise of the feeling of charity and love; as they form the subjects of reading and instruction on the Sabbath, and as we encourage their perusal in our families by our wives and daughters and children, we cannot regard these discussions as suited for a religious journal. The little space that could be spared for such discussions on either side, would scarcely produce conviction on a single mind; at any rate, the evil produced on tempers and feelings, the danger of misrepresentations and consequent retaliations, greatly over balance any good that it can possibly accomplish.

"We have read over the above, to ascertain whether any expression might have escaped our pen that could be construed into personal disrespect toward our brethren whose resolutions have called forth our dissent and our well-meant advice. They are all personally unknown to us, and we have no motive to give them pain. We have been actuated by the sole desire of preserving the unity of the church, both in the North and the South; of strengthening those feelings of love and charity which should characterize us as ministers of the venerable Church of the Reformation, and of preserving that blessed Union of States which should be dear to every American heart. If, however, we have unwittingly said aught that carried us beyond the line of legitimate defence, we shall regret it, and it will only afford another evidence of the danger that may be apprehended when clergymen enter on this debatable ground, whilst there is so much room, and such earnest calls for labor, in a field which we may occupy without dissension, where we will be cheered by the approbation of the good on earth, the smiles of angels in light, and the bright rewards of a God of love.

Fraternally yours,
John Bachman." [40]

It will be seen from the above that the Lutheran Church was from the beginning deeply interested in the religious instruction of the colored people. It only remains to note a few special illustrations of this.

Perhaps no one better typifies the interest of the Church in this work than Rev. John Bachman who served St. John's Church in Charleston from 1810 to 1860. "The Minutes of the year (1860) record 560 communicants, 370 white and 190 black; Sunday School for the whites, teachers 20, pupils 120; for the blacks, teachers 32, pupils 150." [41]

"The two story lecture room, built in 1831 was especially adopted for the use of the two schools. The upper story was occupied by the white school, the basement by the colored." [42]

In 1816, at his request the North gallery of St. John's Church was apportioned to the colored flock. Never was there a more orderly congregation. On Sunday morning the whites took the sacrament first and then the blacks. [43]

Another outstanding Lutheran, Dr. Muhlenberg, was deeply interested in the religious care of the Negroes. The sympathy with which he felt for the colored race is also brought out by the fact that when in 1745, the Augustus Church at Providence was dedicated, three

---

[40] *The Missionary*, Vol. II, No. 46, p. 181.
[41] Wolher, *John Bachman, Letters and Memories of his Life* (Charleston: Evans & Cogwell, 1888), p. 354.
[42] *Ibid.*, p. 354.
[43] Wolher, *op. cit.*, p. 354.

Negroes, slaves of Mr. Rawlings, were at the solemn occasion publicly examined as to their knowledge of the fundamental doctrine of Christianity, and then baptized. Muhlenberg had taken the trouble to properly prepare them for this rite by necessary instruction.[44]

One more simple illustration is the record of the Lutheran Church of Shelbyville, Tennessee, organized in 1820, and in which there appear numerous names of Negroes, who were baptized and taken into full communion of that Church.[45]

---

[44] Mann's *Life of Muhlenberg*, pp. 289, 290.
[45] The Church Record is at present in the hands of G. W. Armstrong, the pastor.

CHAPTER VI

THE ATTITUDE OF PRESBYTERIAN CHURCHES TOWARD THE NEGRO DURING SLAVERY

In order to get a clear picture of the attitude of Presbyterians toward the Negro, it seems wise to briefly sketch the organization of the various branches of the Presbyterian Church in America. This denomination in America dates from the founding of the first Presbytery in 1705 (near Philadelphia) by Frances Makemie. The first synod, composed of four Presbyteries, was organized at Philadelphia in 1717.[1]

The first split came in the denomination when those who believed in methods of revivalism, and in licensing of ministers without full theological training, pulled away from what was called the Old Side Presbyterians in 1741, and established what was known as New Side Presbyterian Churches. Only a short while after this, 1747, Samuel Davies, a New Side Presbyterian, came into Virginia, and began his labors, out of which grew the Hanover Presbytery, which included all Presbyterian churches south of the Potomac. Davies was greatly concerned about the religious conditions among the slaves. In a letter written by him in 1755, to a member of the Society in London for Promoting Christian Knowledge among the Poor, he says: "The poor neglected Negroes

---

[1] Lingle, *Presbyterians, Their History and Beliefs* (Pres. Comm. of Publications, 1928), p. 124. Klett, *Presbyterians in Colonial Pennsylvania,* thinks the date may be 1706—see p. 45f.

who are so far from having money to purchase books that they themselves are the property of others; who were originally African savages, and never heard of the name of Jesus and His gospel until they arrived in the land of their slavery in America. . . . Those poor unhappy Africans are objects of my compassion and I think the most proper objects of the Society's charity." [2]

The Old Side and the New Side churches were reunited in 1758, under the Synod of New York and Philadelphia.[3] In 1788, the Church was divided into four synods, namely, the Synod of Philadelphia, the Synod of New York and New Jersey, the Synod of Virginia, and the Synod of the Carolinas.[4] The first General Assembly grew out of these synods, and was organized in Philadelphia in 1789.

In 1810, there arose another secession movement over the question of licensing ministers without full theological training and the Cumberland Presbyterian Church came into being. This group remained a separate church until 1906, when the larger proportion of them were reabsorbed into the Presbyterian Church, U.S.A.

For many years prior to 1837, the Presbyterians and the Congregationalists worked together in missionary projects. But in 1837, the Old School Presbyterians declared this union as unconstitutional and again brought about a rift in the denomination. By this time the question of slavery was already beginning to give great concern to both branches of the denomination. In 1845, in

---

[2] Harrison, *The Gospel Among the Slaves* (Publishing House of M.E. Church, South, 1893), pp. 50, 51.

[3] *Records of the Presbyterian Church in the U.S.A.*, *Philadelphia*, *1841*, p. 548.

[4] Lingle, *op. cit.*, p. 129.

1846, and in 1857, very drastic resolutions were passed against slavery as will be seen in more detail later.

The New School Assembly split over the slavery question in 1857, and the Old School split over allegiance to the government in 1861.

Those Presbyterians, both of the Old School and the New School who were strongly favorable to abolition gradually came together in 1870, as the Presbyterian Church, U.S.A. Those Presbyterians who were opposed to the abolition movement, and were favorable to the Confederate cause, organized in 1861 a General Assembly, known as the Presbyterian Church in the Confederate States of America, which name was later changed to the Presbyterian Church in the United States.

The United Presbyterian Church was founded in 1858 by the combination of the Associate and Associate Reformed Synods, and among their very first actions was a very strong declaration against slavery.[5]

The Associate Reformed Synod was organized in the South in 1821. The real father of this movement was the spirit of Ebenezer Erskine coming down from the past, after whom Erskine College in South Carolina is named. The withdrawal of this group was partly due to their long distance (they lived in the lower South) from the Philadelphia General Assembly, but perhaps it was much more largely due to the fact that this southern group, being conservative, felt that the general church was far too lax in matters of Psalmody and of Communion. Latham maintains that the slavery issue was not up in this division, and that this Southern Synod was almost unanimously opposed to slavery.[6]

---

[5] Lingle, *op. cit.*, pp. 167, 168.
[6] Latham, *History of the Associate Reformed Synod of the South*, 1882, p. 325.

This, then, is a brief sketch of the divisional organization of the Presbyterian up to the time of the Civil War. We shall now need to trace the issue of slavery in these various groups, and see in detail what the attitude of each group was toward the institution of slavery, and what the attitude of each was toward the welfare of the slave himself.

Latham says that the Synod of the South (Associate Reformed) was decidedly antislavery up to 1830, when the Vesey plot and other influences brought about a somewhat changed attitude. In 1828, the Synod of the South passed strong resolutions opposing the proposed action of the South Carolina legislature, prohibiting education of slaves. Many Associate Reformed Presbyterians migrated west during this period, just as did many Quakers, in order to get free from the influences of slavery. When the Western Synod in 1827 raised the issue of slavery, it was probably largely due to the influence of the Southern Presbyterians who had moved west. The memorial sent up from the church at Hopewell, Ohio, was certainly influenced by these southerners, since this church was almost wholly composed of these South Carolina migrants.[7] In 1834, the Synod of the South made moves to establish a college and theological seminary, because it was "prejudicial to the Southern Church to send its young men north and west." [8] It is altogether likely that the influence which was prejudicial was theological rather than social. At least slavery was not mentioned in the discussion of the project.

One can state rather briefly the position of the Cumberland Presbyterian Church on slavery. First of all, it

---

[7] Latham, *op. cit.*, pp. 359-361.
[8] *Ibid.*, p. 366.

attempted to steer clear of all discussion of slavery, since slavery was, as they held, a civic matter and not an ecclesiastical matter. This they stated again and again in their official documents. Due to this attitude they were able to hold together and not split over the slavery issue, although there were individuals in the church holding strong opinions on both sides of this question.[9] The most notable resolution of the Cumberland Presbyterian Assembly on the question of slavery, passed in 1851, read as follows: "Resolved that inasmuch as the Cumberland Presbyterian Church was originally organized and has ever since existed and prospered under the conceded principle that slavery was not and should not be regarded as a bar to communion, we therefore believe that it should not now be so regarded." [10]

In 1864, when the Civil War was in progress, the Assembly passed the following resolutions: "Resolved that we regard the holding of human beings in involuntary slavery, as practiced in some of the states of the American Union, as contrary to the precepts of our holy religion, and as being the fruitful source of many evils and vices in the social system, therefore: Resolved that it be recommended to Cumberland Presbyterians, both North and South, to give countenance and support to all constitutional efforts of our government to rid the country of that enormous evil." [11]

After the Civil War the colored members of the Cumberland Presbyterian churches continued for some time in active affiliation with the regular churches, but in 1869 and 1870, a move was made by the colored min-

---

[9] Stephens, *The Cumberland Presbyterian Digest* (Nashville, 1899), pp. 341-351.
[10] *Ibid.*, p. 150.
[11] *Ibid.*, p. 350.

isters to establish separate Presbyteries and Synods, and this move was encouraged by the General Assembly. However, in 1883, there was a countermove by the colored church to reunite with the parent body, but the memorial to that effect was not approved. The General Assembly repeatedly voted approval and sympathy for all forward moves of the colored branch of the church, and urged the white churches to make contributions to the educational funds of the colored church. In 1898, the Assembly recommended that colored candidates for the ministry be directed to Fisk University in Nashville, Tennessee, and that the General Assembly undertake to cooperate in seeing that the history, polity, and doctrine of the Cumberland Presbyterian Church be taught to such students.[12]

The United Presbyterian Church, composed of a union of the Associate Synod and Associate Reformed Synod in 1858, has its first General Assembly in Xenia, Ohio, in 1859. The basis of union was the Westminster Confession and what is known as "The Testimony." The fourteenth article of The Testimony reads as follows: "We declare that slaveholding—that is the holding of unoffending human beings in involuntary bondage, and considering and treating them as property to be bought and sold—is a violation of the law of God and contrary both to the letter and spirit of Christianity." [13] To this article is appended three pages of what is called "Argument and Illustration" setting forth the Biblical basis for adopting this article.

No action concerning slavery was taken at the second Assembly meeting in Philadelphia in 1860.

---

[12] Stephens, *op. cit.*, pp. 351-359.
[13] *Confession of Faith* (United Presbyterian Board of Publication, 1869), p. 570f.

The Board of Missions to Freedmen of the United Presbyterian Church was chartered under the laws of Pennsylvania in 1868. In the historical statement appended it is set forth that this Board had been organized in 1863, and that some work had been carried forward on behalf of Negroes even earlier than that. The chief work of this Board seems to have centered in Knoxville College.[14]

Special activities for Negroes in the North were undertaken later on. In 1928, the Board of American Missions was organized to take over the work of the Board of Missions to Freedmen and the work of a number of other Boards of the Church. This Board of Missions has a Negro Department which has close supervision of Knoxville College, and other work with Negroes. This in brief is the summary of the work of the United Presbyterian Church for Negroes.

We now turn to the two main bodies of the Presbyterians, namely, the Presbyterian Church in the Confederate States of America, later called The Presbyterian Church in the United States, and the Presbyterian Church in the United States of America. These bodies are popularly designated as Presbyterians U.S. and Presbyterians U.S.A.

First let us see the background of these two denominations. The Presbyterians had for a long time the problem of slavery to deal with. In discussing the sending of missionaries to Africa as early as 1774, the synod had found the whole question of slavery raised, but since there were "some difficulties attending the discussion of the second part of that overture (namely, that per-

---

[14] *Digest of the Principal Deliverances of the General Assembly of United Presbyterian Churches of North America* (Pittsburgh, 1842), p. 138f.

taining to domestic slavery) the synod agrees to defer the affair to our next meeting." [15] However, when the next meeting was held, the colonies were at war with Great Britain and no mention was made of the Negro or of slavery. The next time the question was raised seems to have been in 1780 when the synod was meeting in Philadelphia on May 17 of that year. At this meeting it was reported that the Hanover Presbytery was not represented.[16] In the minutes of this synod it was noted, "An affair respecting the enslaving of Negroes appears to have been before the Synod of 1774, but by some means passed over by the following synods and not since resumed." [17] "The synod resumed the consideration of that affair and after debating the affair to considerable length, adjourned." [18] There is no further notice of it in the minutes of this meeting, hence, the matter must have been dropped without action.

The next mention we have of the question of slavery comes in the minutes of the meeting held in Philadelphia in 1787. The Committee of Overtures in this meeting brought in the following statement: "The Creator of the world, having made of one flesh all of the children of men, it becomes them as members of the same family, to consult and promote each other's happiness. It is more especially the duty of those who acknowledge and teach the obligations of Christianity, to use such means as are in their power to extend the blessings of equal freedom to every part of the human race.

"From a full conviction of these truths and sensible

---

[15] *Records of the Presbyterian Church in the U.S.A.* (Philadelphia: Presbyterian Board of Publication, 1904).

[16] *Ibid.*, p. 485.

[17] *Ibid.*, p. 487.

[18] *Ibid.*, p. 488.

that the rights of human nature are too well understood to admit of debate, that the Synod of New York and Philadelphia recommend in the warmest terms to every member of this body, and to all the churches and families under their care, to do everything in their power consistent with the rights of civil society to promote the abolition of slavery, and the instructions of Negroes whether bound or free." The consideration of the above overture was postponed until Monday, 28th, at eleven o'clock.[19]

On the following Monday at 3:00 p.m., the following judgment was passed: "The Synod of New York and Philadelphia do highly approve of the general principles in favor of universal liberty that prevail in America, and interest which many of the states have taken in promoting the abolition of slavery; yet inasmuch as men introduced from a servile state to a participation in all the privileges of civil society without a proper education and without previous habits of industry, may be in many respects dangerous to the community, therefore, they earnestly recommend it to all the members belonging to this communion, to give those persons who are at present held in servitude, such good education as to prepare them for better enjoyment of freedom; and they moreover recommend that masters, wherever they find servants disposed to make a just improvement of these privileges, would give them a peculium, or grant them sufficient time and sufficient means of procuring their own liberty at a moderate rate, that thereby they may be brought into society, with those habits of industry that may render them useful citizens; and finally they recommend it to all their peoples to use the most prudent

---

[19] *Records of the Presbyterian Church in the U.S.A.* (Philadelphia: Presbyterian Board of Publication, 1904), p. 539.

measures, consistent with the interest and the state of civil society, in the countries where they live, to procure eventually the final abolition of slavery in America." [20] It is readily seen that these Presbyterians were struggling with a most difficult problem. If they continued to hold slaves they violated their consciences, but if they turned loose crude and untrained people on the community, the second state might be worse than the first. It was the same problem which faced all slaveholders and all the states in which there were large numbers of slaves recently introduced from Africa. As one looks back on it now the easiest way out would have been to stop the inflow of these untrained people, but so far as the record goes there was no thought of such a procedure.

It was at this meeting of the synod that it was resolved to divide into four synods as noted before, namely, the Synod of New York and New Jersey, the Synod of Philadelphia, the Synod of Virginia, and the Synod of the Carolinas; and an Assembly composed of the four synods was set to meet in Philadelphia in 1789.

The Assembly of 1793 reaffirmed the statement of the Synod of New York and Philadelphia of 1787 as reported above, and the Assembly of 1795 went much further and raised the question as to whether a person who held slavery to be a moral evil could have communion with those who held slaves. The Assembly after mature deliberation decided that such a member should live in charity and peace with those who have a different conviction, but they added their deep concern over any vestige of slavery remaining in America, and again referred all the churches to the statement of the Synod

---

[20] *Records of the Presbyterian Church in the U.S.A.*, p. 540.

of 1787.[21] This Assembly of 1795 also raised the question of the morality of selling or transferring of slaves. While they recognized that under certain circumstances, such action might be unavoidable so long as legal slavery existed, they nevertheless insisted that, "the buying and selling of slaves by way of traffic and all undue severity in the management of them as inconsistent with the spirit of the gospel." [22]

The Assembly of 1815 again considered the question of slavery, but a fuller answer to this problem waited until 1818.

The Assembly of 1818 went much more fully into this question of slavery and declared: "Voluntary enslaving of one part of the human race by another is a gross violation of the most precious and sacred rights of human nature, . . . irreconcilable with the principles of the Gospel of Christ." [23] It further pointed out that slavery created a paradox in the moral decisions. It made one human being dependent on others, as to whether they should receive religious instructions, whether husband and wife might live together, and whether they could maintain their own chastity.[24] The Assembly expressed tender sympathy for those who lived under such conditions as made it impossible to be free from slavery, but they urged that they continue, and if possible increase their exertions to effect total abolition of slavery.[25]

---

[21] A Digest Compiled from the Records of the General Assembly of the Presbyterian Church in the United States of America. (Philadelphia, 1820), p. 340.

[22] Ibid., p. 341.

[23] Ibid., pp. 341, 342.

[24] Ibid., p. 342.

[25] A Digest Compiled from the Records of the General Assembly of the Presbyterian Church in the United States of America, pp. 343, 344.

It should be noted with much interest that a spirit of tolerance and Christian forbearance seemed to prevail for they urged: "forebearance of harsh criticism and uncharitable reflection on their brethren" who did live under such conditions. They urged the patronage and encouragement of the recently formed American Society for Colonizing the Free People of Color of the United States (organized January 1, 1817) and they further recommended to all Presbyterians, that they facilitate the instruction of their slaves, giving them the opportunity to attend worship and by organizing Sunday Schools for them where possible.[26] They called upon all Presbyteries to discountenance cruelty and particularly the cruelty of separation of families.[27] The Assembly also forbade a Presbyterian slaveholder to sell any slave who was a member of the Church, without their consent, on pain of suspension from the Church. All in all this was probably the most thorough handling of the question of slavery done by any Assembly either before or later.

The 1819 Assembly affirmed former actions, and fully recommended and approved the American Society for Colonizing the Free People of Color of the United States, and expressed the belief that colonization might be the solution of the slave question, and might also be a means of civilizing Africa.[28] After the full and explicit actions of the Assemblies of 1818 and 1819, it seemed impossible to add anything, so no further reference is made to the matter of slavery until 1836. At that time the Assembly felt itself incapable of rendering judicious

---

[26] *Ibid.*, p. 345.

[27] *Ibid.*, p. 346.

[28] A Digest Compiled from the Records of the General Assembly of the Presbyterian Church in the United States of America, pp. 347-348.

decisions, so it "resolved that this whole matter be indefinitely postponed." [29]

As noted before, the Presbyterians again divided into Old School and New School groups in 1837, but it was not over the slavery question, but it was over the questions of doctrine, evangelism, and the ordaining of nontheologically trained ministers. The New School Assembly was not organized until 1838.

The Old School group in 1845 passed resolutions which plainly said the Scriptures did not justify exclusion of members on the basis of slaveholding but clearly recognized that slavery was an evil and should be abolished by peaceable means as soon as possible.[30] In 1846, this same body declared they had fully spoken on the subject and that no further action was needed.[31] The matter came up again in 1849 through a memorial from the Chillicothe, Ohio Presbytery, but the Assembly again declared it had sufficiently voiced its conviction on the subject. When the matter was raised in 1850, it was laid on the table, and Baird remarks that it was not again brought before the Assembly.[32]

The New School Assembly met in Philadelphia in 1838, and when the memorial on slavery was presented, it was reported that such memorials had been withdrawn.[33] The Assembly of 1839 declared that the question of slavery was not within their province, and they referred it to lower judiciaries.[34] The Assembly of 1840

[29] Samuel Baird, *A Collection of the Acts, Divisions, and Testimonies of the Supreme Judiciary of the Presbyterian Church*, Philadelphia, 1855, p. 822.
[30] *Ibid.*, pp. 822-824.
[31] *Ibid.*, p. 824.
[32] Baird, *op. cit.*, p. 825.
[33] *Minutes of the General Assembly of the Presbyterian Church, U.S.A.*, (Philadelphia: Roberts and Moore, 1894), p. 26.
[34] *Ibid.*, p. 61.

declared that those Presbyteries which had excluded members because they owned slaves, had acted contrary to the Constitution and were called upon to rescind such action. To this decision there was only one dissenting voice.[35] The Assembly of 1843 simply referred to the action of the Assembly of 1839 and refused to take further action.[36] The Assembly of 1846 declared "that many evils were inherent in the system, but that the degree of moral turpitude on the part of an individual participating in it could only be determined by God, and that in view of the embarrassments and obstacles in the way of emancipation they could not pronounce a judgment of promiscuous condemnation, or withhold Christian fellowship from masters of slaves." [37] The Assembly of 1849 passed a resolution saying: "That slaveholding is a sin against God and man, and should be treated by the Church as other gross immoralities." [38] The Assembly of 1850 referred the whole matter back to the sessions and Presbyteries, by a vote of 87 to 16, but some members made solemn protest against this action.[39] In 1851, the fugitive slave law was strengthened which called out a vigorous protest from the General Assembly.[40] Several memorials to the Assembly of 1852 desired the Assembly to "enjoin on the lower judiciaries to bring every case of slaveholding to answer charges" but the Assembly voted that would be unconstitutional

---

[35] *Ibid.,* p. 104.
[36] *Ibid.,* p. 127.
[37] *Ibid.,* p. 162.
[38] *Minutes of the General Assembly of the Presbyterian Church,* U.S.A., (Philadelphia: Roberts and Moore, 1894), p. 224.
[39] *Ibid.,* pp. 269-270.
[40] *Ibid.,* p. 299.

and furthermore no added expression of opinion was demanded at that time.[41]

The Assembly of 1853 reaffirmed the action of 1850, "called for patience and forbearance on the part of critics of slavery and asked the Presbyteries of the slaveholding states to present at the next Assembly, the full facts as to the number of Presbyterian slaveholders, the extent to which this slaveholding was necessitated by state laws, and a full statement of the attitude of southern churches toward the sacredness of family relations among slaves. To this action there was a bitter protest signed by eleven members, claiming the Assembly had no constitutional right to make such inquiries." [42] Another protest headed by Samuel H. Cox of Brooklyn claimed the resolutions were mischievous, would cause trouble and that they falsely implicated twenty Presbyteries and fifteen states. This protest called the crusade against the South a form of monomania. It condemned the abolition idea, and maintained the Church had no business meddling with slavery which was an affair of the state. A committee was appointed to consider these protests, which committee brought in an irenic report, which attempted to discriminate "between the iniquity of a system and the character of individuals, whose circumstances may have involved them therein." [43]

The Committee on Overtures in the Assembly of 1854 recommended that no further action was needed, and this was adopted.[44] The Assembly of 1855 had overtures from fifteen synods, "all couched in respectful

---

[41] *Ibid.*, p. 333.
[42] *Ibid.*, pp. 329-333.
[43] *Minutes of the General Assembly of the Presbyterian Church, U.S.A.* (Philadelphia: Roberts and Moore, 1894), pp. 393-396.
[44] *Ibid.*, p. 433.

language" to which the committee prepared resolutions affirming their opposition to slavery, asking that a pastoral letter be sent to all churches affirming this attitude, regretting the spirit of many who opposed slavery, and calling for a committee to study the constitutional power of the Assembly with reference to slavery, which committee was to report at the next General Assembly.[45]

This committee reported in 1856 that the Assembly "had no power to commence a process" and that the disciplinary function of the Assembly was only appelate and revisionary." [46] The committee so reporting had on it a lawyer and a minister representing the Synod of New York and New Jersey, together with two other representatives whose location was not given. Rev. A. H. H. Boyd of Virginia brought in a lengthy report against the assumption of unconstitutional powers by the Assembly.[47] The Assembly of 1857 reviewed at length all actions of former Assemblies and called upon all members to facilitate the religious instruction of slaves. All churches were urged to prevent cruelty, especially separation of families, and it tenderly sympathized with all who were unfortunately connected with slavery, but it deplored the evil thereof and warned against the making of the legal situation a cover for lack of love and the practice of slavery.[48]

The Assembly of 1858 adopted the following resolution: "Resolved that this assembly, while extending to the memorialists assurances of Christian consideration and regard, can answer their prayer only by referring

---

[45] *Ibid.*, pp. 479, 480.

[46] Ibid., p. 575.

[47] *Minutes of the General Assembly of the Presbyterian Church, U.S.A.* (Philadelphia: Robert and Moore, 1894), pp. 413-525.

[48] *Ibid.*, pp. 473-575.

them to acts of past Assemblies, as being in our judgment all that the General Assembly can properly do on the subject of the memorial.[49] In the Assembly of 1859, the Dakota Presbytery petitioned that missionaries be sent to the southern states, instructed not to receive slaveholders into the church. The petition was referred to the permanent committee.[50] The Assembly of 1860 found no relations or practices with reference to slavery which called for action.[51]

The Assembly of 1861 met at Syracuse, New York, and the absence of all southern synods was conspicuous. Strong resolutions condemning secession and all acts of the southern states were passed and allegiance to the Union affirmed. Thus, the break finally came between Presbyterians of the North and those of the South.[52]

We should now follow briefly the actions of the Presbyterian Church in the Confederate States of America. In 1861, this Church had thirty-eight missionaries working in the home mission field. Presumably most of these were working with and for Negroes. This Church had in its membership a number of very zealous and very able ministers who for a number of years had been giving themselves to the religious care of the slaves. One of the most prominent of these ministers was Reverend C. C. Jones, of Georgia. As early as 1842, Dr. Jones had published at Savannah, Georgia, a little volume called *The Religious Instruction of the Negroes of the United States*. This little book was printed by Thomas Purse in Savannah, is now very rare, and is perhaps the fullest

---

[49] *Ibid.*, p. 612.
[50] *Ibid.*, Vol. II, p. 35.
[51] *Ibid.*, Vol. II, pp. 76-81.
[52] *Minutes of the General Assembly of the Presbyterian Church, U.S.A.* (Philadelphia: Robert and Moore, 1894), Vol. II, pp. 111, 112.

and most accurate statement extant on the early religious work of the churches among slaves. In 1830, he had been instrumental in organizing the Association for the Religious Instruction of Negroes in Liberty County, Georgia. This Association was composed largely of planters who were solicitous for the religious well-being of their slaves. They employed Reverend C. C. Jones as their missionary. In 1834, Rev. Jones prepared a Catechism for use among slaves. In 1845, a very important meeting was held in Charleston, South Carolina, to lay plans for the advance of the religious instruction of Negroes.[53] Daniel Huger, the successor of John C. Calhoun in the United States Senate, was the moderator of this Assembly. Under the influence of men like Reverend C. C. Jones, many groups—often interdenominational—undertook active evangelization of the slaves. Another very prominent Presbyterian was Dr. John B. Adger, of Charleston, S. C. He had been a missionary and when he returned to Charleston, took up work for Negroes, organizing them into a separate congregation, though they still held their membership in the parent church whose pastor was Reverend Thomas Smyth. In 1852, Dr. John L. Girardeau became prominent in this mission work for Negroes.[54] Under his leadership the Anson Street Mission was completely separated from the white Presbyterian Church and became a church in its own right in 1854. Starting with only thirty-six members, it grew very rapidly and had a membership of 1500 by 1860. So popular and powerful was Dr. Girardeau as a preacher that many white people attended his services regularly, occupying the side seats next to

---

[53] *Princeton Review*, October, 1845, p. 590f.

[54] Blackburn, *Life Work of John L. Girardeau* (Columbia, S.C.: The State Publishing Company, 1916), p. 31.

the pulpit.[55] Dr. Girardeau was one of the most powerful preachers of his day. Dr. John B. Adger of the Columbia Presbyterian Seminary once called him "The Spurgeon of America, the grandest preacher of our southland." [56] General Benjamin F. Butler of Massachusetts, who attended the National Democratic Convention held in Charleston, S. C., in 1860, went to hear Girardeau preach on Sunday morning and exclaimed, "Well, I never heard such a man, and I never heard such a sermon." [57] Girardeau established what he called the "Separate System" whereby Negroes were organized into churches where they were the controlling element, though both in theory and in practice whites were permitted to become members of such churches. In 1857, Dr. Girardeau presented this plan to the Charleston Presbytery, and with cogent arguments seemed to answer every objection to the same.[58] Had all the churches of the South followed such a plan consistently, it is possible that the segregation of the two groups in their church life might never have taken place.

Dr. C. C. Jones was one of the preachers at the first General Assembly of the Presbyterian Church in the Confederate States, meeting in Augusta, Georgia, 1861, and of course pled that the Church make every provision for work with Negroes.

In the report to this Assembly on the State of Religion in the Church, paragraph four enlarges on the mission to colored people. It says many pastors and evangelists devote their time to "children as well as parents, to servants as well as masters." It reports several

---

[55] *Ibid.*, p. 33.
[56] *Ibid.*, p. 52.
[57] Blackburn, *op. cit.*, p. 58.
[58] *Ibid.*, pp. 38-51.

large congregations of colored people had been gathered and that large numbers of others had been received into the regular churches.[59] In the General Assembly Address sent out to all the churches, it is clearly stated that one reason for withdrawing from the Philadelphia Assembly, was that being free from abolition tendencies the Church might have free access to Christian work among slaves.[60] Four closely printed pages of this address are given to a scriptural proof that slavery is not a sin and that slaves have been greatly blessed in being brought through slavery into contact with the Christian religion.[61]

In the Assembly held in Columbia, S. C., 1863, the Narrative on the State of Religion closes with a paragraph on the religious instruction of the colored people. It states that the work is more active than it has ever been, and that practically every Presbyterian Church has colored members, including slaves, and it calls upon all ministers to give religious instruction to servants, and urges masters to give funds for work among slaves, and also to grant time to slaves for worship.[62] The number of domestic missions that year was reported as twenty-eight, and money given to carry forward this work, $10.838.67. The hope was expressed that the Assembly might employ an evangelist to give his entire time to this work.[63]

In the Assembly meeting in Charlotte, N. C., 1864, the Narrative on the State of Religion declares: "that the long continued agitations of our adversaries, have

---

[59] Minutes of the General Assembly of the Presbyterian Church in the Confederate States of America, Vol. I, p. 43.

[60] Minutes of the General Assembly of the Presbyterian Church in the Confererate States of America, Vol. I, p. 55.

[61] Ibid., pp. 56-59.

[62] Ibid., p. 158.

[63] Ibid., pp. 159-162.

wrought within us a deeper conviction of the divine appointment of domestic servitude and have led to a clearer comprehension of the duties we all owe to the African race." [64]

The Assembly meeting in Macon, Georgia, 1865, called upon all churches to increase their efforts for the religious instruction of colored people, particularly in the light of their changed status, and appointed a committee to study the best plan of continued service to Negroes.[65] They went on record as believing that white and colored should still remain in the same churches, but expressed entire willingness for the colored members to organize their own church should they so desire.[66] The Narrative of the State of Religion declares that fewer and fewer Negroes are attending worship, due as it was thought to suspicion being spread among them by designing men.[67] The Pastoral Letter pled for redoubled effort to help the Negroes who were now as sheep without a shepherd.[68]

At the Memphis General Assembly of 1866, it was reported that the Sunday School work among Negroes was prospering, that many colored persons had joined the Church and that there seemed to be a decreasing desire among colored people to have separate organizations of their own. The Assembly again put itself on record as believing that separation of the races in churches was inexpedient.[69]

But this question of separate churches would not

---

[64] *Ibid.*, p. 293.
[65] *Minutes of the General Assembly of the Presbyterian Church in the Confederate States of America*, Vol. I, p. 369.
[66] *Ibid.*, pp. 370, 371.
[67] *Ibid.*, p. 380.
[68] *Ibid.*, pp. 385, 386.
[69] *Ibid.*, Vol. II, pp. 35, 36.

down, for in the Nashville Assembly in 1867, there was a long discussion of representation of colored people in the councils of the Church, and there was evident doubt on the part of many white Assemblymen as to the ability of the Negroes to wisely manage their own church.[70] The Baltimore Assembly reported that "the colored people generally still continue in alienation from us." [71] At the Mobile Assembly a committee headed by Dr. John Girardeau reported a plan of work with the freedmen which contemplated organizing colored churches, with colored deacons and elders, but affiliated with white churches, the ministers of which should serve as minister of the associated colored church. It was agreed however that as fast as competent colored ministers could be found they might be ordained and take over such colored churches.[72]

In the Huntsville Assembly, 1871, it was noted that the colored people in great measure held aloof from the white churches.[73] At the Little Rock Assembly of 1873, it was stated that "Endeavors are still put forth to gain the attention and win the confidence of the colored people," [74] but it is very evident that enthusiasm for this work is on the wane.

A number of synods sent overtures to the General Assembly meeting at Columbus, Mississippi, in 1874, urging that a separate church organization be effected for colored people. The Assembly acted accordingly, but maintained that the white churches must still be responsible for the training of colored Presbyterian min-

[70] *Minutes of the General Assembly of the Presbyterian Church in the Confederate States of America*, Vol. II, pp. 145, 154.
[71] *Ibid.*, p. 284.
[72] *Ibid.*, pp. 388, 389.
[73] *Ibid.*, Vol. III, p. 41.
[74] *Ibid.*, p. 341.

isters.[75] A colored evangelist was appointed and a colored evangelistic fund was established. That the Assembly considered the matter of great importance is proven by the fact that eight finely printed pages are given to the subject in the minutes.[76] The St. Louis Assembly of 1875 set aside five per cent of the sustentation fund for colored evangelism.[77] At this same Assembly, Rev. C. A. Stillman presented Overture No. 21, asking that steps be taken to establish an institute for the training of colored ministers.[78] It was noted in the minutes that little was being done, for thirty-five different Presbyteries reported they were doing nothing.

The establishment of Stillman Institute was definitely ordered at the New Orleans Assembly in 1877,[79] the school having run on an experimental basis the preceding year, with six students and one professor.[80] The school was run this first year in a room rented at the cost of $2 per month. The last report of this institute (1943) indicates that an Academic Department was established in 1893, that the school became co-educational in 1922, that a Bible Training School was added in 1924, that a Nurses' Training Course was added in 1929, and that the enrollment in 1943 was 276.[81]

The Louisville Assembly of 1879 reported very small receipts for colored evangelism and stated that no collection for such effort had ever been ordered.[82]

---

[75] *Minutes of the General Assembly of the Presbyterian Church in the Confederate States of America*, Vol. III, p. 517.

[76] *Ibid.*, pp. 588-596.

[77] *Ibid.*, Vol. IV, p. 24.

[78] *Ibid.*, p. 28.

[79] *Ibid.*, p. 438.

[80] *Ibid.*, p. 452.

[81] *Stillman Institute Bulletin*, 1943.

[82] *Minutes of the General Assembly of the Presbyterian Church in the Confederate States of America*, Vol. V, p. 70.

At the Charleston Assembly it was reported that a few white ministers preach to colored people regularly, and that all white churches are open to colored people, and some attend regularly.[83] In 1881, the Home Mission Committee reported having spent only $1,385.83 on colored evangelism.[84] The report on the State of Religion says: "The colored population seem to have passed, for the present at least, beyond our reach." [85] It was agreed that all the Church could do was to search out candidates for the ministry and send them to Tuscaloose to Stillman Institute for training.[86] It was frankly acknowledged that the cause had ceased to stir the enthusiasm of the Church.[87] In the Lexington, Kentucky Assembly of 1883 the Home Mission Board did not even refer to colored work, and the Narrative on the State of Religion says that only eight Presbyteries have done anything about religious instruction of colored people.[88] The Assemblies of 1884 and 1885 report practically nothing done.[89] The amount of money reported for colored work at the Augusta, Georgia Assembly of 1886 was $850.[90] At the St. Louis Assembly in 1887, it is reported that the Church has failed to manifest an abiding interest in colored evangelism, but that they were unwilling not to be represented in the work.[91] The Baltimore Assembly of 1888 reported $6,629 contributed to Stillman Institute and colored evangelism combined,

[83] *Ibid.*, p. 232.
[84] *Ibid.*, p. 381.
[85] *Ibid.*, p. 401.
[86] *Ibid.*, p. 573.
[87] *Ibid.*, p. 579.
[88] *Ibid.*, Vol. VI, p. 65.
[89] *Minutes of the General Assembly of the Presbyterian Church in the Confederate States of America*, Vol. VI, pp. 260, 438.
[90] *Ibid.*, Vol. VII, p. 36.
[91] *Ibid.*, p. 213.

which it was said was less than five cents per member.[92]

Dr. William Crow, Jr., writing in the Union Seminary Review, July, 1940, says that colored Presbyterians (U.S.) in 1861 numbered 31,000, but that by the date of 1916 there were only 1,322. In 1943, the Negroes had five representatives as regular delegates in the General Assembly meeting at Montreat, North Carolina.

Perhaps the personal attitude of southern Presbyterians toward the Negro as a person can best be summed up in the words of C. C. Jones, called the "Apostle to the Negro" when he spoke at the first Assembly of the Presbyterians in the Confederate States. "They are not the cattle upon a thousand hills, nor the fowls upon the mountains, brute beasts, goods and chattels, to be taken, worn out and destroyed in our use; but they are men created in the image of God, to be acknowledged and cared for spiritually by us, as we acknowledge and care for other varieties of the race, our own Caucasian, or the Indian, or the Mongol." [93]

The Church has organized several very successful missions at Louisville, Richmond, Atlanta, and New Orleans. Perhaps the most successful of all of these was the one at Louisville, led by the Reverend John Little, a pioneer, and a most saintly man, who gave a long and strenuous career to developing a really significant work. He was able to interest not only Presbyterians but many others throughout Louisville and set a standard for such work which has borne fruit in other cities. Most of all he gave himself and his fine friendly personality, which has meant much to thousands of Negroes who have known him and his work. The enthusiastic support given

---

[92] *Ibid.*, p. 411.
[93] Mallard, *Plantation Life Before Emancipation*, Richmond, 1892, pp. 199, 200.

him in his work by both his first and second wives, who were sisters, is an indication that the women of the South have a deep and abiding Christian interest in the colored people. If all the funds given by the big educational boards had produced in the same proportion that the meager funds put at John Little's disposal have produced, much greater results might be exhibited at this time. He was a worthy modern successor to John Adger and John L. Girardeau.

Such is the summary of the work of this branch of the Presbyterian Church. The record shows that these Christians were really deeply interested in the Negro people, but they could never quite bring themselves to the place where they would recognize the ability of the Negro to be a responsible agent for his own salvation, and hence they could not give him large enough share in the ongoing of the Church to keep him within the fold.

That part of the New School Presbyterians which did not go with the Presbyterian Church in the Confederate States continued its General Assembly. In the Assembly of 1862, they resolved: first, that they were deliberating in a time of wicked and fearful rebellion; second, that civil government was constituted of God, and in supporting the existing government (the Union) they were friends of good order; third, that they were the constitutional Presbyterian Church; fourth, that the United States was the best government that had ever existed, and probably as good as could be constituted; fifth, that rebellion against that government could find only two parallels in iniquity, namely, the rebellion against the throne of Heaven, and the rebellion which filled the earth with apostates; sixth, that they were of one mind on this rebellion, and that even the most ardent advocates of peace may have an active part in putting down the rebellion; seventh, that they were utterly shocked at the deep depravity of men who had planned this rebellion; eighth, that the one root of the rebellion was African slavery; ninth, that they had great confidence in Abraham Lincoln and the commanders of the Union Army; and tenth, they dedicated themselves and their churches to the cause of a Union victory.[94] Similar resolutions were passed by the Assembly of 1863, and the Emancipation Proclamation was also approved.[95]

The Assembly of 1864 referred to the iniquitous rebellion to preserve slavery, that it was the Anti-Christ opposing the truth, that they recognize the hand of God in all victories of the Union Army, etc., etc.[96]

We turn now in closing to a very brief statement of the work of the Assembly of the Presbyterian Church U.S.A. In the meeting in Philadelphia, 1861, heated discussion was held as to the wisdom of voting full allegiance to the Union, since many members could not conscientiously do so. A resolution was finally adopted, 156 to 66.[97] The Church was spending $130,000 on Home Missions in 1861, but we have no record of what portion of this went to colored work. The Assembly of 1862, meeting at Columbus, Ohio, passed a very bitter and denunciatory paper accusing Presbyterians in the seceding states of treason and fraud. There is only one short paragraph on colored work in the report on the State of Religion, and this paragraph significantly says that one Presbytery "reports work among the colored

---

[94] *Minutes of the Presbyterian Church in the United States,* Vol. XII, Minutes for 1862, pp. 23-25.

[95] *Ibid.,* Minutes of 1863, pp. 241, 245.

[96] *Minutes of the Presbyterian Church in the United States,* Vol. XIII, Minutes for 1864, p. 465f.

[97] *Minutes of the Assembly of Presbyterian Church U.S.A.,* Vol. XVI, p. 330.

race." [98] The report of the Committee on Domestic
Missions makes no reference to colored work. In the
Assembly of 1863 held at Peoria, Illinois, there were
many who wanted to make the denunciatory statement
of the 1862 Assembly even more drastic and pointed if
possible.[99] No attention whatever was given to colored
work. In the Assembly of 1864, the Committee on Domestic Missions dismissed the whole subject of colored
work with the single sentence: "For years the South
will be a mission field to be supplied by the kindness of
the North." [100] The report of 1865 was almost similar.[101]

The Assembly of the Church has provided that any
race in a Presbytery may ask for and obtain a special
Presbytery, and liberalize any Synod, so that Negroes
may have separate organization, but still remain in the
Assembly.[102] The report of 1939 indicates that there
were 24,000 communicants in the Church.

The joint committee appointed to study cooperation
of the two Assemblies (U.S.A. and U.S.) found much in
common, but found the polity of the two Assemblies
quite different. The U.S.A. group believed in keeping
the Negroes in the parent Assembly, while the U.S.
group had in 1888 definitely set the Negroes aside into a
separate congregation.[103]

After the Cumberland Presbyterian Church, or at
least a major part of it, had united with the Presbyterian
Church, U.S.A. in 1906, there was a real desire that the
20,000 Negro Cumberlands should also come into the

[98] *Ibid.*, p. 644.
[99] *Ibid.*, Vol. XVII, p. 60f.
[100] *Ibid.*, p. 357.
[101] *Minutes of the Assembly of Presbyterian Church U.S.A.*, Vol.
XVII, p. 626.
[102] *Digest of Presbyterian Church in U.S.A.*, 1930, p. 141.
[103] *Ibid.*, Vol. II, pp. 100-102.

Presbyterian Church U.S.A.[104] A full discussion of the splendid work of the Presbyterian Church U.S.A. will be found in Chapter IX.

It will be seen from the above narrative that the Presbyterians of all divisions have maintained a permanent interest in the Negro, as a human being and as a possible Christian, but like many of the other churches, they have not proven great statesmen in keeping a vital relation to the Negro through their church activities.

---

[104] *Ibid.*, p. 154.

CHAPTER VII

THE ATTITUDE OF THE CONGREGATIONAL CHURCH TOWARD THE NEGRO DURING SLAVERY

The Congregational Church was later than some other churches in entering the field of work for Negroes, but was very aggressive once it entered upon this work. A very remarkable incident gave to the Church much of its early zeal on the slave question. On August 26, 1839, Lieutenant Gedney boarded a schooner off the coast of Long Island. He found on board 42 Negroes who were sent to jail at New Haven on the charge of having mutinied on the high seas and killed their officers. Investigation proved that the Negroes had been bought in Havana and on the high seas they had mutinied. The Armistad Commitee in New York was formed to defend them and John Quincy Adams and Roger S. Baldwin handled the case, winning for the Negroes a verdict of "free." This incident gave point and much enthusiasm to movements that were just beginning in the Church.

A Committee on West Indian Missions had been organized in 1837, and the Western Evangelical Missionary Society was organized at Western Reserve University in 1843.

The American Missionary Association (A.M.A.) of the Congregational Church was organized in September, 1846, out of a combination of a number of sectional societies such as the Western Evangelical Missionary Society, the Union Missionary Society, and others. The first responsibility of this Society was said to be to carry on missions in Africa, but the first annual report indicates that all of the societies out of which it grew had a common antislavery sentiment; hence, this society was from the beginning the voice of the Congregational Church against slavery. Because it was so clearly the voice of the Church, we will follow its activities first of all. The A.M.A. was up to 1914 an independent, nonsectarian body, but still did represent Congregationalism.

The second annual report mentions a letter from Rev. John G. Fee, of Kentucky, in which he was asking that he be appointed as a missionary in that region. Mr. Fee later became one of the founders of Berea College in Kentucky, an A.M.A. institution for many years. Berea as present is one of the most Christian and one of the best colleges of the South, having an annual enrollment of some fifteen hundred students and an interest-bearing endowment of more than twenty million dollars.

This same report declares that any person professing faith in the Lord Jesus Christ could become a member provided he was not a slaveholder, and provided further that he contributed $30 to the Association.[1] It is further stated that a number of Presbyterian churches of the free synod of Cincinnati—who had withdrawn from the Presbyterian Church on the grounds of antislavery sentiment—were contributing to the A.M.A.[2] Reverend C. B. Ray was the earliest missionary of the Association, A "Slave Bible Fund" was established, and one church in New York contributed one hundred and fifty dollars toward the expenses of a colporteur to the slaves of Kentucky. The report also emphasized the fact that no advocate of caste, slaveholding or polygamy had been

[1] *Report of the A.M.A.* 1848 *1-14*, p. 6.
[2] *Ibid.*, p. 6.

admitted into the society.[3] The land of Calhoun (South Carolina) was declared to be as truly a missionary field as was the land of Confucius.[4] Rev. J. T. Dickinson, a returned missionary from Singapore, read an impassioned paper, in which he pled for missions to the slave country as well as foreign lands, with prior emphasis on the home-land.[5] He really was not opposed to foreign missions, but felt that prior attention should be given to home needs where the territories and young states were in process of building their traditions and character.

The third annual meeting of the A.M.A. was held in Tremont Temple, Boston, 1849. A resolution was passed which asserted that churches in slave states which had excluded slaveholders, had prospered, and called upon the Church to redouble its efforts in strengthening these and establishing others.[6] In commenting on work for colored people in New York, it is interesting to note that they found the white churches in that city refused to admit colored members, so it was necessary to organize separate churches for Negro Christians.[7] This third report goes on to say: "As with the slaveholders of pagan lands, just awakened from his ignorance and sin, so, and much more with the enlightened but persisting slave-holder at home, we cannot, in an official or individual character, do anything that even by implication can be considered as sanctioning his claim for fellowship in God's house." [8] This is the constantly reiterated conviction of A.M.A., and indeed it is specifically stated that the A. M. A. was organized because other missionary

---

[3] *Report of the A.M.A.* 1848 *1-14*, p. 23.
[4] *Ibid.*, p. 25.
[5] *Ibid.*, pp. 24-27.
[6] *Third Annual Report*, p. 8.
[7] *Ibid.*, p. 30.
[8] *Third Annual Report*, p. 31.

societies did not stand squarely for this principle.[9] The eighth article of the constitution of the society set forth this principle most explicitly.[10]

Mr. Fee wrote from Kentucky in 1850 that he was organizing Union Churches and accepting as members those from other denominations who were not happy to be associated with slaveholding members. He reports that on one occasion when he went to his church a slaveholder barred the door and refused to allow Fee and several hundred persons to enter. Mr. Fee said he refused to use violence even though most of the persons present were willing to resort to force.[11] One of the things which aroused the most bitter opposition to the A.M.A. colporteur in Kentucky was the fact that he advocated openly that persons opposed to slavery should withdraw from churches which admitted slaveholders, and establish antislavery churches.[12] They thus drew the line very sharply and carried the fight right into the home community of slavery. Of course the Association was charged with sowing discord in the Church, but the A.M.A. answered through its annual sermon preached on the text: "I came not to send peace but a sword."— Matthew 10: 34. With withering sarcasm the preacher said: "There stands American slavery; that colossus of sin, with one foot on the state and the other on the church, legalized and Christianized. The church has adopted it, popularized it, and pretends to set upon it the seal of God's approval. Conforming her practice to her theory, the evangelical church has invested in slave property $264,000,000 and owns 660,000 bodies and souls

---

[9] *Ibid.*, p. 32.
[10] *Ibid.*, p. 35.
[11] *Fourth Annual Report of A.M.A.*, p. 36.
[12] *Ibid.*, p. 38.

of men, and by their natural increase, produces yearly more heathen on our own soil than her efforts win for Christ in foreign lands." [13] There was certainly no compromise there, and one does not wonder that such preaching should arouse bitter opposition.

The work of Reverend Ray in New York evidently prospered, for in 1851, we find him reporting seven houses of worship and five halls which would seat four thousand nine hundred persons. However, he complains this will not nearly accommodate the twenty thousand Negroes living in New York.[14] It is interesting in the midst of all this agitation and bitter speech about slavery to find one of the strongest opponents of slavery, Rev. John G. Fee, of Kentucky writing in one of his letters that: "Fiery zeal against slavery, with coarse epithets and vulgar abuse will not succeed." [15] This was evidently a rebuke of many of his fellow ministers, and perhaps even of the general attitude of some members of the A.M.A. itself. His non-violent methods, and his more temperate speech was strongly in contrast with the attitude, actions, and words of many who were working to destroy slavery. It would be interesting if we could measure exactly the effect of the respective methods. It might throw some light on the methods of present-day reformers in various realms. The annual sermon at the fifth meeting of the Association was preached by Rev. J. Blanchard, President of Knox College, on the subject: "Were the New Testament churches slaveholding churches?" In this sermon the actions of various churches and church bodies on the question of slavery are reviewed, in order to show that supposed ignorance of the

---

[13] *Fourth Annual Report of A.M.A.*, p. 52.
[14] *Fifth Annual Report of A.M.A.*, p. 41.
[15] *Ibid.*, p. 43.

wrong of slavery is a positive sin. He charges that the
Methodist, Baptist, and Presbyterian churches which had
split over the question of slavery, all continue to tolerate
slaveholding members in *both* branches of each denomination.[16] The statement was inaccurate as to the Presbyterians, for as we saw in the chapter on that denomination, the Presbyterians did not divide on this question
until the opening of the Civil War. It is interesting to
note his belief that both branches of the other denominations did continue to have members who were slaveholders. It shows clearly that the mixing of moral and
political issues poses problems, which, even the most
scrupulous found difficult to untangle.

In order to tighten the net which might catch some
unwary church in sin, the sixth annual meeting resolved: "That to oppose sin in one set of resolutions
while we do not in another, for example, to oppose in-
temperance while we do not oppose slavery, or to pray
against oppression while we vote for it, is to strike down
Christian principles, to deaden conscience, and in the end
to undermine and destroy Christian character.[17] The
annual sermon of this sixth annual meeting was preached
by Rev. Joseph R. Walker, on the text: "If a man say, I
love God, and hateth his brother, he is a liar."—I John
4: 20. One does not need to quote from this sermon to
imagine how completely opposite its spirit was to that
of John G. Fee, who said that fiery zeal against slavery
did not succeed.

In its denunciation of slavery, the Association often
connected the sin up with what they called "Popery."
Here was a group of persons obsessed of a great hatred
of slavery, and therefore bitter toward any person or any

---

[16] *Fifth Annual Report of A.M.A.*, p. 60.
[17] *Sixth Annual Report of A.M.A.*, p. 11.

institution which seemed to them either favorable to or tolerant of slavery.[18]

The annual sermon of the seventh meeting held in 1853 was almost wholly devoted to denunciation of slavery and slaveholders. The eighth annual report of 1854 says there are eight churches in Kentucky and six in North Carolina which are completely free from slaveholding members.[19] It is very evident from this that the two missionaries in these states were finding great difficulty in founding antislavery churches, and once founded, keeping them free from slaveholding members. It was probably about as difficult as it would be at the present time to be sure that no member of a local church held stock in or received profit from the liquor interest, or other traffic which the Church would openly condemn. The reports of John G. Fee, who was the A.M.A. missionary in Kentucky, and of the missionary in North Carolina—himself a native of that state—were full of zeal and of interest in the particular cause which they represented, and they report that many of the people of those states felt strongly against slavery.[20]

In the ninth annual report, the Congregational Home Missionary Secretary introduced some remarks, "In relation to slavery as an obstacle to Christian cooperation in the Home Mission Work, and the progress of the gospel in this country." [21] In these remarks they declare that the New School Presbyterians would have been much stronger and advanced more rapidly had they stood firmly against admitting any into their fellowship who were slaveholders. We have seen in the chapter on Pres-

---

[18] *Seventh Annual Report of A.M.A.*, pp. 75-80.
[19] *Eighth Annual Report of A.M.A.*, p. 71.
[20] *Ibid.*, pp. 73-77.
[21] *Ninth Annual Report of A.M.A.*, p. 99.

byterians that the Church had had dissension over the question of affiliation in Home Mission Work with the Congregational body, and the Old School wing had held such affiliation to be unconstitutional.

The tenth annual report of 1857 was very bitter in its denunciation of slavery, and all those practices which were in any way connected with slavery. At one place it speaks of slavery as "reducing all slaves to the necessity of universal concubinage by denying to them the civil rights of marriage, breaking up the dearest relations of life and encouraging *universal prostitution.* (Italics not mine) . . . involving the violation of every command of the Decalogue, and bringing upon our nation and our churches consenting thereto, the displeasure and the frown of Almighty God." [22] This type of overstatement did not make the A.M.A. popular, even with those who opposed slavery in the South. A Mr. Davies, who for some time served as a missionary in Kentucky, returned to his native state of Virginia and preached often near Woodstock, Virginia, where it was said he was well heard both by slaveholders and by others. He reported that he found there a Mr. Rye, who was trying to acquire an independence so he could give his entire time to anti-slavery work.[23]

Throughout all these records there are constant reminders that no society or church can preach a full gospel, which permits a slaveholder to have membership in such a church or society. It was therefore the constant endeavor of the A.M.A. "to correct the error of the churches, ecclesiastical bodies, missionaries societies, and other religious and benevolent organizations and individuals, who have countenanced slavery, that most for-

---

[22] *Tenth Annual Report of A.M.A.,* p. 22.
[23] *Tenth Annual Report of A.M.A.,* pp. 68, 69.

midable obstacle to Christian missions and the work which is enjoined upon us for the salvation of slaves." [24] There was in all this a note of intolerance, toward other religious bodies, which often smacks of self-righteousness, but one cannot fail to see in it the deep and abiding conviction that slavery and Christianity are unalterably opposed to each other; and these Congregationalists were willing to do something about it.

Rev. John G. Fee wrote the A.M.A. in 1857 that there was needed in Kentucky a college which would be "anti-slavery, anti-caste, anti-rum, anti-tobacco, anti-sectional, a pious school under Christian auspices." [25] This is the first reference so far as I have discovered to what later grew into the idea of Berea College. Mr. Fee held a revival meeting in the little town of Berea in 1857. In this year's reports of the A.M.A. one finds extended references to Mr. Fee's persecution by the mobs, and the great trials and hardships through which he and his family had to pass.[26] The annual sermon for this meeting was preached by Rev. L. A. Sawyer of New York State, and is one of the bitterest and most violent statements of this very troubled period.[27] Conditions were not conducive to the spirit of tolerance, and the attitude advocated by John G. Fee was not often to be found.

In the twelfth annual report one finds a resolution, condemning the American Tract Society, and the American Board of Commissioners for Foreign Missions, for being entangled with slavery sympathy.[28] The report acknowledges that the attitude of the Association has aroused antagonism from other boards, which attitude

---

[24] *Ibid.*, p. 84.
[25] *Eleventh Annual Report of A.M.A.*, p. 65.
[26] *Ibid.*, pp. 67-69.
[27] *Eleventh Annual Report of A.M.A.*, p. 91f.
[28] *Twelfth Annual Report of A.M.A.*, p. 9.

has been construed as "wanton attack upon old boards." [29] The report frankly admits that the society is undertaking to be a missionary to other missionaries, and is trying "to elevate the character of Christian Missions and Missionary Boards to the gospel standard." [30] Of course this attitude was promptly resented by all the other boards, which considered themselves fully as Christian as the A.M.A.

During the year 1858, the A.M.A. entered its third slave state for missionary work, namely Missouri. Although this year's reports recount acts of violence in Kentucky against Fee, Jones, and Davies, all A.M.A. Missionaries, the Rev. D. Worth, who was the A.M.A. missionary in North Carolina reports that he constantly visits slaveholders, and holds services and prays with them and their slaves, apparently without any offense being taken.[31]

The most significant item in the thirteenth annual report is a letter from Rev. John G. Fee telling about the opening of the school at Berea, and raising the issue as to whether colored pupils should be admitted. The contest took the form, he said, of the election of a Board of Trustees. One group was for exclusion—or a caste system as Fee called it—the other group was for anti-caste. The latter he says was elected on a three to one vote. Fee thought this was very significant in a slave state and in a county where there were, he thought, 5000 slaves.[32] It certainly did show that even in the slave states the idea of caste was far from being as prevalent as some believed.

The annual sermon for this year was preached by

---

[29] *Ibid.*, p. 14.
[30] *Ibid.*, p. 15.
[31] *Ibid.*, p. 69.
[32] *Thirteenth Annual Report of A.M.A.*, p. 58.

Rev. George B. Cheever, of New York, and fills thirty-two pages of closely printed material. The subject was "The Great Stumbling Block in the Way of Missionary Enterprise" which was almost wholly directed against slavery. The issues were evidently growing hotter and hotter, and there was little thought of any aspect of missionary work except that directed against slavery.

The greater part of the fourteenth annual report of 1860 is taken up with the expulsion of Fee, Rogers, and others from Berea and neighboring missions. The opponents of the missionaries had met at Richmond, Kentucky, and appointed a committee to notify the missionaries to move. Fee and Rogers appealed to the Governor of the state for protection, but he failed to respond, saying the citizens were determined they should go, and he could do nothing about it. The missionaries therefore withdrew to Cincinnati, and submitted the case to public opinion. The A.M.A., through its official organ, presented the full facts and defended its workers. The public mind at this time had been much inflamed by the John Brown case, and the whole country seemed to be hurrying toward a crisis. Mr. Worth, another A.M.A. missionary in North Carolina, was likewise attacked and thrown into prison, but he was soon released on bond of three thousand dollars, which was later raised in meetings in the North which he addressed.

In the concluding section of this year's annual report it is stated, "The American Missionary Association does not regard slaveholding as the only sin against which the Christian Missionary has to contend, nor does it seek to measure the enormity by comparing it with other transgressions against the law of God, but they find it here in our own land and elsewhere an instance and evidence of man's rebellion against God, from which it is more hard to dislodge him, because of the strong appeal which it makes to his selfishness, to his pride, and to every unholy passion, and because the sin thus deeply intrenched in his natural heart has been authorized and guarded by human legislation, and approved and sanctioned by a portion of the professed Church of Christ." [33] If one reads carefully these reports he finds little reference to any other sins than slavery, however clearly they state that slaveholding is only one of many sins. The attention of the Association was so intensely focused on this one question as to almost completely exclude attention to anything else.

In presenting its fifteenth report, the Association declared: "That the necessity for a labored vindication of its peculiar position on the subject of slavery (namely, non-fellowship with slaveholders) was continually diminishing." [34] In this report it is stated that John G. Fee and J. A. Rogers who had labored at Berea, were still laboring in and around Cincinnati. It is said they were urging a proclamation of emancipation, hoping that such an action would open the door to an active and aggressive missionary work. The discourse of the year was delivered by Rev. C. B. Boynton of Cincinnati, and was almost wholly given to a review of the progress of humanity from slavery to freedom. The address dwells on the class struggle in England, and sets parallel with it the struggle of the slaves in America in trying to throw off the yoke of bondage. It points at length to the degrading influence slavery has had both on the slaves and on the slaveholders, yes, also on all citizens of America. It is a good summary of what the A.M.A. had been fighting to achieve throughout its whole history.

---

[33] *Fourteenth Annual Report of A.M.A.*, p. 65.
[34] Volume of *Annual Reports of A.M.A., 11-20,* New York, Report 15, p. 10.

When the A.M.A. met for its sixteenth session, the Civil War was in full swing. Its report therefore is largely taken up with the work which the Association is doing "with the slaves who have flocked to Fortress Monroe, and who have congregated in other border places." Fee and Rogers are reported as trying to return to Kentucky and work has been started at Newport News, including schools for slaves.[35] It is noted that work has been begun at Port Royal, South Carolina, and that thousands of books including geographies, arithmetics, grammars, had been sent to these points. Thus, the educational work of A.M.A. was launched as what seemed the most immediate and pressing need of the refugee slaves. High hopes were expressed that out of the dramatic and oratorical ability of the slave a great movement for evangelizing the whole South, *white and colored,* would arise. It is almost startling to stumble upon such a sentence as this in the report, "When slavery is abolished, is it too much to believe that at the South, *where prejudice is less violent than in the North* (italics are mine) God will honor such men as preachers and teachers to promote the general elevation of the whole people?" [36]

The seventeenth annual session of A.M.A. deliberately resolved that a disproportionately large amount of all resources should be expended in evangelizing the ex-slaves. Schools were started at Hampton, Portsmouth, Suffolk, Yorktown, New Bern, N. C., and at many other points. More than seven thousand pupils were reported as connected with day and night schools.[37]

The eighteenth report says that sixty-four teachers are working in the vicinity of Portsmouth and Norfolk

---

[35] *Ibid.,* Sixteenth Report, p. 43.
[36] Volume of *Annual Reports of A.M.A.,* Sixteenth Report, p. 47.
[37] *Seventeenth Annual Report of A.M.A.,* p. 49.

alone. It says, "the plantation of Governor Wise and many other proud and aristocratic masters, once cultivated by unrequited toil, and wet by the tears and blood of their slaves, are now cultivated by and for the freedmen, while their children are taught in the parlors and mansions of their fugitive masters." [38] Forty teachers are reported working in North Carolina,[39] thirty-one missionaries and teachers are reported as working in South Carolina; [40] schools were started in Louisiana under the care of General Banks, the A.M.A. sending many teachers to aid in this work.[41] Seven ordained ministers and eight teachers were reported as working in Mississippi, Arkansas, and Tennessee.[42] Fee and others pressed the work of education among colored soldiers in Kentucky. The total of all teachers reported this year working under the A.M.A. for colored people was one hundred and sixty-nine.[43]

The nineteenth annual report—the last one during the period of the Civil War—announces that the National Council of Congregational Churches had set a goal of $250,000 to be used by the A.M.A. in carrying forward this work of education and evangelism among the freedmen.[44]

The report declares, that "when the war began to liberate the slaves, it (the A.M.A.) was seen to be without change of charter or constitution, providentially fitted for and called to the work of clothing, educating,

---

[38] *Eighteenth Report of A.M.A.*, p. 12.
[39] *Ibid.*, p. 15.
[40] *Eighteenth Report of the A.M.A.*, p. 16.
[41] *Ibid.*, p. 18.
[42] *Ibid.*, p. 20.
[43] *Ibid.*, p. 27.
[44] *Nineteenth Annual Report of A.M.A.*, p. 12.

and evangelizing this long oppressed people." [45] The report expresses the hope and belief that the freedmen will when educated become the great missionaries to Africa, their fatherland.[46] It calls attention to the fact that any and all denominations may send missionaries and teachers through their commission, establishing their denominational agencies untrammeled by the Congregational Church.[47] It says nothing about excluding those churches which had formerly held slaveholders, as they must have been considered redeemed by the emancipation proclamation. Thus, the exigencies of the occasion often temper the convictions and actions of even the most ardent.

District offices were to be set up throughout the North for collecting money and workers, and district offices were to be set up throughout the South for supervising the work. Specific provision for sending out 300 teachers—mostly women—was made. All of these were to be prepared to teach day school, night school, and Sunday School.[48] In every group of five-day schools there was to be located one woman missionary, who would go from house to house reading the Bible and giving practical instruction in religion.[49] A Christian minister was to be allocated to every twenty schools, whose business it would be to teach the teachers in the field of religion, and be the general supervisor of all missionaries in the field. Where possible he was to organize churches.[50]

This was a very ambitious program and had it been fully realized it would have been marvelous. It is remark-

---

[45] *Ibid.*, p. 13.
[46] *Ibid.*, p. 13.
[47] *Nineteenth Annual Report of A.M.A.*, p. 14.
[48] *Ibid.*
[49] *Ibid.*
[50] Ibid.

able how much of the program was accomplished. The names of ministers and teachers who had accepted the call to this work appear in this report which makes a most impressive list. They include: for Washington and District of Columbia, 2 ministers and 19 teachers; for Virginia, 11 ministers and 104 teachers; for North Carolina, 6 ministers and 25 teachers; for South Carolina, 9 ministers and 52 teachers; for Georgia, 4 ministers and 10 teachers; for Florida, 1 minister and 4 teachers; for Kansas and Missouri, 3 ministers and 20 teachers; for Illinois, 7 ministers and 10 teachers; forTennessee, 3 ministers and 2 teachers; for Kentucky, 5 ministers and 11 teachers; for Mississippi, Louisiana and Arkansas, 4 ministers and 23 teachers—a grand total of 55 ministers and 280 teachers.

Such a movement was significant in any church, and indicated deep and abiding interest in the religious welfare of the Negro. The annual discourse this year was preached by Rev. E. W. Kirk on the text: "God hath made of one blood all nations of men, to dwell on all the face of the earth and hath determined the times before appointed and the bounds of their habitation."—Acts 17: 26. It was a fitting close to a period of great effort, long sustained interest, and deep and abiding faith.

The period following the Civil War begins with the Association meeting of 1866. In this twentieth session, the A.M.A. reaffirmed its determination to give education as well as religious instruction to the freedmen. It reported $253,045 expended during the year and supplies valued at $118,864. The personnel reported was 89 men and 264 women working in this field.[51] It was during this year that Fisk University in Nashville had its humble

---

[51] *Report of A.M.A. 15-26*, Twentieth Report, pp. 10-14.

beginning, under the tutelage and support of the A.M.A. The account of the opening of Fisk with Governor Brownlow and Chancellor Lindsay of Peabody College is most interesting.[52] Light is thrown on the way in which the A.M.A. and its agents worked by an article from the Nashville correspondent of the Cincinnati Gazette, telling about the starting of a school on the famous Belle Meade estate of General Harding. It runs in part as follows: "Yesterday General Fisk went out to General Harding's to talk to him and the colored people about a school. When the matter was first broached Mr. Harding expressed himself in strong terms against it. . . . However, a meeting was called and General Harding introduced General Fisk, told who he was, what his business was, and sat down . . . After hearing the General and beholding the enthusiasm of the blacks, Mr. Harding gracefully surrendered." [53]

The Association reported 528 missionaries and teachers in 1867 and reported on expenditures as $334,582. It claimed 200,000 colored had learned to read in two years, and that many normal schools had been established.

That the A.M.A. workers were successful in gaining the confidence and friendship of many southerners is proved by such an incident as that at Dudley, N. C. At this place, the Rev. John Scott had erected a combined church and school for the Negroes. On February 21, 1871, this building was burned, evidently the work of an incendiary. The citizens of the community immediately called a meeting presided over by the leading citizen of the community. They condemned the lawless act, offered a reward of $100 for the apprehension of the

---

[52] *Ibid.*, pp. 36-37.
[53] *Twentieth Report of A.M.A.*, p. 38.

criminal, and contributed $500 in cash toward the erection of a new building.[54]

In 1872, the A.M.A. could report seven chartered colleges, nineteen normal schools, and the beginnings of four theological seminaries.[55] The annual report of 1882 says the Association was then administering eight chartered colleges, 11 high and normal schools, and 38 common schools, with a total enrollment of 9,608 pupils, under 241 teachers. It also reported theological departments in Howard, Talladega, and Straight. White students were reported as enrolled this year in the Medical Department of Howard University, and in the Law Department of Straight, while many colored students were enrolled in Berea, considered a white school.[56]

In 1884, the A.M.A. reported 8 chartered colleges, 14 normal schools, 43 common schools, with 319 teachers, and 9,758 pupils.[57] This same report claims that 10 normal schools and 423 common schools once operated by the Association had been discontinued.[58] This number added to the 65 which were active this year, would make a grand total of 503 schools which up to this date had been operated by A.M.A. This seems to be the highest number of schools ever operated by the Association though the number of normal schools did increase later. In the thirty-ninth report it is clear that the high tide of work had passed—at least as to numbers—for it is clearly stated that A.M.A. should not try to compete with the state in public education, but should foster the advanced training of leaders, and when a college such as Hampton should become entirely self-supporting, the

---

[54] *Twenty-fifth Report of A.M.A.*, pp. 28, 29.
[55] *Twenty-sixth Report of A.M.A.*, p. 18.
[56] *Twenty-sixth Report of A.M.A.*, p. 40.
[57] *Thirty-eighth Report of A.M.A.*, p. 40.
[58] *Ibid.*, pp. 67-70.

A.M.A. should cease to list it as one of their institutions.[59]

This item is very interesting in that it reveals two things: First, the liberal policy of the A.M.A. of giving any institution, which it had founded, freedom to go its own way whenever such institution was able to carry its own financial load. Secondly, it revealed the fact that the A.M.A. was now convinced that the South was taking seriously its obligation to give common school education to all of its people, black as well as white.

Having thus reviewed the actions of the A.M.A., which was the chief and most active agent of the Congregational Church in work for the Negro, it might be well to look briefly at the other Congregational Church agencies as spokesmen for the Church.

Dr. C. M. Clark in his little book *American Slavery and the Maine Congregationalists*[60] shows that some early Congregational ministers owned slaves, either purchased, or acquired by gift from their congregations. A Father Samuel Moody had a slave given him in 1732, but his services either proved unsatisfactory or else the preacher developed scruples against holding a slave, for the assessors were ordered in 1736 to dispose of the Negro *to the best advantage*.[61] At Aurundel the Rev. Thomas Prentice had a slave bought for him and his successor, presumably by the Church. In 1741-1768, Rev. John Havey owned a slave,[62] and several other ministers of the Congregational Church are known to have owned slaves.[63]

A State Colonization Society was organized in Maine

---

[59] *Thirty-ninth Annual Report of A.M.A.*, p. 43.

[60] Clark, *American Slavery and the Maine Congregationalists* (Bangor, Maine, 1940).

[61] *Ibid.*, p. 6.

[62] *Ibid.*, p. 6.

[63] *Ibid.*, p. 7.

in 1831.[64] William Lloyd Garrison and his Liberator attacked the Society as impractical, and drew forth some bitter reaction from Maine Congregationalists.[65] In 1843, Amos Phillips, a Congregational minister published lectures on "Slavery and its Remedy." In 1833, the Kennebeck Conference of Congregationalists passed a strong resolution against slavery.[66] A convention in Augusta, Maine, in 1834, was called to discuss antislavery and immediate emancipation. There were names of twelve Congregational ministers signed to this call.[67]

As early as 1836, the Illinois Congregational Association passed resolutions which read as follows:

"I   Resolved that slavery as it exists in our country is a heinous sin and calls for the united efforts of the church and every patriot for its immediate removal.

"II   That as a nation we owe the oppressed among us every possible reparation for the wrong heaped upon them, and that we can make that in no way so effectively as by furnishing them along with emancipation, every possible facility for moral and intellectual improvement.

"III That it is the duty of the several state governments within whose jurisdiction slavery exists in our country, to abolish it within their respective limits as speedily as possible.

"IV   That the opposition in the law in any community to emancipation does not justify the holding of human beings in bondage, and that every slaveholder is implicated in the guilt of upholding and perpetuating such laws.

"V   That no individual who is disaffected with slavery and about to leave a slaveholding state is justified under any circumstances in selling his slaves.

---

[64] *Ibid.*, p. 22.
[65] Clark, *op. cit.*, p. 30.
[66] *Ibid.*, p. 40.
[67] *Ibid.*, p. 42.

"VI   That slaveholders ought not to be admitted to our
pulpits and communion tables." [68]

These Illinois Congregationalists passed other resolutions against slavery in 1838, in 1840, and at other
times. Flavel Bascom, a pioneer preacher in Illinois, 1833-
1840, gives interesting accounts of problems of slavery
and its discussion in the individual churches.[69] Lovejoy
was another opponent of slavery in this western country,
who paid with his life for his convictions. The question
of refusing the pulpit and the communion table to slaveholders was discussed in many other conferences of Congregationalists, but it seems unnecessary to repeal all of
these. The resolutions passed by Illinois Congregationalists represents on the whole the attitude of members of
this denomination throughout America. Of course sentiment against slavery, and the bitterness of the resolutions
passed were not unanimously approved by Congregationalists. But they were fairly representative of the
majority.

With so splendid a record as this Church had on the
subject of slavery, it is rather disconcerting to find the
harshness so often expressed following the Civil War.
In 1865, a Congregational Council was called to discuss
ways and means of meeting the emergency left by the
Civil War. Those who had worked long and faithfully
to help the South seemed as harsh as any others in their
denunciations. Resolutions were passed which branded
secession as worse than treason. Against these resolutions
Henry Ward Beecher spoke—pleading for moderation.
In answer to him, Hon. Mr. Pomeroy of Kansas said:

---

[68] Sweet, *Religion on the American Frontier* (Henry Holt, 1931),
pp. 177-178.
[69] Sweet, *op. cit.*, passim, pp. 246f.

"It is not to be supposed that in a single resolution or two resolutions the Committee could report what would be acceptable to everybody. Our only effort was to hit upon some general topics on which we could all agree and report them to the Council. The fact is the report would suit me better if we spoke out a little more plainly about hanging somebody. (applause). I am very willing to mingle our justice and mercy to the common people of the South, as has been suggested by our friend, Henry Ward Beecher, but it does seem to me it is time somebody was hung. (applause). Some wholesome hanging, I think, would have settled this question in the minds of the American people long ago, and I do not believe a convention, even of this character, composed largely of clergymen,—men who love forgiveness and mercy— would be harmed if it adopted a little stiffer resolution on this question." [70]

In this council Mr. Sturtevant of Illinois advocated the planting of a Congregational Church in every southern community, believing as he said he did, "It is the best instrumentality to achieve this"—namely, the evangelization and education of all the people.[71] Mr. Pomeroy of Kansas was sure that "society must be organized by beginning at the bottom and turning it bottom side up because it has heretofore been so constructed as to need this overturning." [72] Prof. Bartlett of Illinois reminded the Council that the amount of money they were proposing to spend ($750,000) on this great campaign of evangelizing a section of America was just half the annual cost of a single cavalry regiment.[73]

---

[70] *Minutes of the National Council,* Boston, 1865, pp. 244, 245.
[71] *Ibid.,* p. 267.
[72] *Ibid.,* p. 271.
[73] *Ibid.,* p. 273.

Mr. Thorne of Ohio pled earnestly for the poor whites and for the freedman, and paid high tribute to the work of the A.M.A.[74]

Henry Ward Beecher again took the floor and pled for practical results. He said he was more interested in the $750,000 than he was in the reports of Committees. He was very impatient of the amount of time given by the Council to matters of church policy, and other such subjects, since he thought the one real business of the Council was to devise ways and means of meeting a great crisis in the religious life of America.[75] Had the Church had more men of the caliber and spirit of Beecher, much more might have been accomplished and much less antagonism aroused.

This then is in brief the story of the Congregational Church, in its attitude toward the institution of slavery and in its attitude toward the slave himself. It is a record of high ideals and of splendid achievement. It is too bad that the record is marred again and again by bitterness and what seemed to be almost vindictiveness. But human nature seems to be like that—we rear our heads into the clouds, but our poor weary feet still cling to the muddy earth. There have been few times in history when sharp differences of opinion have not brought out the worst in human nature as well as the best.

[74] *Ibid.*, pp. 288, 289.
[75] *Minutes of the National Council*, p. 292f.

CHAPTER VIII

THE ATTITUDE OF THE ROMAN CATHOLIC CHURCH TOWARD THE NEGRO DURING SLAVERY

The century or more preceding the Protestant Reformation found all Europe seething with new thought, beginning with Dante and his *Divine Comedy* in the first half of the fourteenth century, coming on down through the social message of Langland's Piers Placamon about the middle of that century on into the reform preaching of Savanorola in the second half of the fifteenth century and the moralizing of Sir Thomas Moore in his Utopia during the early years of the following century. All Europe was astir with a new intellectual and moral life. The work of Gutenberg in bringing in movable type, and broadening influence of Columbus' voyages, all conspired toward a new spirit.

Within the Church itself there were stirrings of new life. Cardinal Xamines was striving to purify morals, and enlighten the ignorant Spanish Clergy. In France Ignatius Loyola together with Francis Xavier was founding the Jesuits. The Benedictines were revived, the Capuchins were organized, the Franciscans and Dominicans took on new life. While all this was going forward, Luther in Germany was bringing on the Reformation. In the light of all this stirring of life, both in the Church and out of it, the time was ripe for a far-flung missionary campaign which should be a part of, and even at times should be the dynamic behind the opening up of the new continent of America.

In the sixteenth and seventeenth centuries Spain, Portugal, and France, all predominantly Catholic, were most active in American exploration and colonization; consequently Catholicism was early established in American life.

Since the early Catholic explorers and colonists practically all brought Negroes with them, and since the motivation was partly missionary, it will be necessary in order to see the full picture of Catholic work for Negroes to look at their whole picture of Indian and Negro missions together.

The first concern of the Catholic Church was to see that the faith was proclaimed to the Indians whom they found in the new discoveries. Columbus on his second voyage, 1493, had seventeen ships carrying fifteen hundred men, including missionaries, soldiers, laborers, etc. A Benedictine friar, Bernardo Buil, was one of the missionaries.[1] When Nicalos de Ovando arrived in Hisponiola, April 15, 1502, no less a personage than Las Casas, the future apostle to the Indians, landed with him.[2] When the Indians, because of ill treatment, refused to have any dealings with the Spaniards, the sovereign in a letter dated December 20, 1503, directed Avando to compel the Indians to have dealings with the Spaniards. Avando therefore gave encomienda of so many Indians to each of his men with the specific order that they should "teach them the things of our Holy Catholic Faith."[3]

Queen Isabella, a most devout Catholic, bequeathed her interests in the new world to King Ferdinand and

---

[1] Wilgus, *The Development of Hispanic America*, p. 76.
[2] Helps, *The Spanish Conquest of America*, Vol. 1, p. 133.
[3] *Ibid.*, pp. 138, 139.

her daughter, Juana, with the specific injunction that the conversion of the Indians should be the principal end.[4]

The first Dominicans to arrive in Hispaniola came in 1570, under the governorship of Don Diego Columbus, and there were probably twelve or fifteen of them.[5]

In an expedition sent out from Darien to explore the South Sea (the bay south of Isthmus of Panama) Helps notes that there was a Franciscan priest named Francisco de San Roman in the company.[6]

A Cedula was signed by the sovereign to Diego Vilazquez, February 28, 1515, in which he is much praised: "The principal thing I recommend you is that you have great care for the conversion and good treatment of the Indians of the island, and endeavor in every way that the Indians be taught and indoctrinated in the Holy Catholic Faith, because we would be without burden of our conscience." [7]

It is clearly seen therefore that early Spanish conquests were undertaken in the spirit of religion. That they gave such little moral content to their religious treatment of the Indians only reflects the other-worldliness and practical conception of religion of the day.

The issues of Negro slaves soon was prominent in the Spanish Conquest, for most of the voyagers took with them Negroes as workers or slaves. Prince Henry the Navigator had introduced many Negro slaves into Portugal in the early part of the century, and Spain also early had many Negroes.

Although Ovando asked that Negroes should not be sent to Hispaniola because they were hard to control,

---

[4] *Ibid.*, p. 151.
[5] Helps, *op. cit.*, pp. 168, 175.
[6] *Ibid.*, p. 286.
[7] *Ibid.*, p. 319.

there is a letter from Ferdinand dated September, 1505, saying: "I will send more Negroes slaves as you request, I think there may be a hundred." [8]

Negroes must have been imported rapidly, for on September, 1514, the declining Ferdinand wrote to the Bishop of La Conception in Hispaniola refusing to send Negroes because there were already many (Negroes) and it might cause inconvenience should he send more. [9]

It is well known that Hernando Cortes had Negro slaves with him when he went on his voyage from Cuba to the mainland in 1518. [10] When Lucas Vasquez de Ayllon set sail from Hispaniola in 1526, he carried with him Negro slaves, Dominican friars, among the latter being Antonio de Montesenos, the opponent of Indian slavery. [11]

When Vasco Nunez journeyed westward across Panama to the Pacific in 1573, Helps tells us he had thirty Negroes with him. [12] Presumably he had with him Jeronimite Priests.

When Cabeca de Vaca, who had entered Florida with Narvaez, pushed his way inland in Florida, he had with him a Negro who acted as a kind of scout to find out all he could about each Indian tribe. [13]

When Ponce de Leon entered Florida in 1512, he brought with him colonists, men at arms, secular priests as chaplains, and monks as missionaries. A new patent was given to Ponce de Leon later which carried explicit orders that all natives must be required to submit to the King of Spain and the Catholic Church. De Leon sailed

---

[8] Helps, *op. cit.*, p. 135.
[9] *Ibid.*, p. 340.
[10] Wilgus, *op. cit.*, p. 88.
[11] *Ibid.*, p. 92.
[12] Helps, *op. cit.*, p. 293.
[13] *Ibid.*, Vol. IV, p. 293.

with two vessels in 1521, and carried with him secular priests and Dominicans.[14]

In 1528, Pomphello de Narvaez led an expedition which had in it at least one Negro Estovan, five Franciscan fathers and one lay brother.[15] Hernando de Soto sailed for Florida in 1538, having 600 men, among them eight secular priests and four religious. The cedula under which de Soto acted specifically commanded that he take religious leaders with him to convert the natives.

Father Luis Barbastro sailed for Florida in 1549, with a band of Dominicans, unprotected by soldiers, hoping to win the natives to the Catholic faith.[16] This expedition failed miserably, but in 1555, Tristron de Luna was sent out with fifteen hundred men, among them four Dominican fathers and a lay brother.[17]

In 1565, Menendez de Aviles was given a grant to make permanent settlements in Florida, one condition being that he must maintain at his own expense twelve religious and four Jesuits.[18] He landed at St. Augustine and laid the foundation for the oldest settlement in the United States. It is claimed that the work of building this foundation was largely done by Negro slaves. Menedez sent settlers north to the Chesapeake, who were accompanied by Jesuit priests.

Negro slaves accompanied practically all these Spanish expeditions, and Gillard claims that from the beginning they were given religious instructions by the Catholic priests.[19]

---

[14] O'Gorman, *A History of the Roman Catholic Church in U. S.—Amer. Ch. Hist. Vol. 9*, p. 18.

[15] *Ibid.*, p. 22.

[16] *Ibid.*, p. 26.

[17] *Ibid.*, p. 28.

[18] *Ibid.*, p. 30.

[19] Gillard, *The Catholic Church and the American Negro*, p. 11.

Florida as known by the Spanish was not simply the peninsula which is now known by that title, but all the land south of the 40° latitude. This included what we now know as Texas. It was to this section of Florida that Narvaez sailed in 1528, where he was wrecked and the Negro Estavon wandered northwest into what is now New Mexico. De Soto, Coronado Onati, and other Spanish explorers crossed Texas territory; Franciscans accompanied some of these expeditions, and it is known that Negro slaves were present. French settlements began with Cortier in 1541 the express purpose being stated as discovery, settlement, and conversion of the Indians. The French had attempted a colony in the Carolinas under Ribovet, but the colonists had been captured and murdered by the Spanish under Menendez.

In 1608, Samuel de Champlain laid the foundation of Quebec, and Franciscans were brought in. Jesuits came to Quebec in 1625, and this city became the center of their future activities in America. In 1644, Montreal was founded and this settlement became the headquarters for the Sulpitians.[20] The King of France was following the same rule as the Spanish Sovereigns in requiring the colonies to take priests for the conversion of the natives.

La Saussage established Port Raga in 1613 with Jesuit priests in charge of religious instruction.

In 1633, Cardinal Richelieu gave over the Acadian mission to Capuchin priests, and furnished them money to establish schools.[21]

Every school child knows the story of the spread of French Conquest and Catholic Mission work in a westward wave across the Great Lakes and then down the Mississippi to New Orleans. This movement has left its

---

[20] O'Gorman, *op. cit.*, p. 119.
[21] O'Gorman, *op. cit.*, p. 130f.

mark in the names of scores of cities, such as Detroit, Duqesne, St. Louis, and New Orleans.

In 1666, La Salle started on his important journey to the Mississippi and a company of Sulpitians started with him. In his final arrangements he carried Recollects and not Jesuits or Sulpitians. In order to press his plan for a series of settlements down the Mississippi looking to holding the interior country for France, La Salle made several journeys back to the home land. In 1684, he sailed from France direct to the Gulf of Mexico. With him went Father Membre, a Recollect, with two other priests of the same order, and three Sulpitians. The expedition was destroyed and La Salle died, so the Recollects seem to have done little or no missionary work. After La Salle's failure, French interest seemed to lag with reference to the Mississippi, but when it became known that the English were planning to occupy the mouth of the river, France sent Iberville in 1698 to form colonies. He first settled Biloxi, then Mobile, and in 1717, the present site of New Orleans was selected for a colony.[22] Father Douay, a Recollect priest, accompanied Iberville. When Iberville returned from France in 1700, he brought with him a Jesuit, Father Du Rhu, who ministered to the Indians at Biloxi and Mobile. About this time the King of France decided that this whole territory should be the special responsibility of the Bishop of Quebec. It will thus be seen that in the early days, Recollects, Sulpitians, Jesuits and Capuchins and also Franciscans had some share in missionary work, besides Dominicans, had been brought to Florida and they may have had some share in the missionary work of the lower Mississippi.

In 1717, the Duke of Orleans transferred the pro-

---

[22] *Ibid.*, p. 207.

prietorship of Louisiana to the Commercial Company of the West. "The fifty-third clause of the transfer obliged the company to build at its expense churches at the places where it should establish settlements and to maintain the necessary number of approved ecclesiastics, all under the authority of the Bishop of Quebec, who had the nomination of the priests of the colony." [23]

Soon after this the territory of Louisiana was divided into three sections. The first section was the territory north of the Ohio, which was committed to the care of the Jesuits. The second section was the mouth of the river, and all territory lying west of the river from the mouth to the Ohio. This section was turned over to the Capuchins. The third section was all the territory east of the Mississippi from the mouth of the river to the Ohio, and this section was turned over to Carmelites and Capuchins. But the Capuchins soon turned over that part of the third section lying north of Natchez to the Jesuits. By this arrangement the Jesuits became the leading missionaries to the Indians with the Capuchins a close second. [24]

O'Gorman tells us there were between six and seven thousand Negro slaves in Louisiana when the Spanish took back this territory in 1769. [25] To these Negro slaves, of course the Catholic priests ministered.

Sir George Calvert, afterwards Lord Baltimore, undertook to establish a colony in Newfoundland in 1622, but was not very successful. In 1629, he moved his whole colony down to Jamestown, but due to religious differences (Baltimore had become a Catholic) he was not hospitably received. He returned to England and applied

---

[23] O'Gorman, *op. cit.*, p. 209.
[24] *Ibid.*, pp. 209-210f.
[25] *Ibid.*, p. 212.

for a charter to lands north of the Potomac. The grant
was issued to his son, Lord Cecil, for the first Lord Baltimore died just before its issuance. The land thus cited,
the Virginians claimed was a part of their patent rights.
Be that as it may, the second Lord Baltimore, at elaborate expense, set out to colonize his newly granted territory. The two vessels used, the Ark and the Dove,
carried three hundred laboring men and some twenty
gentlemen, and at the Isle of Wight they took on two
Jesuit fathers, although Bacon claims it was a Protestant
emigration under Catholic patronage.[26] Whatever the
motives, Lord Baltimore insisted on religious tolerance,
and notified the head of the Jesuit order that he could
offer the clergy sustenance. They could take up lands
just as any other adventurers. O'Gorman says that these
lands and others acquired for the Indians were the support of the Jesuits down to their disestablishment in
1767.[27] The work of these Jesuit missionaries and others
who came to join them seems to have prospered and extended into parts of Virginia, what was later Pennsylvania and also what was later to be New York. Due to a
quarrel between Lord Baltimore and the Jesuits, secular
priests were introduced into Maryland in 1642, and the
Jesuits were forced to give up all lands ceded from the
Indians. In 1673, two Franciscan Fathers arrived to
establish a mission, and to their number was added three
more Franciscans in 1677.

Father Harvey, a Jesuit, came into the New York
Colony in 1682, and was soon joined by two other
Jesuits, Fathers Harrison and Gage. Liberty of religion
was enacted in this colony in 1683, and about the same
time William Penn started his colony of Pennsylvania

---

[26] Bacon, *A History of American Christianity*, p. 56.
[27] O'Gorman, *op. cit.*, p. 222.

as a land of religious freedom. But the status of the religious freedom was not yet fully established. After the overthrow of James II in England in 1689, William of Orange sent out to Maryland Protestant governors who turned the tide of toleration, and the colony became a royal province with an established church.

Having taken a rapid survey of the entrance of Catholic representatives into America, one is led to contrast these various streams of influence. The Spanish whose chief work lay in the southern and southwestern region of America had two primary motives: 1. the finding of gold; 2. the conversion of the Indians. Since mining was a most arduous task, it was but natural that these Spaniards should enslave the Indians at first, and then finding them unsatisfactory workers, should look elsewhere for labor, which was most easily supplied from the Negroes, who were already in considerable numbers in Spain and Portugal, and later that they should turn to Africa for more numerous recruits. Their interest in evangelizing the Indian also led some of their most devout leaders such as Las Casas to try to shield the Indians from too strenuous labor, and to bring in more able-bodied Negroes.

In the North, where France was exploring America, the motive was largely commercial. The fur trade was the great source of wealth. Since the Indian trappers further west were more successful in finding pelts, the French were drawn farther and farther west. They did not set up permanent communities, but what better be called trading posts, and they were very eager to hold the monopoly of the whole interior; hence, their eager desire to establish posts from the mouth of the St. Lawrence to the mouth of the Mississippi, in a great semicircular ring that would hem round the English colonies on the Atlantic Seaboard. Naturally these traders were individualists. They did not need numerous laborers. Hence, they would not have introduced Negro labor even if the climate had been more propitious.

The Maryland and New York colonies were largely English and Dutch, who came with the desire to establish homes and to find a degree of freedom both political and religious. Here, too, labor was at a premium and Negroes were early introduced. Our story from here on must be the story of the organization and development by the Catholic Church for all those peoples among whom it worked, giving special attention to their interest in the Negro.

The development of Catholic work for the Negro in Louisiana was certainly not very encouraging as it is set forth somewhat at length in a recent book by a Catholic—"*Colored Catholics in the United States.*" [28] Gillard tells us there were just 172 Negroes in the New Orleans population when Iberville moved his capital to that spot in 1718. He feels the priests were eager to do all possible for the Negroes, but the environment was not very favorable. He quotes Boudier as saying:

> "The Colony was a new province where life was in the raw, where few of the inhibitions of civilization found place in tedious and discouraging pioneer life. The excesses that were common in early years quickly grew worse and appalled the missionaries. When the Capuchins arrived (1722) they found scandalous conditions prevailing at New Orleans and at the various posts. Beyond any possibility of contradiction, the boat loads of street scrapings and jail clearings dumped into Louisiana brought no angels of morality and religious paragons of perfection, nor did their example in the colony tend to ameliorate conditions." [29]

---

[28] John T. Gillard, *Colored Catholics in the United States,* 1941.
[29] Boudier, *History of the Catholic Church in Louisiana,* p. 33.

When Charlevoix made the journey from Quebec to New Orleans visiting the various points of Catholic effort, he arrived in New Orleans in 1722. "He described it as a place with a hundred houses, scattered about without any order." [30]

As indicated in the above quotation, the first contingent of Capuchins arrived in New Orleans in 1722. This section of the Church was then under the direction of Coadjutor, Bishop of Quebec, Duplessis de Mornay, who was himself a member of the Capuchin order. Hughes, in his history of the Jesuits, remarks that Vallier and Mornay arranged matters as they chose, by which we infer they were not very favorable to the Jesuits. But four years after this territory was assigned to the Capuchins, they resigned their Indian work to the Jesuits and allowed the latter a residence in New Orleans.[31] Hughes reports that by 1754, Louisiana had thirteen Fathers (Jesuits) and four Brothers working either at the residence in New Orleans or in the Illinois Missions, or at divers places among the Arkansas, Choctaws, etc.[32] He further tells us that each Jesuit worker had an annual income of only twenty-six sterling and that the Louisiana Mission had no estates worthy of notice.[33]

In 1727, the Church in New Orleans had its influence greatly increased by the entry of the Ursulines who came from France in that year. They set up a convent and an institution for higher learning for girls, the first

[30] O'Gorman, *op. cit.*, p. 209.
[31] Hughes, *The History of the Society of Jesus in North America*, Vol. 2, p. 258.
[32] *Ibid.*, p. 353.
[33] *Ibid.*, p. 354.

such institution established by the Catholics in America.[34]

To combat the immoral and irreligious conditions of the times, Bienville drew up his Code Noir in 1724. This code of Bienville followed rather closely the Code Noir of Louis XIV issued in 1685 for French West Indies. This code called for all slaves to be baptized and instructed in the Apostolic Roman Catholic religion; that slaves should not be called upon to work on the Sabbath or any festival days of the Church; that concubinage must be heavily punished; that slaves should have regular marriage rites; and that Christian slaves should be buried in the colony at the time.

The strenuous interdicts against concubinage speaks volumes as to the lax moral situation which maintained in the colony at the time.

The Ursulines had a long struggle to establish their girls' school, but finally in 1734, their first building was dedicated and the order was able to begin a marvelous work which has lasted down to the present time.[35]

The jealousy and conflict between the Capuchins and the Jesuits was very tense and greatly retarded the advancement of religion.[36] The purpose of religion was further retarded by the uprising of the Indians at Natchez in which most of the Capuchin priests who were laboring with the Indians in the lower Mississippi were killed.

In 1763, France by a secret treaty transferred Louisiana to the sovereignty of Spain. Louis XV wrote Governor d'Abidie: "In consequence of the friendship and affection of his Catholic Majesty, I trust that he will

---

[34] O'Gorman, *op. cit.*, p. 210.
[35] Shea, *History of the Catholic Church in America*, Vol. 1, p. 570.
[36] *Ibid.*, p. 579f, passim.

give orders to his governor and all other officers employed in his service, in said colony and city of New Orleans, to continue in their functions the ecclesiastics and religious houses in charge of the parishes and missions as well as in the enjoyment of the rights, privileges, and exemptions granted to them by their original titles." [37]

The Capuchins therefore were not disturbed in their work, although one of the Fathers was accused of exciting the people against the Spaniards.[38]

In 1772, the Bishop of Santiago de Cuba, under whose jurisdiction Louisiana now falls, sent Cyril de Barcelona to New Orleans with four Capuchin Fathers. They found the Church in not too good condition, since the priests, according to Shea, had thrown off all allegiance to Bishop or superior and "led lives that were a public scandal." [39] As a result, "religious duties were everywhere neglected; Negroes were not instructed, and did not receive the sacraments when dying." [40] Father Cyril evidently labored earnestly to reestablish the Church. Under his direction and cooperation the Ursulines in New Orleans found new help and took on new life.

The plan of administering Louisiana from Santiago proved unsatisfactory, so the Pope appointed Father Cyril de Barcelona, Bishop of Tricoli, and Auxiliary of Santiago de Cuba in 1781, and Cyril proceeded to New Orleans as the first resident Bishop.[41] At this time there seem to have been some fifteen local posts filled by parish

---

[37] Shea, *History of Catholic Church in America*, Vol. II, pp. 540, 541.

[38] *Ibid.*, quoted from Gayarre History of Louisiana, Vol. II, p. 165.

[39] Shea, *op. cit.*, Vol. II, p. 543.

[40] *Ibid.*

[41] *Ibid.*, p. 547.

priests in Louisiana. Reports of Bishop Cyril setting forth
the neglect of the Negroes had the King of Spain to
issue a Spanish "Code Noir" which "provided for the
establishment of chaplains on the plantations to give
spiritual ministration to the slaves, it called for segregation of the men from the women, regulation of amuse-
ments on Sundays and Holy days, elimination of manual
labor on these days, and insisted upon marriage for
slaves." [42]

One of the steps taken to advance the work in
Louisiana and Florida was to bring in Catholic priests
from Ireland, which it was thought would have a good
effect on the English remaining in this country. Shea
remarks that the "Register shows a series of Baptisms of
adults, White and Colored." [43]

Bishop Cyril was succeeded by Bishop Penalver who
made his first official visit to Louisiana in 1795 and
found much laxness, particularly with reference to religious care of Negroes. When Bishop Penalver was transferred to Gustemalo in 1801, Louisiana was left without
a resident Bishop until 1815, when Louis William
Dubourg was appointed to the See of New Orleans.
Catholic historians agree that this was the darkest period
of Catholic history in Louisiana. During this period,
Louisiana passed into the possession of the United States
in 1803, and the disorganization affecting the govern-
mental change naturally affected the Church. Also there
was somewhat of a change in the view taken of the
Negro. The French and Spanish codes had given the
slave at least some personal standing in theory, if not in
practice, but the American code gave him little or no

---

[42] Gillard, *Colored Catholics in the United States,* p. 54.
[43] Shea, *op. cit.,* Vol. II, p. 555.

standing either in theory or in practice. Also the prevailing religion of the United States was Protestant and that meant that many Negroes dropped away from the Catholic Church. Bishop Dubourg was slow in returning to Louisiana and when he did visit New Orleans it was after that city had been without the personal presence of a Bishop for nineteen years.[44] When Bishop Blanc was consecrated in 1835, there were only six Catholic Churches in all Northern Louisiana and at the opening of the Civil War, the Diocese had only seventeen priests, nineteen parish churches and thirty-five out missions.[45] O'Gorman estimates that in 1894, there were 50,000 Catholic Indians as the result of two centuries of work on the part of the Church.[46]

In all these changing vicissitudes of the Catholic Church in Louisiana, there had been much earnest solicitude for the religious care of the Negro. The success in winning Negroes to membership in the Catholic Church seems meager. So striking is this fact that Gillard in a recent book calls attention to this fact: "and gives as an explanation the meagerness of contact with Negroes; the rivalries between Catholic immigrants and Negroes; and other circumstances over which the church had no control, greatly limited the results of Catholic effort." [47]

Lataurette, in his *History of the Expansion of Christianity*, seems to think the Catholic Church was greatly retarded in America by the fact that it was too closely supervised and controlled from Europe, and hence the spirit of independence so evident in America was not given any large expression in the early Catholic Church.

---

[44] Gillard, *op. cit.*, p. 58.
[45] *Ibid.*
[46] O'Gorman, *op. cit.*, p. 212.
[47] Gillard, *op. cit.*, p. 59.

The second center where Catholic work for and with the Negro people was most prominent was Maryland. We have seen earlier that Lord Baltimore, a Catholic, brought with him two Jesuit priests, Father White and Altham, when he came to colonize Maryland. These were early increased by Father Black and Father Fisher. Father White was instrumental in converting one of the Indian Chiefs to Christianity and receiving considerable grants of land from the Indians.

Gillard tells us that as early as 1636, mass was said at Leonardtown for Whites, Negroes, and Indians.[48] The Jesuit priests were themselves slaveholders, though they tried to ameliorate this status by calling their slaves: servants, servant men, servant women, laborers, etc.[49] These Negroes belonging to priests were often referred to as "Priest Negroes" which some thought meant they had exceptionally good treatment[50] while others thought it meant they were poorly controlled and hence inefficient.[51] In one respect the priests were scrupulously careful; they were unwilling to permit the separation of families. Thus, a Father Mosely reports having married his Jerry to a Negro woman belonging to Charles Blake, named Jenney, whom he was forced to buy.[52] The Negroes were allowed to have their own gardens; they were given more ample provisions than ordinary; and they were allowed to make small change on the side.[53]

Mobberly commented on the profit of slaves rather

---

[48] Gillard, *op. cit.*, p. 62.
[49] Hughes, *op. cit.*, Vol. II, p. 560.
[50] Gillard, *op. cit.*, p. 62.
[51] Hughes, *op. cit.*, Vol. II, p. 560.
[52] *Ibid.*, p. 560.
[53] *Ibid.*, p. 562.

discouragingly, believing that indentured boys would be much more profitable.[54]

Father Mosely reported that "The Negroes that do belong to (Catholic) gentlemen of our persuasion are all christians and instructed in every christian duty and care."

The number of Negroes in Maryland and neighboring colonies was greatly increased by the migration from San Domingo at the time of the French Revolution, possibly a thousand Negroes, many of whom were slaves or ex-slaves. Most of these were Catholics since they came from the French West Indies. The Sulpicians had opened a seminary in Baltimore in 1791, and it was to these priests that the French speaking immigrants turned for religious instruction. In the basement of this seminary known as "Chapelle Basse" a catechism class was organized for colored adults. Dubourg, afterwards Bishop of New Orleans, was the teacher. When Dubourg left Baltimore, M. Tessier took over the class and continued it for thirty years. In 1827, M. Tessier chose M. Jaubert to take over this work. He it was who discovered that many of his pupils could not read the catechism, so he felt it necessary to establish a school, particularly for the girls. He found four Negro young women who wanted to consecrate themselves to this work, and with the consent of Archbishop Whitfield, these were organized into the Oblate Sisters. These were the teachers of the first convent school for colored girls. Later it also became an orphanage for colored girls.[55] These Oblate Sisters have been very outstanding in serving colored people through all the years.

In 1785, Father John Carroll estimates there were

---

[54] *Ibid.*, p. 563.
[55] Sherwood, *The Oblates' Hundred and One Years*, passim.

3,000 Negro Catholics in Maryland.[56] At the time of Emancipation, Bishop William Russell claimed there were 16,000 colored Catholics in Maryland.

Catholics were, of course, scattered through the South, but in few places were they numerous enough in colonial days to form churches. It was not until 1820 that a Bishop in the person of John England was located in Charleston, South Carolina, and in one of his earliest letters, England declares he has only six priests in his whole diocese. Bishop England was always interested in the religious instruction of the Negro, and in 1835, he opened a school for Free Negroes. His biographer remarks, that "No action of his career was considered more imprudent by his friends in the city." [57] The abolition movement was very active at this time and thousands of leaflets were being mailed into the South. January 29, 1836, the Charleston "Southern Patriot" announced that the mail was crammed with these papers, so a mob gathered, the post office was entered and the accumulated papers were burned near the Citadel, the old military school of South Carolina. Dr. England reports that some of his members were in this mob and heard talk that as soon as this business was finished, they meant to go to the Catholic Seminary, where Bishop England lived, and give him the benefit of Lynch law. At two o'clock in the morning, the Irish who formed one of the Volunteer Corps of the city militia were sent for and the place was thoroughly guarded. Bishop England put himself at the head of this group and told them if necessary they would fire on any intruders. After keeping guard for two nights, the mob seems to have disappeared. A group of leading citizens then requested Bishop England to discontinue his school.

---

[56] Gillard, *op. cit.*, p. 87.
[57] Guilday, *Life and Times of John England*, Vol. II, p. 151.

This he agreed to do if all other denominations would do likewise. All schools were closed.[58] This action was fully in accord with ideas expressed by England in a letter to officers of the South Carolina Association, through Alex H. Brown, its Chairman, in 1835.[59]

Bishop England made a trip to the Pope in 1833 for the express purpose of pleading for more active Catholic effort among the Indians and Negroes. It was due to this great interest that he was sent to Haiti to reorganize the Catholic Church there.[60]

Bishop England evidently held the prevailing Catholic opinion that slavery was a political issue and not a matter in which the Church should dabble. This is made clear even in the political campaign of 1840. Forsyth, Van Buren's secretary, in a speech in Georgia quoted a letter from Gregory XVI in such a way as to make it appear that the Pope was an abolitionist. Bishop England came forward in defense of the Pope. He said that far from condemning domestic slavery the Holy Father endorsed it. He quoted an interview with the Holy Father in which the Pope said: "Though the southern states of your Union have had domestic slavery as an heirloom whether they would or not, they have not engaged in the Negro traffic, that is, the slave trade."

Bishop England then proceeded to say: "I trust I have succeeded in showing that this letter of his Holiness which you describe to be an apostolic letter on slavery does in fact regard only that slave trade which the United States condemns and not that domestic slavery which

---

[58] *Ibid.*, p. 152.
[59] *Ibid.*, pp. 154, 155.
[60] Guilday, *op. cit.*, p. 276.

exists in our southern states." [61] Stephen L. Thebald, an ardent Catholic, comments: "That the Bishop indirectly contributed to the hardships of the Negro by participating in the political upheaval over the question of slavery as I have shown above seems true enough though painful to tell." [62]

Bishop England wrote Forsyth: "Slavery then, Sir, is regarded by that church of which the Pope is the presiding officer, not to be incompatible with the natural law, to have been established by human legislation, and, when the dominion of the slave is justly acquired by the master to be lawful not only in the sight of the human tribunal, but also in the eyes of heaven." [63]

That this was the attitude of many more than one official of the Church is clear from a statement of Archbishop Hughes. In a letter to Mr. Cameron, Secretary of War in 1861, he wrote: "There is being insinuated in this part of the country an idea to the effect that the purpose of this war is the abolition of slavery in the south. If that idea should prevail among a certain class it would make the business of recruiting slack, indeed. The Catholics so far as I know, whether of foreign or native birth, are willing to fight to the death for the support of the constitution, the government and the laws of the country. But if it should be understood that with or without knowing it, they are to fight for the abolition of slavery, they would turn away in disgust from the discharge of what would otherwise be a patriotic

---

[61] Guilday, *op. cit.*, pp. 471, 472. Also Stephen L. Thebald in *Catholic Missionary Work Among the Colored People of the U.S., 1766-1866*, printed in Am. Cath. Hist. Soc., Vol. 35, p. 333.

[62] Thebald, *Catholic Missionary Work Among the Colored People of the U.S., 1766-1866*, Vol. 35, p. 337.

[63] *The U. S. Catholic Miscellany*, October 10, 1840.

duty." [64] That this was the official attitude of the Catholic Church can hardly be doubted. A study of the Baltimore Catholic Mirror seems to reveal this.

"Never has the church condemned slavery, and equally never has she condoned it. There are many things in this world that have to be taken as they are, not as they ought to be, and among them the church has reckoned slavery. The Catholic Church looked upon the lot of slaves as accidental. This unfortunate people was indeed human and possessed human rights, but circumstances out of the control of slaves or master forced the former into an inferior social position, and made him economically dependent on the latter. In many cases, this situation was to the mutual advantage of both." [65]

The Catholic Mirror declares: "Our Clergy and Press have been true to their mission. Our priests in the North, whatever their private opinions about slavery, have not desecrated their pulpits by slavery harangues. Our clergy in the south, who have a true appreciation of the facts, preach to the slaves obedience, and to the masters clemency." [66] Archbishop Spalding writes: "No political discussions have been allowed in our ecclesiastical councils, whose deliberations have been exclusively conformed to questions connected with faith, morals and the discipline of the church. So far as we have been able to ascertain, no Bishop nor priest of the church has ever thought of bringing up such matters in our councils, so general and deep was the conviction that these subjects

---

[64] John R. G. Hossard, *Life of the Most Reverend John Hughes*, p. 437.

[65] C. E. Allen, OSB, *The Slavery Question as Seen in the Freeman's Journal and Baltimore Catholic Mirror*, 1850-1865 (Catholic Univ., 1935), p. 20.

[66] *Baltimore Catholic Mirror*, June 5, 1858.

belonged to politicians and would be wholly out of place in ecclesiastical meetings." [67]

The attitude of the Catholic Church was in some ways parallel to other churches in that it did not attempt to influence political opinion on slavery. It was first and foremost interested in religious instruction of slaves. In this work it was most diligent. Of this I think we have found ample evidence. A few sporadic references however might strengthen this conviction. Paul de Jeune, a Jesuit missionary rejoiced that he was teaching a little Negro boy whom he hoped to baptize when he had learned enough. [68] In 1800, Dr. Carr, the famous Augustinian received a Negro slave into his church in Philadelphia. [69] In 1805, Father Badin, a Sulpician, was preaching to slaves in Kentucky. [70] In 1811, Bishop Flaget, also a Sulpician, was preaching in Bardstown, Kentucky. [71] Both Badin and Flaget owned slaves. Archbishop Carroll also owned slaves, [72] but he freed one, prayed with others, and united regularly with the colored members of his household in religious worship. [73] Archbishop Marechol preached to slaves, "throughout his entire episcopate until the time of his death; he gave untiring assistance to the Catholic Negroes in his diocese." [74] And a great number of such references have been given, showing that while the Catholic Church took no political stand on slavery, it was the consistent policy of the Church to

---

[67] *American Catholic Historical Society,* Vol. 35, p. 333.

[68] Miriam T. Murphy, *Catholic Missionary Work Among the Colored People of the United States, 1776-1866,* p. 104.

[69] *Ibid.,* p. 108.

[70] *Ibid.,* p. 114.

[71] *Ibid.*

[72] *Ibid.,* p. 117.

[73] *Cathedral Records from the Beginning Catholicity in Baltimore to the Present Time,* p. 46.

[74] Murphy, *op. cit.,* p. 119.

impart spiritual knowledge to all slaves to whom they had access.

At the present time the Catholic Church is very active in religious work among Negroes, the order of Josephites giving very special attention to this work. We have given some account of this present-day work in Chapter IX.

CHAPTER IX

PRESENT ACTIVITIES AND PROGRAMS OF THE CHURCHES

The student of the churches in their attitudes toward the Negro is surprised, if he is not amazed, at the very obvious fact that every church, particularly in the South, was much more active in preaching the gospel to the slaves before 1860 than it has ever been since the Civil War in making Christian teaching available to all the Negro population. This statement seems so strange that many people refuse to believe it. But the full facts about the leading churches set forth in the chapters preceding are proof of the truth of the statement. Various explanations have been given. Some have claimed that masters had definite responsibilities for the religious state of their slaves resting on them, and they could not by any possible subterfuge escape that responsibility. Since many of these masters were themselves deeply religious, they did not desire to escape this responsibility, and public opinion would be a powerful incentive to those masters who were not themselves very religious.

A more cynical explanation is that masters found their slaves were better satisfied and therefore more easily controlled if they were given full opportunity to share in religious services. The recent imports from Africa were accustomed to emotional expressions in their religious life, and would be restless and unhappy without opportunity for some such expression. A more charitable view of this would be that since Christianity taught good will and all the virtues of manhood, it made better persons of the slaves, and as such they were more amenable to the conditions under which they lived and worked. It was not an infrequent thing for masters—even those who were not themselves religious—to say that Christian teachings made their slaves more valuable.

Another explanation given for the activity of all the churches before the Civil War, in the religious instruction of the slaves, is that the slaveholders found themselves under the severe condemnation of the abolitionist, and as a matter of self-protection, and salving their consciences, they were bound to do all they could to make the lot of their slaves seem a happy and helpful one. In other words, they justified their legal attitude of holding slaves by their religious attitude of being solicitous for the religious instruction of their slaves. It was a kind of escape mechanism by which they eased their consciences. Perhaps there were masters to whom each of these motives could be applied, and in some cases, all of them might apply to a single master. Careful reading of the original records convinces one that most of the masters were thoroughly honest and genuine in their desire to see their slaves instructed in matters of religion. It seems amazing to us, living in a more social-minded time, that these slaveholders did not see the inconsistency of teaching the Christian principle of the value of persons and at the same time holding such persons in a state that precluded the full development of personality. But self-interest has a way of blinding people to the real truth of many a situation. In my college days I knew a very ardent Methodist who worked hard to develop the Sunday School in his church in order that children might be developed, but at the same time he worked scores of other little children in his factory to the utter destruc-

tion of their personalities. He was not a bad man—he was
deeply concerned about justice and good will, but his
selfish interest blinded him to the needs of his mill
workers. Was he not giving them a livelihood? Did they
not eat because he gave them steady work? In some such
way many an honest slaveholder saw to it that his slaves
were well-fed, well-clothed, and religiously instructed,
and he honestly felt that he was a blessing to them, and
that they were better off under his paternal care than
they could possibly be if left to themselves. There are
plenty of men today who feel that they must dominate
those whom they choose to call the weaker masses.
Plenty of persons who think they must be guardians of
the less trained—and they would carry their guardianship
to the point of shutting the less advantaged out of all
self-direction, hence out of self-respect. The paternal
attitude of the planter has taken on different form, but
it is far from dead. I believe the careful reading of the
records of the slave period will convince any open-
minded person that these slaveholders were sincere, honest and well-intentioned men, eager to do what they felt
was their Christian duty. That they were often blind
to human values none of us can doubt.

After the load of personal responsibility for the slaves
was lifted from their shoulders many felt less personal
concern. Also, the whole relationship between master
and slave was so changed by reconstruction that there
actually grew up a bitterness between white and black,
which was not essentially the fault of either, but was
surely due to the bungling way in which the whole reconstruction period was handled. The gradual loss of interest on the part of white people in the welfare of
the Negro is one of the tragic aspects of the post Civil
War period. Many of the churches struggled valiantly

to maintain interest in the religious life of the colored people, but the tide was against them. Interest on the part of the churches and the church members grew steadily less and less, until in 1887, one annual gathering could report that "The church has failed to manifest an abiding interest in colored evangelism." The southern Methodists had three hundred and thirty-five missionaries giving their time to religious work among Negroes at the opening of the Civil War, but by 1900 they were hardly giving five cents per member to the support of any efforts for the Negroes' well-being. The Presbyterians, very active during the slave period, again and again insisting that every minister give as nearly as possible half his time to work for slaves, had by 1886 reduced their contribution as a denomination to $850 and only a "few white ministers were preaching to colored people." The Baptists and Episcopalians were no more active.

The Congregational Church which was almost wholly northern in its membership and which began its work for the Negro at a comparatively late date, increased its activities after the war, as did some of the other northern churches such as the Northern Methodists (M. E. Church) and the Northern Baptists. Gradually since 1900, the tide has been turning and more and more the southern churches have taken up their responsibility to the neglected groups of both races.

Obviously, it will be impossible in the space allotted to this chapter to go into full details of the attitudes and activities of any one denomination, but certainly the highlights must be given.

Activities of the Baptist Denomination

F. B. Matson of the Southwestern Baptist Seminary wrote a pamphlet in 1956 which is my authority for saying that there were in 1855 only 45,000 Negro members, and 50,000 white members of the Baptist churches of Virginia. The same authority states that in 1865, there were 600 Negro members and only 300 white members of the First Baptist Church of Montgomery, Alabama. Prof. Matson found what this study has frequently stated —that in many cases before the Civil War, both in Methodist and in Baptist churches, white and colored members sat indiscriminately in their churches.

This unity of membership was, however, soon altered after the bitter struggle and during reconstruction days when political methods engendered feelings of suspicion and even hatred where formerly there had been trust and good will.

It has been a slow process, but the Baptist denomination has slowly taken up its task with and for the Negro.

The Southern Baptist Convention of 1950 reports it is carrying on interracial work along many lines. First of all, the Home Mission Board of the Southern Baptist Convention supplies a teacher missionary to twenty-four schools and colleges, whose duty it is to teach courses on Bible and religion in those colleges. In 1950, there were twenty-nine teacher missionaries serving in these twenty-four colleges. Second, there were nineteen southern cities in which Negro centers were conducted. Each of these centers had paid directors, who conducted classes for Negro ministers, and for laymen who desired training for Christian service. The report says that 311 institutes and extension classes were conducted, with an enrollment of 9,618. The amount spent on this work in 1950 is not given, but in 1943 it was said to be about $50,000.

Third, the Sunday School Board of the denomination gives annually a series of scholarships to the American Baptist Theological Seminary and to the Woman's

Training School, both located in Nashville, Tennessee. This Board also distributes a large amount of literature free to Negro Baptist churches which are recognized as needy. The American Baptist Theological Seminary in Nashville founded through the cooperation of the National Baptist Convention and the Southern Baptist Convention. Some $200,000 was contributed by the Southern Baptist Convention for the erection of the original buildings, and a goodly share of the annual budget is borne by this same convention.

Fourth, the Woman's Missionary Union cooperates with a similar organization in the National Baptist Convention in furnishing free literature to needy Negro churches.

Fifth, all publications of the Southern Baptist Convention and its Home Mission Board give attention to the Negro Church and Negro Missions. The amount of space given to Negro work as compared to Spanish, Cuban, and other phases seems meager. To illustrate, in the report of 1943, out of fifty-three pages, the work for Negroes occupied only one small section, and in 1950 a page and a half out of forty-four pages of report was given to the report of Guy Bellamy, Secretary of Negro work. This is not criticism, for the denomination deserves much credit for its aggressiveness in this field. It only points to the fact that the Southern Baptist Convention, representing one of the most powerful and aggressive religious agencies in the world, had not at that time waked up to its tremendous responsibilities in this most needy field. Mr. Bellamy, in a pamphlet entitled *Negro Missions,* quite frankly acknowledges that the Church has not in any sense adequately occupied the field.

The agency at present (1956) under which this work

is directed is known as the Advisory Council of Southern Baptists for Work With Negroes. This Council is composed of representatives from all agencies of the Southern Baptist Convention—namely, the Home Mission Board, Sunday School Board, Educational Commission, Promotional Committee, W.M.U., Christian Life Commission, all Baptist Seminaries; and the report of Dr. Guy Bellamy, the Secretary, says they are asking (1955) representatives be appointed from the Foreign Mission Board and the Southwide Brotherhood.

This report of Dr. Bellamy (October 1955) says they had during the year 45,075 students in their training centers, preparing for church leadership. It reports 9,579 Negro preachers in regular classes; it reports 772 extension classes, enrolling 13,029 persons, many of whom were Negro ministers. It reports the Council helped 60 ministerial students go to school who could not have gone without help. The report indicates that the Council as of this year has 31 teacher missionaries in Negro colleges, whose task is to help christianize all students in these colleges. It reports 20 mission centers for evangelizing Negroes, and the Council is looking forward to the time when each state in the territory of the Southern Baptist Convention would have on its staff a man to promote cooperation with Negroes of that state.

A group of representatives white and Negro members of Baptist churches in the South was invited by the Advisory Council of Southern Baptists for work with Negroes to express themselves on their attitude toward race relations in the South. Two of the most significant of their findings were:

1. "All true Christians are brothers in Christ, and Children of God."

2. "We commit ourselves to see new insights as to

our Christian duty, and to seek more grace in manifesting Christian love toward all men."

The Southern Baptist Convention of June, 1954, only a month after the Supreme Court decision on desegregation in the schools declared: "We recognize the fact that this Supreme Court decision is in harmony with the constitutional guarantee of equal freedom to all citizens, and Christian principles of equal justice and love for all men." They then called upon all Christian statesmen and bodies to use their leadership in preventing bitterness and prejudice, and proclaiming a democracy that will command freedom for all people.

All of this shows a great interest on the part of Southern Baptists for the religious welfare of Negroes, but it must be said that this powerful denomination has not yet measured up to its great possibilities and responsibility with reference to the Negro.

Methodist Activities

The Methodist Church, which is now the largest Protestant church in America (since the union of the Methodist Episcopal Church, the Methodist Episcopal Church South, and the Protestant Methodist Church), is very active in work with and for the Negro. This church has a colored membership of 360,000. Years ago this Church adopted the Social Creed of the Churches, which includes a declaration of the sacredness of marriage; the family relation and the home; protection of women and children as regards labor and labor conditions; a national economy which guarantees plenty for all; the full training and employment of youth; reasonable hours of labor; the right of employers and workers alike to organize; the right of private property, with the Christian stewardship for the same; the Sabbath as a rest day for all; the proper treatment of criminals and delinquents; etc. Having set forth this creed, the Discipline adds: "We stand for the rights of racial groups and insist that the above social economic and spiritual principles apply to all races alike." [1] The Board of Social and Economic Relations of the Methodist Church is the official body set up by the Church to implement the Social Creed of the Churches. This Board is of comparatively recent creation and has not at the present writing fully matured its working plans.

The former Methodist Episcopal Church was very aggressive in sponsoring education among the Freedmen, immediately following the Civil War. They established two medical colleges, a theological seminary, and a number of liberal arts colleges. At the present time, the United Church sponsors and supports twelve educational institutions, eight of which are senior colleges, two junior colleges, one medical school, and one theological seminary. It cooperates with and gives funds to numerous other institutions, which are under branches of the Colored Methodist Church, such as the Colored Methodist Episcopal Church, the African Methodist Episcopal Church, et al. The property value of these institutions runs into the millions, and the endowment is something of the same proportions. The boards of trustees of most of these institutions is interracial.

The Discipline of the Church orders Race Relations Sunday in all 25,000 or more of its churches "in order to educate its people in regard to better race relations and the needs of Negro schools." In each of these churches a collection is taken for Negro work which funds are administered by the Board of Education for the "promotion of educational institutions for Negroes re-

[1] *Discipline of the Methodist Church*, 1940, pp. 766-769.

lated to the Methodist Church, and for religious education of Negro youth and adults." This department op-
erates hospitals, homes, and community centers for the
improvement of health and family life; it holds schools of
Methods for Negro ministers; sponsors vocation Bible
schools for Negro youth, and has a liberal budget at its
disposal for such work.

Perhaps the most vital and aggressive effort of the
Methodist Church for bringing about better race relations is put forth by the Women's Division of Christian
Service. The very central effort of this Division is to
create a climate of opinion that would make possible
progress in this field.

Up to 1944, according to Miss Thelma Stevens, Secretary of the Department of Christian Social Relations
and Local Church Activities, it had hardly been admitted
that there was such a thing as segregation in the Methodist Church. But of course everybody knows that the
Jurisdictional organization is clearly segregational in
operation and possibly in interest. So the women of the
Church set about making clear to the Church that all
elements of segregation were unchristian. Perhaps it was
in part due to their effort that made it possible for the
General Conference at Minneapolis in 1956 to pass resolutions declaring: "There must be no place in the Methodist Church for racial discrimination or enforced segregation" which finally was modified to read: "that
churches were urged to eliminate discriminatory practices whether by conference structure or otherwise with
all reasonable speed." The conference went on to *ask
churches to admit members without regard to color.*"
The conference then proposed amendments to the
church constitution which would permit individual
churches or whole Negro conferences of the Central

Jurisdiction (the Jurisdiction composed of colored churches) to transfer into geographical units or Jurisdictions by a two-thirds vote of the conferences involved. This action makes possible (though not clearly probable) the ultimate elimination of the Central Jurisdiction, which is the most obvious work of segregation in the Church.

In 1948, the Women's Division of Christian Service created a committee known as the "Committee on Racial Policies and Practices." This committee has drawn up a *Charter for Racial Policies* which contains six articles of belief, the fifth of which reads, "We believe that the Women's Division as an agency of the Methodist Church must build in every area it may touch a fellowship and a social order without racial barriers."

To implement this belief there are specific practices called for as: "Workshops, seminars, and institutes should be set up on a geographical basis with full opportunity for initial participation by all racial groups in the making and execution of the plans." They call for all Jurisdictions and conferences to study the plan with the hope that all would sooner or later adopt this charter as a working principle. Up to this date, eighty-five conferences out of something over one hundred have so ratified. In addition to the conferences, many local societies of the Women's Division have ratified this charter.

The Women's Division of the Church has made a compilation of "States' Laws on Race and Color" which has been used widely and has enabled women of the Church to carry on an intelligent campaign against all forms of segregation.

Mr. R. B. Eleaser, one of the best informed men in the Church on Race Relations, was for some years employed as Race Relations specialist by the Board of Education. He wrote a most significant article for church papers called "The Touch That Makes the Whole World Kin." In this he gives the simple story of one of these racial women's societies: "It was in a small town of Georgia of 3500 inhabitants. The society helped a colored woman attend a leadership school at Payne College, Augusta, Georgia. This led to interest in a mission study course on interracial understanding, which in turn led to a survey of their own Negro community. The principal of the colored school was called in to tell the group about conditions as the Negroes saw them, and make recommendations for improvement. Some results of this growing interest of the white women of this church are: A county health unit serving Negroes; a school-feeding program for undernourished children, white and colored; a course in domestic science for colored girls; a course in manual arts for colored boys; a public playground; a community house; and as a cumulative effect, a new school building for Negro children." While this may be an exceptional case, it illustrates the kind of dynamic activity these women's societies can carry forward. As I say, they are the hope of the Methodist Church.

The Board of Education has from time to time issued textbooks on Race Relations which have had wide use and have helped to make church members intelligent on racial issues.

The Women's Division conducts a number of Wesley Houses in cities, and recently several of the theological seminaries of the Church have opened their doors to colored candidates for the ministry. So far as I have been able to learn, there have been no untoward happenings in connection with this forward step.

By way of summary, one can say that many of the leaders of the Church have waked up to the tremendous issues at stake and are exerting every effort to lead the Church in a great forward movement. One wonders how long it will take to bring as large a body of church members as this Church has, to realize how tremendous are the issues, and how important that they act promptly, intelligently, and with genuine Christian spirit.

Work of Presbyterians

As we saw in the chapter on the Presbyterian Church and its attitude toward the Negro during slavery days, this Church tried hard after the Civil War to retain its Negro membership, but gradually most of them pulled away. The Church as late as 1941 had a small Negro membership organized into four Presbyteries united in the Snedicor Synod. At that time they were represented in the General Assembly of the Church by commissioners who had full voting rights. Up to that time, however, there was not full fellowship with all members of the Assembly, for the Negro commissioners were segregated in the dining room and housed in a separate building from the other members of the Assembly. On inquiry I found this treatment of the Negro commissioners was not only distasteful to the Negro commissioners, but also to many of the forward-looking white members.

In 1945, the Presbyterian Assembly U. S. appointed an Ad-interim Committee to "make an exhaustive study of the whole field of our Assembly's evangelistic and educational work among the Negroes within the bounds of our Assembly."

The Ad-interim Committee was a very able one, and set about making a real study. In their report to the

Assembly of 1946, they declared: "Our churches, pastors, and people have always recognized this claim to Christian equality and brotherhood" (this in spite of the situation mentioned above); they called for maintaining righteousness and justice between the races; they called for preaching which faced major social problems, "including glaring injustices in our treatment of Negroes," etc.

To meet this situation, they called for a great forward movement to be implemented by the Assembly through an agency known as "The Assembly's Committee on Negro Work." They asked that this committee should have a full time executive, and that $100,000 annually should be provided as the budget to sustain the program. The program was to include evangelism, establishing of new churches, Christian education, and particularly higher education. Stillman Institute, which had served the Negroes for years, was to be enlarged and reorganized; a school of religion was to be developed; and a campaign for $1,000,000 was to be undertaken to develop Stillman Institute into a college.

Dr. Alexander R. Batchelor became the Secretary of the Assembly's Committee on Negro Work, and served most efficiently and faithfully until his untimely death January 8, 1955. Dr. Batchelor was able to capitalize on the background work of men like Dr. C. A. Stillman, Dr. J. R. Howerton, Rev. A. L. Phillips, Rev. James G. Snedicor, Dr. D. Clay Lilly, and others.

Dr. Batchelor and his committee had the belief that there was a growing number of educated Negroes who were dissatisfied with the old emotional type of church service, and also dissatisfied with the living conditions in the Negro sections of the towns and cities. They felt as these persons moved out into better living sections, a new type of church life should be afforded them. Hence, new churches must be built and a better trained ministry should be furnished. By 1953, new churches had been organized in Jackson, Mississippi; in Richmond, Virginia; in Beaumont, Texas; in Memphis, Tennessee; in Elberton, Georgia; in Pine Bluff, Arkansas; and other places.

Two other very significant forms of service to Negroes have been carried on by Presbyterians U. S. The first of these had its origin in Louisville, Kentucky, where John Little, while a student in the Presbyterian Seminary, organized a Sunday School for Negro children which ultimately grew into two or more important mission churches with institutional programs. These were supported by contributions from many friendly white people of all denominations. John Little was a real Christian who honestly loved all people. Born in Tuscaloosa, Alabama, of one of the fine families of the Old South, he gladly gave his whole life to the Negro people of Louisville. In so doing he not only served hundreds of Negro families in Louisville, but he set a pattern which the Presbyterian Church has followed in other cities, notably in Richmond, Virginia, and in New Orleans in Louisiana.

Another special phase of work by the Presbyterians U. S. was that for women inaugurated by Mrs. W. C. Winsborough at Tuscaloosa, Alabama, in connection with Stillman Institute. In 1917, Mrs. Winsborough writes, "The Woman's Auxiliary held at Stillman Institute, Tuscaloosa, Alabama, a conference for Negro women of our church, the first of its kind ever held by any denomination for Negro women." [2] By 1921, this idea had taken root and other synods began holding women's conferences for Negroes. By 1944, the First

---

[2] Batchelor, *Jacob's Ladder*, p. 104.

Auxiliary Training School for Presbyterian Negro Women was held.[3] The heads of these synodical conferences for Negro women now attend the regular training schools of the General Assembly held annually at Montreat, North Carolina.

Soon after the Supreme Court handed down the decision about desegregation in the public schools, the Presbyterian Church U. S., through its authorized Assembly, spoke as follows: "Having in mind the recent decision of the Supreme Court of the United States concerning segregation, the Assembly commends the principle of the decision and urges all members of our churches to consider thoughtfully and prayerfully the complete solution of the problems involved. It also urges all of our people to lend their assistance to those charged with the duty of implementing the decision, and to remember that appeals to racial prejudice will not help but hinder the accomplishment of this aim." Dr. Malcolm Calhoun, Division of Christian Relations, Board of Church Extension, Presbyterian Church U. S., speaking before a group of church women concerned about the schools of the South, said, "Let us be grateful for the privilege of sharing in an undertaking which we believe has been initiated by the spirit of the Almighty God working within our hearts and minds."

The membership of Negroes in the Presbyterian Church U. S. was in 1940 probably not over 3500, but had almost doubled by 1953, and is growing steadily. The Negro has really become a part of the life of this denomination. With the growing importance of Stillman College as a training center, the development of the Alex Batchelor Memorial Fund to help train ministers, and the well-known habit of Presbyterians in supply-

[3] *Ibid.*, p. 105.

ing funds for philanthropic and religious causes, one can readily believe that this denomination will be an increasing factor in better relation between the races in the South.

The United Presbyterian Church, with headquarters in Pittsburgh, has one very important venture on behalf of the Negro people of the South—namely, Knoxville College, at Knoxville, Tennessee, established in 1875. It is a coeducational college which has had a large share in training leadership for the Negro Church.

The Presbyterian Church, U.S.A., began work in 1864 by directing their Home Mission Committee to "seek to effect arrangements through which the institutions of the Gospel may be given to the large and increasing number of Freedmen." [4]

By 1865, they had established a Negro church in Knoxville, Tennessee, which they claim is the oldest Negro Presbyterian Church organized after the Civil War. Soon they had churches at Maryville and New Market, Tennessee, and at Jacksonville, Florida.

Mission day schools were early established, and sixty-one such schools were reported in 1868, with 185 teachers. [5] By 1870, Scotia Seminary for Girls and Biddle Institute (later Johnson C. Smith University) were established. In 1891, Biddle elected a Negro, Dr. Daniel Jackson, as President and was one of the earliest colleges to have Negro leadership. By 1931, there were seventy-six day schools and twenty-seven boarding schools under the Presbyterian Church U.S.A. [6] and all the old slave states had such schools, save Missouri and Maryland. This was the peak of schools by number.

---

[4] *Climbing Jacob's Ladder*, Board of National Missions, 1952, p. 35.
[5] *Climbing Jacob's Ladder*, Board of National Missions, 1952, p. 39.
[6] *Ibid.*, p. 63.

The Church soon began discontinuing schools where they felt the public schools were adequate. Coulter Institute at Cheraw, S. C.; Haines Institute at Augusta, Ga.; Brainerd Institute at Chester, S. C.; Barker-Scotia College, Concord, N. C.; Harbison Junior College, Irmo, S. C.; Swift Memorial Junior College of Rogersville, Tenn.; Mary Homes Junior College of West Point, Miss. have all been efforts of the U.S.A. Church to help the Negro people. Gillespie Selden Institute and Hospital at Cordele, Georgia; Boggs Academy, Keysville, Georgia; and Mary Porter Academy, Oxford, N. C., have all been efforts of the Presbyterian Church, U.S.A. Philander Smith College has been and still is the church's chief educational institution.

The Church fosters a community center program for Negroes in larger towns and cities.

In 1932, a Committee on Negro Work was created by the Board of National Missions, and about this time they began electing some Negroes to church boards. In 1938, a Negro, Dr. Albert Byron McCoy, was elected Secretary of the Unit of Work for Colored People.[7]

By 1938, there were four synods with 385 churches and 24,421 church members.[8] The Catawba synod has four Presbyteries with 116 ministers and 161 churches, and 14,270 communicant members.[9] This is the largest of the four synods. The Church lists the following items in its advance movement: 1. Training Program for Ministers; 2. Larger Parish Development; 3. The Workers Conference; 4. Young People's Activities; 5. Institute on Racial and Cultural Relations.[10]

---

[7] *Climbing Jacob's Ladder*, Board of National Missions, 1952, p. 74.
[8] *Ibid.*, p. 80.
[9] *Ibid.*, p. 89.
[10] *Ibid.*, p. 92.

Work of the Catholic Church

The year after the Civil War in America, an English Catholic priest, Rev. Herbert Vaughn, obtained permission to organize a Foreign Mission Society of Mill Hill, England, and to train priests to carry out its work. The first priests sent to America to evangelize the Negroes were commissioned in 1871. For twenty-two years, this society continued to send workers to America, but in 1893, the American Catholic Missionary Society for the Evangelization of the Negro Race was organized as St. Joseph's Society of the Sacred Heart. For sixty years this group has worked with great earnestness to win the Negro to Christianity and to the Catholic Church. The third Plenary Council of the American Church in 1884 made provision that a collection for the work of the Josephites should be taken up in every Catholic church in the United States on the first Sunday of Lent each year. This council also decreed that priests who were to serve the Negro were to devote themselves to this work exclusively, for as Archbishop Janssens of New Orleans said, "It is almost impossible, a few cases excepted, as far as my experience goes, to do much good for the salvation of the Negroes whilst engaged in the ministry for the whites." [11] In 1888, a seminary, named in honor of St. Joseph, was established to train American priests for this work, even before the society was a separate organization from that in England.

The first Superior General of the Society of St. Joseph was Father Slattery, who held office from 1893 to 1904, and was succeeded by Rev. Thomas B. Donovan who served four years. Father Justin McCarthy and Father Louis B. Pastorelli have been later incumbents of

---

[11] *The Colored Harvest,* Vol. XXXI, No. 2, 1943, p. 5.

this office.   In 1927, the Society had grown until its workers numbered eighty-four priests and it carried on seventy-eight missions.   The Society then had 55,968 persons under its care, and during that year administered 2,686 baptisms.   On the basis of this splendid record, the Society was granted the status of a Pontifical Institute.   In his letter of praise, Pope Pius XII wrote, "As a pledge of heavenly favors, we gladly impart the Apostolic Blessing to our Beloved Children, the Superior General and Members of the St. Joseph's Society of the Sacred Heart, to the Friends and Benefactors of the Society in its work on the Negro Missions, to those in the Missions and Institutions of the Josephite Fathers and to all the Members of the The Colored Harvest." [12] In 1948, "there were 320 missions for Negroes with resident pastors.   Attached to these Mother Missions were 103 attended missions, i.e. mission plants to many of which schools are attached, but they have no resident priest.   This makes a total of 423 missions operated especially for Negroes.   There were also 45 mission stations, i.e., places where the missioner regularly said Mass and administered sacraments, but which had as yet no mission plant." [13]

The largest single congregation of colored Catholics is that of Corpus Christi in New Orleans with 12,000 members.

The 1955 report shows continuing progress.   The net gain of parishioners for the Josephites was 2,092 and converts numbered 1,954, with 1,008 preparing to become Catholics.   They had 24,637 pupils under the care of 412 sisters and 140 lay teachers.   *The Colored Harvest* for April 1956 lists at least eight new churches,

---

[12] *The Colored Harvest*, Vol. XXXI, No. 2, 1943, cover page.
[13] *The Negro American*, p. 67.

schools or rectories, finished in Josephite Missions during the year. Fifteen new priests were ordained.[14]

The Catholics of course have other agencies than the Josephite Fathers working for and with the colored people, such as the Oblate Sisters, the Sisters of the Blessed Sacrament, the Society for the Divine Word, the Catholic Board of Mission Work Among Colored People and others. Cardinal Gibbons was one of the most ardent advocates of better treatment of Negroes and was hailed by Dr. Booker T. Washington as a friend of the race.

In the early 1940's Father John T. Gillard completed and published a very careful survey of Catholic activities in the United States. He found at that time of 296,998 colored Catholics, 189,423, or 63.7 per cent, were members of colored rather than mixed churches. He calls attention to the fact that all Catholic churches are open to all Catholics regardless of race or color, but that "it is agreed by all impartial observers, that in the South where there are large concentrations of Negroes the only practical plan is for Negroes to have their own churches." He goes on to state, "It is a matter of experience that under present conditions whites and colored benefit from separate church units." [15]

So aggressive have been the Catholic efforts among Negroes that at the present time (1956) the number of Negro Catholics is fast approaching the half million mark. Of course this is a very small proportion of the Catholic membership—only 1 out of every 63, but it is a growing percentage.

The Catholic Interracial Council has put itself squarely behind the Supreme Court decision in the following

---

[14] *The Colored Harvest*, April 1956.
[15] Gillard, *Colored Catholics in the United States*, p. 138.

language: "We are confident that throughout the country thoughtful citizens will support with appropriate efforts this historic reaffirmation of the principle of equality of all men before the law."

Latourette thinks the results of the Catholic work have been meager, compared to the very widespread effort, and he thinks that this may be due to several facts: first, that the Negroes themselves had so few priests, there being only four ordained before 1914; second, that the Negroes lived in a predominantly protestant section of the country, and hence considered the Catholic Church as alien; and third, the Negro desires to control his own church which obviously he cannot do as a Catholic.[16]   That the Catholic Church is seriously and earnestly trying to win the Negro to the Christian faith, no one can doubt who reads the records given in an earlier chapter of this volume. Whether the Negro will ever turn in great numbers to this form of worship may be a question, but results already achieved clearly indicate that this Church has a real appeal to some members of the race.

Work of the Episcopal Church

The Protestant Episcopal Church, according to Episcopal authorities, lost many of its members at the close of the Civil War because the Negroes seemed to think they could get larger freedom in the Methodist and Baptist churches. The Church of course resisted this tendency and organized the Freedmen's Mission to deal with the problem. Although some independent churches were organized, and some were admitted into union with the Convention, the work did not go well and was soon abandoned. As we saw in the main chapter

---

[16] Latourette, op. cit., Vol. IV, p. 331.

on the Protestant Episcopal Church, there was a long fight over the question of Suffragan Bishops and the giving of the colored representatives full privileges in the councils of the Church. The latest report I have been able to secure through Mr. Harris, at the time in charge of the colored work of the Church, indicates that there were in 1937 one hundred and seventy self-supporting churches, three hundred and fifteen ordained clergymen, fifty-four thousand five hundred and twenty communicants, and something over seventeen thousand church school scholars. Diocesan budgets show that the Church is spending $103,833 on its Negro work, but Mr. Harris feels that the results are quite inadequate. Mr. Harris thinks the reasons for this small showing are fairly clear.

First, the colored Episcopalians have never been quite clear about their welcome in the Church either in the North or in the South. Thus, St. Philip's Church in New York remained, after organization, outside the Convention for thirty-four years. When St. Stephens of Petersburg, Va., applied for membership in the Convention, a storm of protest arose, and other such incidents tended to make the Negro Church dependent rather than independent, and hence has discouraged growth. Third, he thinks the Negro churches have had inadequate supervision. The Bishops are loaded with responsibilities for the white churches and there is not an adequate number of authorized colored men to discharge these duties. Fourth, he thinks there are not enough trained clergymen, and lastly, he thinks the membership has been drawn too exclusively from the so-called upper strata of the Negro population; hence, the Church has gotten the reputation of being "snooty." [17]

---

[17] Harris, *A Study of Our Work*, a pamphlet, passim.

In 1906, the Protestant Episcopal Church organized the American Church Institute for Negroes, which has under its supervision ten schools. The two oldest of these are Bishop Payne Divinity School at Petersburg, Virginia, and St. Augustine's College, at Raleigh, North Carolina. Each of these institutions date back to the first days after the Civil War, and has had a long and useful career. There are technical schools such as Calhoun School in Alabama; Voorhees Normal and Industrial School, Denmark, South Carolina; Okalona Normal and Industrial School in Okalona, Mississippi; and St. Paul's Polytechnic in Virginia. Also, there are the Nurse Training School at St. Agnes Hospital, Raleigh, North Carolina, and College Center at Fort Valley, Georgia. These schools enroll more than three thousand students and have an annual budget of nearly half a million dollars, about ten per cent of which is contributed by southern dioceses.[18] Mr. Harris, in the pamphlet referred to above, calls upon the Church to inaugurate a plan of general church work comparable to the educational program of the American Church Institute, and he would make it interracial, but distinctly controlled by the colored members of the Church. Should some such statesmanlike program be adopted, the Protestant Episcopal Church might greatly increase its hold upon the Negro people of America.

Work of the Quakers

The American Friends, or Quakers, were the first group in America to develop a keen conscience on the question of slavery, as set forth fully in the chapter on this group. They have always maintained interest in the welfare of the Negro people. Like many other churches,

---

[18] Patton, *Negro Education in War Time,* a pamphlet, 1942.

however, their active participation in work with the Negro population lagged somewhat after the Civil War. It was not until 1944 that a Race Relations Division was organized under the Social Industrial Section of the American Friends Service Committee. The Committee has been doing considerable work in this field for a number of years. Perhaps the most outstanding contribution has been made through its work camps, a number of which are interracial. These camps are just what the name implies, groups of young people who live together in groups for a period of several weeks, sometimes three months, and who undertake to do some piece of actual community work, which would not likely be done otherwise, such as the building of a park or playground, or sometimes the building of a schoolhouse or community center where funds are not otherwise available for the purpose.

All the young people in these camps (mostly college students) give their time and in many cases pay for their food and maintenance. The interracial camps undertake tasks which will be specially helpful to communities which are either mixed white and colored or distinctly colored. The boys and girls, white and colored, who work and live side by side in these camps learn to know and respect each other, and hence lay a foundation for better racial understanding. The first such interracial work camp carried out in the South was conducted at Nashville, Tennessee, in 1944, in cooperation with Fisk University.

The Friends also conduct certain houses such as Flanner House, in Indianapolis, where work with Negro youth is given special attention.

One distinctive feature of the Friends' work has been their willingness to cooperate with other agencies or denominations in work for and with the Negro people. They have been perfectly willing to lose themselves in a cause, and have in so doing found their soul. They take part in many meetings or groups without ever being known as the supporters of that work. The volume of work done by these Friends is not nearly so large as that done by some other groups, but the spirit and attitude of their work is quite out of the ordinary.

Work of the Lutheran Church

The United Lutheran Church in America carries forward its work for Negroes under the direction of The Board of Social Missions. The Church still has a few members scattered among the various regular churches, and a few exclusively Negro churches have been organized. In Washington, D. C., the Church of the Redeemer was founded in 1885; the Church of the Transfiguration was founded in New York City in 1923 to care for West Indian Negroes of the Virgin Islands; in 1934, the Church of the Holy Trinity was organized in Jamaica, Long Island, and in 1942, the Church of St. Paul's was organized in New York City.

The Lutheran Church's mission to the Negro really began in Baltimore, Maryland, around 1890. In that year, a Rev. Mr. Heuer, a layman, started a Sunday School for Negroes on Ivy Lane, Baltimore. From this beginning the work spread to other sections, particularly to the South. Work in the South usually started with a Christian Day School and gradually developed into a church. The United Lutheran Church now has work for Negroes in thirty-four Alabama communities, in two communities in Florida, one in Georgia, one in Kentucky, ten in Louisiana, two in Mississippi, eight in Missouri, fourteen in North Carolina, one in South Carolina, three in Tennessee, three in Texas, and three in Virginia.

Special emphasis has been laid on training Negro ministers and teachers, the central institution for which work among Negroes in the South being The Lutheran Bible Institute, Montgomery, Alabama. According to Ervin E. Krebs, who writes the history of Lutheran Negro Missions, the denomination has spent $890,299 on this work in the last sixty years.[19]

In 1951, the Board of Social Missions drew up a statement of Human Relations to guide Lutheran churches on racial issues. The significant paragraph in this statement reads as follows: "Since the Church is the body of Christ, it must free itself from those cultural patterns of prejudices and discriminations which persist in our society and must manifest in its own life the principles and attitudes of Jesus. The Church must seek to be true to its own nature as a community of Children of God inclusive of every race, nation, and class who confess Christ as Lord." "The Church's agencies and institutions should seek to serve all people fairly without distinction because of racial or cultural background. All its congregations should be centers of action to develop Christian fellowship across human barriers, and to instil the spirit of equality and Christian brotherhood. To this end the United Lutheran Church in America calls its pastors and people to earnest study and remedial action. As indicative of this spirit which prevails in the Lutheran Church, Krebs in his outline of work for the American Negro says: "There is no thought today of developing a separate Afro-American National Church

---

[19] For full information see Krebs, *The Lutheran Church and the American Negro* (Columbus, Ohio: Board of American Missions, 1950).

body. All pastors, congregations, and conferences in the American Lutheran Church are a part of the districts and the National Church body, regardless of race or nationality." [20]

In the light of such action as this, Lutherans, after the Supreme Court decision, needed only to reconfirm one of the above paragraphs and to add "Christians have special responsibilities as citizens to make society's law and practices conform to God's order." Various synods of the Church have taken positive action. The Virginia Synod went on record as favoring "the integration of Negroes into the full church life of the synod at the earliest possible date"; the West Virginia Synod recommended that "all churches of our synod plainly state that their altars, pews and membership are open to men of all races"; the Maryland Synod resolved (1) that pastors and lay delegates encourage their congregations to move toward racial integration in Congregational life and (2) that the synod call upon its pastors and congregations to exercise constructive community leadership in the transition to racial integration in public schools"; the Central Pennsylvania Synod urged that all congregations "take the necessary steps toward integrating Christians of all races and ethnic backgrounds into their congregational life"; it also urged affirmative action to eliminate discrimination in housing, education, and employment.

The Board of Social Missions prepared in April 1955, a folder for information of their congregations on social matters, a statement which declares: "There is a growing tendency for our congregations to reach out and draw into their fellowship men, women, and children of all racial and ethnic backgrounds who live in their

---

[20] Krebs, *The Lutheran Church and the American Negro*, p. 51.

neighborhoods." [21] Ervin E. Krebs declares that the National Lutheran Council and synodical conference bodies have some 170 congregations of predominantly Negro membership, with a total of more than 20,000 members.[22]

It can thus be seen that this denomination has taken advanced ground in its declarations concerning race relations. It will be wonderful if in the near future its declarations can work out into active practice.

As we wrote this, information comes that the United branches of Lutheran churches will join the World Council of Churches and will thus take with them this high sense of brotherhood of all peoples, into this influential World Council.

The Work of the Congregational Church

In the chapter on the Congregational Church, we have set forth rather fully the remarkable work which this Church did following the Civil War. The American Missionary Association which is the chief representative of this denomination in its work with the Negro has fortunately come into rather large resources through the Hall (Aluminum) Fund, and is therefore in position to carry forward a rather remarkable program. It continues to cooperate with a group of colleges, such as Talladega in Alabama, Le Moyne in Tennessee, Atlanta University in Georgia, Tougaloo in Mississippi, Tillotson in Texas, and still holds cooperative and helpful relations to such schools as Fisk in Tennessee, and Hampton in Virginia, which the Church sponsored in the earlier days. But they are building or founding no more

---

[21] *Desegregation, Basic Considerations for Christian Action,* published by Board of Social Missions, 431 Madison Avenue, New York.
[22] Kreb, *Lutheran Church Work in Interracial Communities,* p. 3.

colleges now, and they are encouraging all institutions to become independent and self-supporting as rapidly as possible.

The A.M.A. still cooperates with and largely supports a few demonstration schools, such as Avery Institute in Charleston; Fessenden Academy in Martin, Florida; Ballard School in Macon, Georgia; Lincoln Academy at Kings Mountain, North Carolina; The Lincoln School at Marion, Alabama, Trinity School at Athens, Alabama; Cotton Valley School at Fort Davis, Alabama; and Bricks Rural Life School in North Carolina. These schools the Association is trying to develop into community agencies, which are much broader and more practical in outlook than simply an ordinary school.[23]

In 1942, the Association assembled a very significant group in New York to study racism in America and ways and means of "doing something tangible toward establishing human solidarity in the days to come."[24] This group made the following recommendation, "It is the sense of this assembly that the American Missionary Association be encouraged to carry forward its contacts working toward a closer integration of existing agencies in interracial work, correlating their studies and surveys, and using cooperatively their expert staffs in coming to close grips with problems of racism in America and in the world at large, and, should it be desirable, taking the initial step in creating a general commission with which to implement such work."[25] In April of 1942, the Executive Committee of the Board of Home Missions and its Policy and Planning Committee of the Congregational Christian Churches, adopted the follow-

---

[23] See *Shackled Still*, a pamphlet issued by the A.M.A., 1943.
[24] *Shackled Still*, p. 14.
[25] *Ibid.*, p. 14.

ing resolution: "That the American Missionary Association Division concentrate its attention on the field of race relations, particularly in the Negro-white area, and that as funds become available, the Association develop a non-institutional type of pioneering work which would send competent representatives into various communities to work by such methods as the local situation shall suggest and make possible." [26]

The report goes on to explain, "Our purpose is to begin an era in the Association's history of more direct cooperative service, looking first toward the securing of the full rights and privileges of citizenship to American Negroes, already guaranteed by amendments to the constitution of the United States, and second, not to build more schools, colleges, and churches for a disadvantaged people, but rather to work with them in utilizing private and public institutions, movements and agencies, which seek to establish just and peaceful relations." [27]   "With conviction and courage we are therefore determined to move more directly toward the elimination of racial discrimination in all human relations everywhere." [28]

This new Social Action Group has assembled trained research and activity persons and is attacking the problem with great vigor. It publishes a small journal called *Social Action*, and month by month publishes *A Monthly Summary of Events and Trends in Race Relations*. It has held a significant seminar in Nashville during the summers of 1944, 1945, 1946, and 1947, etc. on Race Relations, and is cooperating in publishing some of the most significant researches in the field. It is perhaps the

[26] *Ibid.*, p. 14.
[27] *Shackled Still*, p. 15.
[28] *Ibid.*, p. 16.

most ambitious and promising effort yet made in bringing in a new day of interracial good will.

Through last minute reports just received we find that this denomination has worked out several new techniques through its department of Race Relations, headed by Mr. Lester M. Long—such as the following:

A. Special emphasis is being placed on helping communities such as San Francisco, Minneapolis and numerous smaller communities, to make complete surveys of their own racial problems, and helping them develop programs to meet such problems. This gives a sense of responsibility to the local community for its own problem and seems to guarantee long time efforts in this field. Such programs have led in many cases to employers in their communities giving responsible jobs to capable Negroes, which not only aids able Negro workers, but also helps the local community to put a new valuation on Negroes as members of the community.

B. The Race Relations Department is rendering direct service to schools that are seeking a more full integration of Negro and white students, by helping them reshape their educational programs so as to do a more thorough democratizing job. They have also helped these schools do a better job of educating their community leaders in intergroup relationships. They have even helped develop new units of study better fitted to study by mixed groups.

C. This department has made careful studies of exclusive clauses in real estate transfers in cities both North and South, which closed large areas of cities to Negro homes. Such studies have eventuated in remedial legislation in some cases, whereby Negroes were permitted to buy homes in the better sections of the cities.

D. This Department of Race Relations has concerned itself in the larger aspects of Negro life such as housing, recreation, employment, education and church relationships. It works at the local level in all these fields. Its watchword is action.

E.   The Institute at Fisk University has been continued and latest reports indicate that 1,300 to 1,500 community leaders have been trained to go back to their local communities to help guide long time programs of better life for Negroes—hence better race relations.

The Race Relations Department of the Congregational Church has done and is doing a most aggressive work which should set a pattern for many other denominations. Their publications will be most helpful to many other religious groups.

Work of Smaller Denominations

Other small denominations are doing what they feel they can to meet the present need of good will, but the above record of eight of the larger denominational groups shows the trend of interest at the present time. One cannot fail to be impressed with significant activities of these groups, but if one is Christian, or even if one is interested in democratic processes, he must see how inadequate the present program is.

Some of the newer and smaller denominations also are carrying on active work with and for Negroes. Thus the branch of the Church of God, with headquarters at Montgomery Ave, Cleveland, Tennessee, through their Assistant General Overseer, Dr. James A. Cross, report that they have 140 Negro Churches, with a membership of 3,056; that they have 114 Negro Sunday Schools; that there are 265 ordained Negro preachers in their church and that they maintain in Florida a Bible Training School for Negro ministers;

and that they appoint an evangelist for every state in which they have Negro churches. Other of the younger churches are doing similar work.

The record of the older denominations outlined above shows strong and definite interest, and one must be impressed with the total volume of such work, but if one is really interested in democracy, and much more if one is deeply concerned about Christian influence, one cannot fail to have the feeling that efforts so far in this field are quite inadequate.

Work of the Y. M. C. A.

This summary would not be complete if it did not give some account of the work of another religious organization, namely the Y.M.C.A. While not a church, it is the servant of all the churches and has had a remarkable share in the development of racial good will. Mr. Hoover's Commission on Recent Social Trends in the United States pays tribute to the Y.M.C.A. and Y.W.C.A. in their activities in this and kindred fields.[29]

In 1909, Dr. W. D. Weatherford, who was then the Southern Student Secretary of the International Committee of the Y.M.C.A., called together a little group of persons in Atlanta, Georgia, to discuss ways of bringing about better understanding between the races. Among those present were Dr. Walter Lambeth, later Bishop of the Methodist Episcopal Church South; Dr. Steward Roberts, a brilliant young physician of Atlanta, who had been a teacher at Emory College; Mr. John Wesley Gilbert, who had accompanied Dr. Lambeth in the founding of the Southern Methodist Mission in West Central Africa; Mr. Watson, a representative of the National

---

[29] *Recent Social Trends in U.S.* (McGraw Hill, 1933), Vol. II, pp. 1036-1039.

Y.M.C.A. work among colored men, and Dr. Weather-ford himself. After a full day's conference, Dr. Lambeth insisted that Dr. Weatherford be commissioned to pre-pare a textbook to be used by students, both white and colored, to better inform both groups on the present conditions. The final result of this commission was a little volume called *Negro Life in the South*,[30] which went through several editions, was sold in numbers of more than 30,000 copies, and was studied by upward of 30,000 white students. It made the first real break in the dead indifference of the time. Mr. Cleveland E. Dodge, then Chairman of the Student Committee of the Y.M.C.A., was so impressed with this little book that he offered to raise a fund of $50,000, half of which he himself gave, to push this work in the colleges and other fields in the South for a period of five years.

Under the direction of Dr. Weatherford, Dr. Chan-ning H. Tobias was called from Payne College in Augusta, Georgia, to begin a more aggressive work among colored students, and Rev. A. M. Trawick was associated with Dr. Weatherford in carrying on a more aggressive education of white students in racial good will. Other volumes followed,[31] one of which was *Present Forces in Negro Progress*, dealing with race leadership, population movements, the Negro farmer, the rural schools and what the churches were then doing in race relations. This volume was sent to every Farm Demonstration agent in the South by Mr. Julius Rosen-wald, with a covering letter from the Secretary of Agri-

---

[30] W. D. Weatherford, *Negro Life in the South* (New York: Association Press, 1909).

[31] These volumes were: *Present Forces in Negro Progress* (New York: Association Press, 1912); *The Negro from Africa to America* (Doran, 1924); *Race Relations* by Weatherford and Johnson (New York: D. C. Heath, 1934).

culture. These various volumes had much to do with changing the attitude of college students and some church leaders from one of indifference to that of advocates of good will and understanding.

When World War No. I broke out, W. D. Weatherford was asked to conduct at Blue Ridge, North Carolina, a school for training secretaries for the Y.M.C.A. in the Army and Navy camps. The day the Armistice was signed, Mr. L. Wilbur Messer, General Secretary of the Y.M.C.A. at Chicago was at this Blue Ridge School. Dr. Weatherford raised with him the question of how the way could be prepared to reintegrate the returning soldiers into American life. In particular he pointed out that Negro soldiers would not be happy in their old relationships after their experience in France. He suggested that the Blue Ridge School be continued, not to train secretaries, but to prepare laymen to receive these Negro soldiers back into their communities, with due recognition for their services. Mr. Messer, who was a real statesman, saw the importance of this move and agreed to back an appeal to the War Work Council of the Y.M.C.A., of which he was a member, for funds to carry forward this work. He and Dr. Weatherford went to New York and made the appeal to the War Work Council, and secured $100,000 with which to carry forward twelve ten-day schools of about one hundred men each, to be held at Blue Ridge, N. C. A similar series of schools was set up for colored men in Atlanta under the direction of W. W. Alexander. When this series of schools—training men in spirit and outlook to receive the colored soldiers back into civilian life—had been finished, and growing out of this experience, a group of nine men met in Atlanta to discuss ways and means of developing good will and understanding be-

tween the races. This group included John J. Eagan,
M. Ashby Jones, R. R. Moton, Plato Durham, S. A. Ack-
ley, J. H. Dillard, W. W. Alexander, W. D. Weatherford, and Dr. Wallace Butrick of the General Education
Board as guest. In this meeting the Commission on Interracial Cooperation was organized, and John Eagan
elected chairman.

The Commission first asked the War Camp Community service to help finance the program, but were
turned down. They then turned to the War Work
Council of the Y.M.C.A. and secured a grant of $20,000
per year for five years as the nucleus of a budget. Every
State Secretary of the Y.M.C.A. in the South acted for
a period as a field agent for this Interracial Commission,
thus helping it to get on its feet. Most of the Y.M.C.A.
secretaries of the South were members of the various
state commissions on Interracial Work. It is hardly
necessary to outline the tremendous contribution toward
better understanding made by this Commission.

After twenty-two years of service, the Commission
resolved itself into, or was absorbed by, the Southern
Regional Council which still holds as one phase of its
work the development of good will between the majority and minority groups of the section. This new
organization included all members of the old Interracial
Commission desiring to serve and a large number of new
members. It started its work with two coordinate ex-
ecutives, one white, Dr. Guy Johnson, and one colored,
Dr. Ira D. Reid.

The facts here outlined show a great awakening in
the last twenty years. Practically every denomination
has a commission on Racial Understanding, and many
of the social organizations taking their bearings from the
Church have taken steps to see that white people shall

be intelligent on this great issue. Practically every leading denomination has declared itself as strongly in favor of church integration, if only these declarations can become operative. But the end is not yet. Interest, intelligence, even justice in education, economics, and politics are not enough. We are at the parting of the ways. The Christian forces of America simply must see to it that the Negro is accorded a full status of a citizen and a man. This demands a new spirit, a new attitude, a new fellowship. If this cannot be attained, then we have fought the second World War in vain. A full discussion of the spirit and attitudes which the times demand will be found in the closing chapter of this book, along with some practical suggestions of the next steps to be taken. It is to be hoped that all who have any interest in the future peace of America will read and ponder that chapter. The number one problem of America for the next twenty-five years will be that of interracial good will. We must either solve that question or make shipwreck of our democracy and also of our Christianity.

Chapter X

THE ATTITUDE AND PROGRAM WHICH THE HOUR DEMANDS OF THE CHURCHES

The preceding chapters have revealed a deep and abiding interest of the churches in the religious welfare of the slaves. Most of the churches, in particular the Baptists, the Presbyterians, and the Catholics, took the position that slavery was an institution of the State, and, on the principle of separation of Church and State, the Church had no business attempting to change the order of society. Its business was to ameliorate conditions and mitigate all the hardships and cruelties of slavery. For a defense of this position they turned to the Scriptures. Literally read, their documents seemed to justify slavery. Indeed, many of the divines of the period found in the Scriptures a complete justification of this institution. They believed that slavery was God's method of bringing the savage people of Africa under the influence of the Christian gospel. Hence, they felt the Church was duty bound to see that every slave had the benefit of religious instruction. We have seen that in the later years of the slave period, a veritable crusade for religious instruction of slaves had set in. If the Church could not interfere with the political institution of slavery, it could and must serve the slave to the utmost of its ability. Only thus could a Christian reconcile the state of slavery with the teachings of Christianity.

As this tension grew the Church searched more earnestly to find a fuller justification of the institution. One of the seemingly solid rocks on which the argument rested was the story of the cursing of Ham in the ninth chapter of Genesis. Because Ham had broken taboo, his father, Noah, cursed him, and said he should be a servant to his brethren. It, of course, called for a very literal interpretation to twist this story into the curse of God upon Canaan. But that very literal interpretation was in accord with the strict religious thought of the time; hence, the story seemed to justify slavery. But since the institution of slavery seemed to be a part of the plan of God, it made a religious attitude toward the slave, all the more incumbent upon the church member. The Negro was a son of God, even if he was a son who rested under a curse. Indeed, it was the business of the Church to so train and nurture him that ultimately he would come from under this curse. Such was the churches' thought.

We have seen that this conception of slavery opened the way for a deep sympathy and solicitude for the slave. Just as a parent is apt to be more drawn to a disadvantaged child, so the master was often drawn to his slave as one who through no fault of his own was living under a terrible curse, so that personal relationships between master and slave were often of the kindest and most considerate temper. This opened the way for the exceptional slave to attain real standing, and respect. We have seen that the Baptist Church in Patsmoth, Va., called a Negro pastor. To the religious slaveholder there would be no incongruity or inconsistency in this. We have seen that twenty-eight of Charleston's most prominent white citizens joined a Negro Presbyterian Church, and agreed in advance never to take the leadership out of the hands of the Negroes. We have seen that the first Methodist Church organized in the territory of Mississippi had, as charter members, two planters and their wives and three slaves, and that all seven were of equal standing in the Church. We have seen old St. John's Lutheran Church in Charleston with a Negro membership almost as large as its white membership, and all communing at the same table. Bishop William Capers of South Carolina, one of Methodism's great souls, often took Henry Evans, a full-blood Negro with him on his preaching tours, allowing Evans to preach to white congregations. It is said that many whites even preferred the preaching of Evans rather than that of the Bishop himself, one of the South's great preachers. In other words, the antebellum white Christians looked upon the Negro as a possible son of God who had a right to every privilege of the Church, and it did not offend them to see him partaking of all these privileges; but, politically and economically, the slave rested under the curse and had no standing. *We of the present time have reversed the attitude. We claim that the Negro has full rights to economic, civil, and political freedom, but we are sure that socially and religiously he must be completely separate and segregated.* We not only would not call a Negro pastor to our church, however able and brilliant, but in most churches it would be at the cost of his position that a white pastor invite a Negro minister to fill his pulpit. We not only would not think of joining a Negro church as did some of the most prominent whites in Charleston, but we make a great fuss if a few well-dressed, well-behaved, and Christian Negroes presume to attend a service in one of our white churches. A great many white Christians, and not a few white ministers, still ignorantly twist the curse of Noah into a curse of God, resting on the colored people, and make that a justification for a belated race prejudice. The present-day prejudice is worse than that of the ante-bellum planter. We are willing to grant economic justice, which the planter did not, but we are not willing to grant the dignity of manhood, which the planter took for granted. The planter joined the same church with his slave and partook of the same communion elements, because he believed the Negro was the son of the same God which he worshipped; but the present church member seems to have fallen into the error of thinking that the Negro is not a child of God but a kind of stepchild. In the matter of good will toward the Negro we are probably more backward than were the more enlightened slaveholders. We can look back to them as more open-minded and more Christian than many of our present-day church members. It would be almost sacrilegious to attempt to compare the attitude of most modern Christians to the attitude of those superb and knightly leaders of the Old South, Stonewall Jackson and Robert E. Lee. This thought should sober the modern Christian and prepare all of us to think in larger and more Christian terms.

Indeed, the times demand a new tempo and a broader outlook. We are at the parting of the way. The world wars have brought us into a different time and the old patterns of race relations will no longer serve as a basis of national culture. The Negro has made tremendous progress since emancipation. He has produced many gifted and talented leaders, such as Washington in education, James Weldon Johnson in literature, Roland Hayes and Marian Anderson in musical art, and hundreds of less known, but equally useful citizens. The Negro is no longer satisfied, and should not be satisfied, to be patronized. He wants to be a man in his own right, and those of us who have come to know their brightest and ablest youth, know full well they can and will become independent and efficient citizens. Surely the Church cannot take lower ground than does the State. We cannot as Christians hold our colored fellow Christians as less worthy than the State holds these same persons as citizens. The issue is clearly drawn—we must either have a new attitude as church members, or we must confess that Christianity has failed to follow Christ. The Supreme Court decision of 1954 has dramatically high-lighted this hour of crisis. Of course many people have not yet accepted the decision of the Supreme Court on desegregation of the schools, but they will. Americans are essentially a law-abiding people. In spite of all the difficulties—and they are many—if given time and allowed to work with a reasonable degree of patience, all sections of America will ultimately come to accept the ruling of the Supreme Court.

But where does this leave the churches? If our children can be educated in desegregated schools, surely mature Christians cannot be overwhelmed by the idea of some colored people wanting to join white churches which may be near to their place of residence. If the Church cannot set the pace in race relations, it would seem it ought to at least remain in calling distance of the State in any advanced thinking and action.

Besides, our ideals of democracy force us to give a fuller and more meaningful status to the Negro. We of the South, in particular, have prided ourselves on our Jeffersonian ideals. We have claimed that we were the democrats of democrats. But Jefferson long ago said: "We hold these truths to be self-evident: that all men are created equal; that they are endowed by their Creator with certain unalienable rights; that among these are life, liberty, and the pursuit of happiness." Do these statements apply to the Negro, or do they not? If we are really democratic, they apply to all alike. On any other interpretation we are not a democracy. Nazism and Fascism have forced the world to face this fact realistically. We must be democratic or we will be fascistic. We must be followers of Jefferson, or we will be followers of Hitlerism. Surely there cannot be any hesitance in our choice. Theodore Roosevelt once said: "A man who is good enough to shed his blood for his country is good enough to be given a square deal afterwards." The recent wars have driven all fair-minded men to realize that we cannot fight for democracy in the world at large and then deny it to some of the people back home. We might paraphrase Lincoln by saying: "Our country cannot be half democratic and half fascist," for any state divided against itself must fall. All this, plain political insight is teaching us.

Furthermore, the world situation is making it equally clear that America cannot take her rightful place in the fellowship of nations if we do not treat fairly the minority group within our gates. The recent world war was clearly a war for the rights of the oppressed and less privileged. If the English were willing to go to war to protect the Poles and other smaller nations; if the sympathy of America from the beginning was with the English and we were really at war with Germany long before we declared war; if we were scandalized by the German treatment of her minority group, the Jews; surely, we cannot keep faith with our better selves if we do not do complete justice to our own minority group, the Negro, nor can we expect to continue in the leadership and respect of the world. It is well known that Japan rejoiced during the second World War in every evidence of racial friction in America. She published it abroad as the attitude of the white race toward the colored race, and her propaganda could not but undermine our standing with the smaller nations. Due partly to our great wealth; due partly to our prodigious organizing energy in producing the greatest war equipment in the history of the world; due partly to the hope, if not to the full confidence that we have no motives of aggrandizement; and due partly to the honest and straightforward leadership of our officials in this world; our nation today stands in a position of unchallenged leadership. We can, if we will, become one of the most powerful forces in the world today. But there is a weak spot in our armor, and that is our race attitudes. The colored nations of the world—China, Japan, India, and those of Africa—and they are overwhelming in the majority as to population, these nations will not continue to trust any people which does not deal with its minority groups on a basis of full and fair equality. Our world leadership depends on our racial fairmindedness.

But there is a far deeper appeal to the Christians than democracy or world leadership. That which should appeal to us as Christians and members of the Christian Church is that our leader, Jesus Christ, set himself with heart and soul against all discrimination against persons. If one will read the New Testament with care he will see that the most frequent moral teaching of Jesus is the value and sacredness of persons. (Mark 2:27; Mark 10:14-15; Mark 9:42.) In the great struggle of early Christianity with the mystery cults of the Roman Empire, two elements, more than any other, helped Christianity to win a real victory—first, the matchless personality and leadership of Jesus himself; and second, the constant and persistent emphasis on the value and worth of all persons. What a message! Coming to a weary and disillusioned people such as the Romans were, it made a profound impression. The mark of true Christianity has always been the appreciation of all persons. If Christianity ever loses this distinctive note, it will lose its soul. It is just here that the race issue is such an acid test of Christianity. Will the Church prove that she really is Christian?

To be Christian does not mean mere preaching and platitudes about brotherhood. We have had plenty of generalities and benevolent talk. What the Church and its members need now is to prove, in action and in living, that they really mean fellowship and brotherhood. This must take concrete form. It must, of course, mean that all Christians really do want economic equality, equal pay for equal work, and no discrimination in employment on account of race or creed. It means equal justice before the law, without reference to one's influence or one's race. It means equality of educational opportunity whether the child be white or black. But it means more than this. *It means equal respect and courtesy to all men, white and black.* It means that the Church must no longer be a closed corporation open only to the respectable few; it must be a society of friends, equally interested in all persons. Such an attitude the Church and the churches have not assumed. Rather, as one writer puts it: "Religious beliefs are brought into play to support prejudices, and good Christian men stand in church pulpits to preach their doctrines of racial superiority with no feeling of hypocrisy or anachronism. Their congregations expect nothing else from them, and would be profoundly shocked if they challenged a system which has given ministers and people a common set of attitudes and prejudices." A recent writer suggests that these prejudices are a cocoon in which men are wrapped, and they must open this cocoon if they would be free. Thus, it comes about that the Church itself in many places sanctions and supports the program of a caste system in which it is entangled. In very few places is the American Church interracial. It conforms to the pattern of caste rather than to the teachings of Christ, and it does so with complete self-righteousness. Once again this is not a sectional matter; North and South, East and West, the Christian Church conforms to caste, only occasionally breaking down the middle wall of partition and recognizing that Christ has made all one.[1] This is a withering indictment which the Church must answer with real action if the Church is to remain Christian.

It is hopeful that gradually the Church has realized this truth. At a meeting of eight interdenominational bodies in Cleveland, Ohio, in December 1942, consideration was given to the spiritual implications of Race and Culture in our Democracy. Finding Number Twelve of this gathering reads: "As an institution, we, the Church, must cleanse our own temples of the sin of race discrimination, segregation and 'Jim Crow' and thereby make ourselves more fit to minister to the soul and spirit of man, not the white man, not the yellow man, or the brown man, the red man, the black man, but Man." [2] That is by far the most significant finding of that conference.

The Federal Council of the Churches of Christ in America*, in its Columbus, Ohio, meeting of 1946, declared that segregation "with some differences of emphasis is accepted *in all sections of the country*." The report declared that "in the greatest crisis of our history, segregation made it impossible to utilize fully large sec-

---

[1] *Social Action*, published by the Congregational Christian Churches (January 15, 1941), p. 18.

[2] *Ibid*. (January 15, 1943), p. 45.

* Later this became the National Council of Churches of Christ in the United States of America.

tions of our manpower in the armed services and in war production." "Segregation subjects sections of our population to constant humiliation." "Segregation handicaps the Nation in international relations and the pattern of segregation is given moral sanction by the fact that churches and church institutions as a result of social pressure have so largely accepted the pattern in their own life and practice." This report then goes on to state: "Either the Church will accept the pattern of segregation in race relations as necessary, if not desirable, and continue to work within this pattern for the amelioration of racial tensions, or it will renounce the pattern of segregation as unnecessary and undesirable.

"The Federal Council of Churches of Christ in America hereby renounces the pattern of segregation in race relations as unnecessary and undesirable and a violation of the Gospel of love and human brotherhood. Having taken this action, the Federal Council requests its constituent communions to do likewise. As proof of their sincerity in this renunciation, they will work for a non-segregated church and a non-segregated society." This report goes on to say that the two-fold function of the Church is to "Create new men with new motives" and "To create a new society wherein such men will find a friendly environment within which to live their Christian convictions." [3]

The World Council of Churches, meeting in Evanston, Illinois, in 1954, was led in one of its most powerful sessions to raise such questions as these—how can the Church contribute to the correction of racial prejudice and injustice, and how can the message of the Gospel

---

[3] *The Church and Race Relations,* Federal Council of the Churches of Christ in America, March, 1946.

be presented so as to affect the deep springs of race prejudice? Prof. Mays, who was the leader of this session, suggested that it might turn out that the Church was the last bulwark of segregation, following slowly or not at all such secular forces as education, labor, big league baseball, and other agencies. The assembly formally resolved: "That segregation in all its forms is contrary to the Gospel and incompatible with the Christian doctrine of man and with the nature of the Church of Christ."

The Methodist Church (the largest protestant denomination in America, with between nine and ten million members) in its Minneapolis General Conference of May, 1956, declared: "There must be no place in the Methodist Church for racial discrimination or enforced segregation." They set up a 70-man committee to study ways and means of making that statement come true.

The Presbyterian U.S.A. General Assembly Meeting during May, 1956, in Philadelphia, even dared to commend to its members that they should be absolutely unbiased in the selling of residential property, making it available to "all qualified perchasers, without regard to race."

First of all, the ministers must know the facts and preach them in the spirit of Christ. Most ministers are muzzled. They are afraid of their boards or sessions. They dare not speak the real truth about the pagan elements in our caste system. If they are to have free souls they must speak the truth in humility, *but speak the truth*. The Church will never rise higher than the courage and unselfishness of its ministers will carry it. Like priest, like people. The time has come when the minister who would save his soul must do so through dealing honestly with his people on this sin of caste in race relations.

Many of our ministers could be of real service if they would cease to practice caste in their ministerial meetings. All the ministers of a city are supposed to come together once a month to discuss the common problems of Christianizing the city. Why have the white ministers so long forgotten that the colored people of the city are a part of that city, and if the city is ever to be Christian the colored people must be considered? Why should not the colored ministers be brought in at regular stated times to consider the religious welfare of the whole city? This has been tried in some few cities and with good results. It is good for the white ministers to find out that the "color" won't rub off, and that there is real ability and consecration among the Negro ministers, and it's good for the colored ministers to find out that all white ministers are not cowards and lacking in Christian attitude. Again, our white churches must be willing to have the best of the Negro ministers preach from the pulpits of white churches. How can we know each other until we are willing to hear what each race has to say for itself through its most able spokesmen? If Rev. A. (White) should invite Rev. B. (colored) to fill his pulpit some Sunday morning, how many of the deacons, or elders, or vestrymen, or stewards would resign immediately? How many of them would insist on Rev. A.'s resigning? As long as such questions as these can be asked with real meaning, just so long the Church has not mastered the caste system in its own membership. We cannot really be Christians as long as we despise or refuse fellowship to any Christians.

Does this mean that our white churches would immediately be crowded with colored members, and our colored churches would at once be dominated by ambitious white members? Not at all! A graduate student at Fisk some time ago wrote a thesis on the attitude of Negro Christians toward membership in white churches, and the general conclusion to which his studies led him was that both groups were fairly satisfied with their present membership, *if chosen on a voluntary basis.* Dwight W. Culver, in a recent study of segregation in the Methodist Church (1953) finds that Negroes say they prefer to worship in their own churches rather than in white or mixed churches because they fear they will not be welcome in white churches, but with this qualification practically all "agreed that colored Methodists prefer to worship in churches separate from whites." (page 30.) But the colored Christian does not feel it is a Christian church which would tell him he cannot attend simply because he is colored. He wants to see all Christian churches hang out the sign: "All Men Welcome" and mean it.

The Catholic Church has an Interracial Council in New York and certain other cities such as Boston, Detroit, Kansas City, Los Angeles. The purpose of this Council, which is composed of laymen is: "To promote in every practicable way relations between the races based on Christian principles of interracial justice and charity which uphold the God given dignity and destiny of every person." This Council carries on lectures, furnishes information and holds a semimonthly seminar in which white and colored people take part. "Symbolical of the Council's wholehearted dedication to interracial harmony and understanding is its participation with the Catholic Layman's Union in a bimonthly Communion Breakfast."

"These breakfasts, addressed by representative

Negro and white speakers on pertinent aspects of the race question, are preceded by a Dialogue Mass in the Chapel of St. Peter's Church, sometimes celebrated by a Negro priest, at which Negroes and whites kneel together in worship." [4] If the Catholics can thus meet together as white and colored on a basis of complete Christian equality, why cannot Protestant churches overcome their prejudices and meet the Negro half-way in Christian activities?

In a very significant article in the *Christian Century* for May 20, 1956, Ralph Lord Ray makes a comparison of the Methodist Church with the Catholic Church in their respective attitudes toward racial fellowship. It is clear when all factors are considered, thinks Ray, that Protestants are probably just as open-minded and as cooperative in racial matters as are Catholics. And there are cases of Protestant churches, as widely separated as Chicago and the deep South, which have become completely interracial. (See the *Christian Century*, April 11 and April 18, 1956.)

The supreme job of the Church is to develop human personality into a God likeness. To this one great purpose every effort must be made. The Church must seriously and honestly ask what forces are destroying personality, and what can be done to eliminate these forces. It would not be too bold a statement to claim that race prejudice and race hatred are probably doing more to destroy character than any other single influence in the nation. Miss Lillian Smith of the Old South has set forth in a full article in the *New Republic* for September, 1944, her conviction that racism is destroying character both for white and black people. Her statement is from a psy-

---

[4] *A Story of Achievement*, a pamphlet issued by the Catholic Council, 20 Vesey Street, New York.

chological standpoint, where mine is from simple practical observation. But the two methods arrive at the same conclusion. Gunnar Myrdal, in one of the most exhaustive studies ever made of the effect of racism, points out that the present caste system in America is one of the most costly experiments ever tried by any people. It keeps all Americans in high tension. We know that caste is wrong, and our American creed calls for the integrity and worth of all men. But we will not rise up and destroy this monster, so we live in constant tension.[5] In the South in particular this tension is most destructive. Who can estimate the disproportionate amount of time we of the South have spent, thinking about, condemning, defending, trying to overcome or practicing this caste system? Probably one reason the South has found itself belated in the intellectual and cultural race of the day, is because we have had to spend so much time on this one social issue. During the slave period, the North outran the South in accumulation of wealth because the South held to her slave labor, which in the nature of the case was less efficient labor. So now we allow the North to advance faster than does the South, not because the people of that section are more capable than are the southern people, *but because we harbor a caste system which absorbs a disproportion of intellectual and cultural energy.* Caste certainly is an expensive luxury, and what man can be at his very best when he is hemmed in by a social system which forces him constantly to violate his conscience? We as Christians claim that all men are equal in the sight of God, and yet our caste system makes it impossible to live up to our Christian convictions. We must hedge and defend and justify at every

---

[5] Gunnar Myrdal, *An American Dilemma* (Harper's, 1944), closing chapter.

turn of our lives. If this does not make hypocrites of us, it may make cowards, and if not cowards, at least it may make men and women of split personalities. If the Christian is really honest, he wants to do what his religion demands; namely, respect and serve every person he meets. He surely struggles to do so. But on every hand he finds himself thwarted. He cannot pay full respect to the womanhood of the Negro race without being accused of being a Negrophile and without being shut out from many of the opportunities of normal life. He cannot stand squarely for the Negro adult being given full political rights, without being called a mugwamp or a traitor to his own "white supremacy." The Conference of White Southerners meeting in Atlanta, April 8, 1943, recognized that there were many and flagrant injustices, but they were not able to work out a program which had any promise of amelioration within any reasonable time. Every man who faces this problem finds himself baffled in some such manner. When people live under such constant frustration, what must happen to their inner souls? Surely to ask the question is to answer it to any really thoughtful person. In the interest of the development of robust, honest, frank, and straightforward character, the Church must do something about this race issue. We cannot develop full personality in the South, or for that matter in America, so long as white people are forced to hold a position of dilemma. This in reality gives the title to Myrdal's able volumes.[6] The keynote of those volumes seems to be: "The moral struggle goes on within people and not only between them. As people's valuations are conflicting, behavior normally becomes a moral compromise." [7]

---

[6] Myrdal, *op. cit.*, Introduction.
[7] Myrdal, *op. cit.*, p. XLIV.

This is precisely the most serious aspect of Racism as it affects the building of character. Christianity as a religion is opposed to opportunism, compromise, and subterfuge, but racism develops all of these to the nth degree. Hence, the Church must enter the battle to destroy racism if it ever hopes to develop a full-fledged Christian experience in its members.

But the influence of racial antagonism on the white people is not the only price we pay for holding to our caste system. It is probably impossible for any white person to put himself completely into the position of a Negro, or for a colored person to completely understand and put himself into the place of a white man. But it ought not to be impossible for a white Christian to understand how a colored Christian must feel when he faces the many frustrations of daily life. Imagine for just an hour how one would feel if one could not be addressed with the respect indicated by the simple title of Mr., or Miss, or Mrs. How would one feel if he was always "Jim Crowed" in his travel; how would he feel if he could not enter the chief hotels or theaters; how would one feel if he could not enter even many of the churches of his community? What would be the effect on one's personality if he was constantly reminded that he was considered inferior, that he could not have all the privileges of being a real man? Surely we can understand that we would become sick of soul if we did not become desperate and bitter. When men become desperate or bitter, character ceases to grow. The Church has a definite responsibility to see to it that every Negro as a human being has a chance to grow in richness of character. But this cannot happen so long as a caste system controls the destiny of thirteen million Negroes.

The future of Christianity in America depends on

what Christianity can do to make real Christian people. We as Christians cannot tolerate any evil which stands in the way of the development of Christian character. The hour has struck. The crisis is at hand. The Church must do more than talk; it must pray; it must consider; it must act.

How could one make a better plea for a forward look than was made by one of those capable Negro souls who had often felt the steel of racism as it cut into his own quivering flesh?

O Southland! O Southland!
Have you heard the call
The trumphet blown, the word made known
To the nations, one and all
The watchword, the hope-word
Salvation's present plan
A gospel, new, for all—for you
Man shall be saved by man.

O Southland! O Southland!
Do you not hear today
The mighty beat of onward feet
And know you not their way?
'Tis forward, 'tis upward,
On to the fair white arch
Of Freedom's dome, and there is room
For each man who would march.

O Southland, fair Southland!
Then why do you still cling
To an idle age and a musty page,
To a dead and useless thing?
'Tis springtime! 'Tis work time!
The world is young again!

And God's above, and God is love
And men are only men.

O Southland! My Southland!
O birthland, do not shirk
The toilsome task, nor respite ask,
But gird you for the work.
Remember, remember
That weakness stalks in pride
That he is strong who helps along
The faint one at his side.[8]

---

[8] Poem by James Weldon Johnson in *Saint Peter Relates an Incident;* published by The Viking Press.

INDEX

A

B